TWO FOR THE MONEY

D0862714

Other Avon Books by
Mike and Jacqueline Powers

HOW TO OPEN A FRANCHISE BUSINESS
HOW TO START A BUSINESS WEBSITE
HOW TO START A FREELANCE CONSULTING BUSINESS
HOW TO START A MAIL ORDER BUSISNESS
HOW TO START A RETIREMENT BUSINESS

TWO FOR THE MONEY

A Couples Complete Guide to Money Management

MIKE AND JACQUELINE POWERS

A Third Millennium Press Book

AVON BOOKS ◆ NEW YORK

56042996

AVON BOOKS, INC.
1350 Avenue of the Americas
New York, New York 10019

Library of Congress Cataloging in Publication Data:
Powers, Mike.
Two for the money : a couples complete guide to money
management / Mike and Jacqueline Powers.
p.   cm.
Includes index.
1. Married people—Finance, Personal. I. Powers, Jacqueline K.
II. Title.
HG179.P64   1999   99-38189
332.024'0655—dc21   CIP

First Avon Books Trade Paperback Printing: December 1999

AVON TRADEMARK REG. U.S. PAT. OFF. AND IN OTHER COUNTRIES,
MARCA REGISTRADA, HECHO EN U.S.A.

Printed in the U.S.A.

OPM   10   9   8   7   6   5   4   3   2   1

To our parents,
who taught us the basic tenets
of financial responsibility,
and to our children,
who made us practice them.

CONTENTS

INTRODUCTION

Like most couples who have been married more than twenty years, we agree on some things and fight over others. We share some interests and pursuits and prefer to strike out alone after others. By and large we've reached these accommodations quietly and painlessly.

There's one big exception: money. It has taken us the better part of our more than two decades together to negotiate a lasting cease-fire from the constant financial battles that plagued our marriage, day in and day out, from the moment we said "I do." That's because we were totally—it seemed hopelessly—financially incompatible. We battled over how much to spend, what to spend it on, when and where and how much to save, and, later, what kind of investments to make.

Jacquie: *Mike's a rational, organized, even-tempered man. But I love him anyway. Right from the start he wanted to establish a household budget, to sit down regularly and discuss household finances, and to plan for major expenditures. I flat-out refused. For reasons we'll get into later, I was incapable of talking about money, declined to listen to his "sermons on spending," and refused to participate in budgeting or financial planning. You can imagine the decibel level of our financial discourse. Besides, Mike had his own financial idiosyncrasies. More on that later, too.*

Mike: *When I met Jacquie her attitude was basically that money unspent was money wasted. In seventh grade economics she learned that money was a medium for exchange, and from then on she exchanged it with a vengeance. Unfortunately, her financial attitudes hadn't advanced much further. Her basic economic theory could be summed up in one thing she said to me shortly after we were married: "How can I be out of money? I still have all these checks!"*

Don't get me wrong. I certainly wasn't a paragon of financial virtue, either. I can drop a buck just as fast as she can, and during our first two or three years together, before we had kids, I happily jumped on the spending bandwagon. Expensive dinners out, weekend trips at the drop of a hat, clothes, electronic gizmos, sporting goods, home furnishings—you name it, we bought it.

But at some point I got bit by the responsibility bug and decided we needed to set up a budget and begin to divert some money into investments. That's when it got ugly. Despite her acknowledgment that this was indeed a good thing to do, Jacquie couldn't quite pull it off. If I managed to put money aside, it was always without any help from her. And if I did protest over her spending, I was accused of "lecturing." It led to many arguments, bitter silences, and long nights of trying not to bump into each other in bed. (Fortunately, we have a king-size bed— another acquisition from our free-spending days—so avoiding each other was easy.)

Jacquie: *Saint Mike, patron saint of financial fortitude and forgiveness. See how irritating he can be? But okay, he has a point.*

Now, we've been reborn. Our days of fighting over finances are over. And in the true spirit of the reformed we want to share with couples and would-be couples the secrets of our success in achieving fracas-free financial compatibility. It wasn't easy, but then we had no easy-to-follow path to guide us. We were pioneers. But if you read this book and follow the strategies we map out, we guarantee you can avoid all (okay, most) of those battles over money that spell disaster for millions of marriages nationwide.

Better yet, this book will help you and your partner develop your own strategies for investing in your future and for future investing that will ensure the financial success of your long, happy, richer lives together. We'll explain fully the importance of establishing a financial partnership, then tell you how you can marry your disparate money styles. We'll describe how to establish a household budget and give you tips on establishing joint and separate credit. We'll help you draft a life plan for investing that will take you from "I do" to "It's time to retire."

We'll also lead you through what for many couples becomes a financial minefield—identifying insurance needs and sifting through the many insurance products offered by the industry. We'll advise you on selecting financial planners and advisers if you decide that's the way to go. And we'll give you sound advice and tips on starting those essential family funds: the house fund, the college fund, and finally, the retirement fund.

In addition to giving you expert advice on the specifics of financial planning and investing, we'll teach you the fine art of compromise. It sounds easy. "Sure, I know how to compromise," you might say. But as you begin your journey together as a couple—whether you're married or unmarried, newly remarried and merging two families, or same-sex partners—you'll find that in your financial challenges you face stresses and strains, decisions and dilemmas that cut to the core of your relationship in ways other shared concerns can't match. For these truly are the decisions that shape the quality and comfort, the very viability of your future together.

So read on, and let us help guide you on the path to

a happy, healthy financial future. If you read this book and practice what we preach, not only will you find financial compatibility, stability, and perhaps even prosperity, but you'll also be able to turn what for many couples is a cause of unending friction into a unique source of pleasure that enriches your relationship. Let's get started.

PART ONE

COMING TOGETHER: DOLLARS AND SENSE

1

Why Do Couples Fight over Money?

Congratulations, you're a couple now. Or maybe you've been together for some time. Whether you're newlyweds or longtime partners, you've obviously decided it's time to quit squabbling about money and start accumulating some. Whatever your age, you realize you need to plan—together—for your shared future. And to do that, you need to learn how to forge a full financial partnership. You've probably already realized it won't be easy.

Most couples fight about three things: money, sex, and how to raise the children. There are good reasons for that. Generally, couples don't determine their long-term compatibility in these key areas before they tie the knot. In fact, many couples don't even discuss these three topics—critical to the heart of every relationship and around which their lives revolve—in a thoughtful, open, analytical way until it's far too late. Usually they're only talked about when the vows have faded, the gloves are off, and their knuckles are bloody, figuratively speaking.

Take sex, for example. Let's face it—when two people are in the full bloom of an intense relationship, sex is the last thing they think they'll ever have a problem with. They're so hot for each other that their ears emit steam at the mere thought of their beloved, and it's impossible to imagine that fire cooling down.

Then there are the kids. Before they take the ceremonial plunge, most couples discuss whether or not they want children and what size family they'll feel comfortable with. But most don't think to sound each other out on their equally important parenting styles. After all, the little darlings are so far in the future at that point that the awful reality of potty training and tantrums haven't yet hit home.

Finally, there's that mysterious, mystical, mythical, mega-marriage-mutilator—MONEY.

MONEY—THE BIGGEST MARRIAGE MUTILATOR

Some five million Americans will head to the altar this year. Most will be entering their first marriage. But a surprising number—around 40 percent—will be getting married for the second or third time. Many will never have discussed with their soon-to-be spouse their basic money styles: whether they like to spend freely or save, whether they like to buy on credit or insist on paying cash, whether they prefer risky or conservative investments, whether they're immune to debt or if it gives them physical pain to pile up debt.

These couples will marry blissfully ignorant of each other's financial profiles, and chances are good they'll soon discover they're just plain incompatible in money matters. Experts agree that money is the primary battleground for most couples in the United States. The divorce rate in America is now a whopping 50 percent, and the sad fact is that fully 57 percent of divorced couples pointed to financial problems as the major reason their marriages failed.

Thousands of other couples who are still managing to

hang on are in therapy over their money miseries, while many, many others are duking it out daily, just a few battles away from divorce court, with its own unique kinds of financial distress.

A Casualty of the Money Wars

Beth and Adam Moore agree on one thing only: they got divorced because they couldn't agree on money matters. First, they had different spending patterns. Beth was a saver, Adam a spender. Moreover, Beth says, Adam would spend money on big-ticket items like cars and state-of-the-art computer systems without so much as consulting her.

"He didn't even have the courtesy to ask whether I preferred a blue or beige interior, much less whether I wanted a Bronco or a Pathfinder or even if I thought we could afford a new car at all," she says.

Finally, despite Beth's pleas and against the advice of his father, sister, brother, and just about everyone else he consulted, Adam abruptly quit his job in Ohio and bought into a boat business in southern California. He put all their joint savings into the business, even though the two partners he was joining were total strangers to him and California was in the third year of a drought that had virtually killed the boating industry. By the time the business—and the Moores—went bankrupt a year later, the marriage was emotionally bankrupt as well, Beth says.

"The constant bickering over money and our inability—mine as well as his—to come to any agreement over how to handle our finances put the finishing touches on the relationship," Beth says. "But in truth it was the lack of commitment to me as a full partner, including a financial partner, that doomed the marriage for me."

No One Is Immune

It seems that even the righteous and reformed aren't immune to backsliding. Here's a true confession—an instant replay of a conversation we had as we were dressing for work just this morning.

> **Mike:** (*picking up a new book lying on Jacquie's bureau*) *Did you buy this?*
>
> **Jacquie:** (*starting to wander off in search of her coffee cup*) *Yes.*
>
> **Mike:** *When?*
>
> **Jacquie:** (*getting irritated at the inquisition over a $13 book, but trying to stay calm*) *Last week. It's for my book club.*
>
> **Mike:** *How did you pay for it?*
>
> **Jacquie:** (*turning to him, hands on hips, tapping foot*) *American Express. What's the big deal? It was only $13.*
>
> **Mike:** (*throwing his hands up dramatically*) *Why didn't you pay cash or write a check? It doesn't matter if it was only $13, it all adds up. I asked you not to use any credit cards right now. I'm trying to keep track of our expenses. How can we manage our money if you keep sticking things on credit cards and not telling me about it?*
>
> **Jacquie:** (*guilty, but with heels now dug in deep*) *Okay, I'm sorry. Just shut up about it, will you!*

So here we are trying to tell you how to get your financial house in order, and even we're not immune to the little financial skirmishes that are so common in marriage. The point is it's natural to backslide occasionally. But there are ways to minimize the problems and the backsliding. Understanding the reasons for the problems is the first step. Read on.

Money Is the Last Taboo

There are many reasons why a lot of people just can't get along when it comes to money matters. First, as we mentioned earlier, many couples don't analyze each other's financial styles before making a commitment. For some reason, they just find it too uncomfortable.

Although those same people may not hesitate to share intimate revelations about their previous lovers, their families, their jobs, and even their skin conditions, they fear that probing about finances might make them appear greedy and insensitive. Ask about assets and debts? Income and inheritance? No way. Some even go so far as to hide purchases or debts from each other.

The truth is, money may be the last taboo, as Freud pointed out. In our rush-to-reveal, let-it-all-hang-out society, we tend to retain the lessons of our childhood in money matters, and the first rule is to seal our lips. Remember how Dad always frowned and refused to reveal his salary if you were rude enough to ask? And didn't Mom remind you of your manners if you forgot in your enthusiasm and asked how much a gift cost?

So, during the lovely discovery days of courtship, we do what we learned as children and keep our lips tightly buttoned about money. Then, because opposites attract, many of us end up marrying someone whose money management style is completely incompatible with our own. And then we fight. Over money. Over and over again.

Even if couples share the same attitudes about money, they frequently polarize as time goes on. If a spender marries a spender, for example, they often begin to subconsciously compete over who can spend the most. But then an odd reversal occurs. At some point, one person will concede and do a 180-degree turn and become a skinflint. Then real problems occur. The same thing can happen when two financial conservatives get together. Over time, one will often become a spendthrift.

Couples Freak Out over Money Because Individuals Do

The bottom line, though, is that couples have problems dealing with money issues because individuals do. We've already explained that couples fight over money because they haven't overcome the great communication taboo and talked about their money styles. But that's not necessarily the result of a deliberate choice. The fact is that many of you haven't given a thought to figuring out your own money style. And until you do that, you won't be able to understand how and why you and your partner's styles are so incompatible, much less what to do about it.

So why do so many of us have such problems coming to terms with money matters? The root of the problem is that most people suffer from a condition authors Stephen M. Pollan and Mark Levine, in an article in *Psychology Today*, called "money myopia."

Pollan and Levine defined money myopia as "the inability to recognize that money has no intrinsic value and is simply a tool to be used to meet rational needs and achieve realistic goals." But money is essential to our survival and helps determine the quality of our lives. Therefore, they noted, "its very prominence in our lives has caused us to make money a sort of totem: a neutral substance upon which we project fears, desires, attributes, and characteristics. As a result, it has become our psychological manna."

Thus, money often is at the core of who and what we are. The emotions and anxieties we experience over money matters really relate to our very identities, our sense of ourselves and of our self-worth. Naturally, then, when you join your finances with those of another person you are in many ways risking your own identity and self-worth. And when that other person is your spouse or life partner, with whom you are vulnerable in so many other areas, the risks are compounded and involve much more than mere coinage.

Our Attitudes about Money Are Deeply Rooted

Most psychotherapists and sociologists believe we develop our attitude about money as we develop our identities, from infancy. Freud equated money with feces, and postulated that at a very early age we learn to barter emotionally with our parents by using feces as the means of exchange. We are praised or criticized, rewarded or punished, loved or hated based on whether we release or withhold feces. When we later grow up and use money as the means of exchange, Freudians say, our actions still are dictated by the emotional responses carried over from our potty-training days.

Other experts, however, take a broader view about the origins of our money myopia. Yes, early interactions with parents matter. But so do a host of other factors, including education, family socioeconomic background, culture, ethnicity, gender, and home environment.

Whatever the roots, we bring our individual money myopias with us when we unite as a couple, and the potential for marital discord over money is therefore amplified geometrically.

Different Personality Types Have Different Money Styles

Kenneth O. Doyle, a financial psychologist at the University of Minnesota, believes all a person's money-related motivations derive from a single source—"the drive to avoid isolation. Money is fundamentally a talisman that people use to protect themselves against the fear of isolation."

Doyle believes fights about money derive from differences between the four classic personality types. These types comprise the analytical person, for whom money means control; the driven person, for whom money means competence; the expressive person, for whom money means esteem; and the amiable person, for whom money means love.

The analytical person "learned to use order to avoid further isolation . . . stresses order to the extent that one suspects a deep-seated fear of losing control," Doyle writes. "The analytical gains confidence by experiencing order and suffers anxiety at the loss of control. He or she uses money as a talisman against the loss of control, saves money to protect against unnamed threats and engages in behaviors such as bargain hunting and hoarding and those that suggest indecisiveness, cautiousness, stubbornness, and unusual ability to defer gratification."

The driven person, according to Doyle, "gains confidence by demonstrating achievement and suffers anxiety at the possible loss of competence . . . uses money as a talisman against the fear of being found incompetent, spends money on things that will 'prove' his or her success to other people . . ."

The expressive person "learned to use appearances to avoid isolation . . . stresses appearances and self-expression to the extent that one suspects a deep anxiety about what other people think," Doyle writes. "He or she uses money as a talisman against loss of self-esteem, spends money to buy respect, and engages in behavior that indicates feelings of privilege and possessions."

Finally, he writes, the amiable person "learned to use relationships to counteract feelings of isolation. . . . Thus the amiable gains confidence by receiving affection and suffers anxiety at the thought of loss of relationship. He or she uses money as a talisman against the fear of losing affection, saves money to hold on to people and engages in behaviors that indicate feelings of low self-esteem and low potency, that money is evil and that center in excessive giving, sharing, and the inability to say no."

If an analytical person marries an amiable person, for example, their different attitudes about money could cause a serious breach in the relationship. When the analytical person inevitably exerts control and withholds money, albeit for a good reason, the amiable person may conclude the spouse doesn't love him or her sufficiently.

The Financial Personality Struggle

Barbara and Sarah are just such a couple. They're both in their thirties and, after two years together, have concluded after much soul-searching that they would each like to bear a child and be parents together. They love each other deeply, they say, and feel they can withstand the social pressures faced by gay parents. What they're not sure they can surmount are the financial battles that already disrupt their lives and which will only be exacerbated by the presence of children.

Using Doyle's analysis, Barbara describes herself as the analytical type. She says she's very conservative about spending her money, doesn't like to use credit, and needs to always feel in control of her finances and her life. Sarah, on the other hand, is very much an amiable financial personality, a free spender who spends a great deal of money on other people.

They share a joint household account, and each has a separate account, for personal spending. Their problems are twofold, Barbara says. First, she's a lawyer and makes quite a bit more money than Sarah, who's a teacher. Second, Sarah spends freely, buying gifts she can't really afford for herself, for Barbara, and for friends and relatives. So she dips into the household account to stay afloat. When Barbara tries to talk to Sarah about her spending and the need to save for a house and children, Sarah not only gets upset at the immediate suggestion of wrongdoing but she also feels unappreciated, even unloved.

Sarah says that at first their money squabbles seemed like such a small thing, and easily rectified. But as the stakes got higher with the discussions of children and a house, and as their finances became more intertwined, the fights became more intense and protracted. Now, both say, they aren't sure what to do.

Money Can Be a Weapon, Too

In a relationship, money can be a weapon that involves issues of power as well as control, whatever your gender and basic personality traits. Even if you're both conservative with money, for example, you can argue over what kind of investments to make or what kind of vacation to take. And those kinds of arguments may have more to do with who wants or needs control and who wants or needs to be the decision maker than with the relative merits of the investments or the vacation spots and costs.

Jacquie: *I admit that one of my basic problems with money is the issue of power and control. Except at work, or in a situation in which my hierarchical position is clearly of lesser rank, I can't stand to have anyone tell me what to do. That stems from my childhood, when my father held all the power and control, and most clearly in the area of money. I identified with my father because I refused to accept the subservient position my mother held. So when Mike tries to talk to me about my spending or our finances, even if he's right, that old control trigger switches on, and my ears switch off.*

Then, too, my father spoiled me rotten. I was used to getting pretty much anything I wanted and wasn't taught to consider the cost or timing of a purchase. In desperation, in high school and college my parents tried a clothes allowance, but it was generous. In addition, I learned quickly that if I spent all my allowance and "desperately needed" something, I could wangle it. My father thought it was "cute."

Mike: *Jacquie's recognition of the reasons for her attitudes toward money was important in helping us learn to communicate and get our finances under control. She's learned to be more analytical about her behavior, although she still can't help trying the "cute" routine sometimes. When that happens, I simply point out that I'm not her father.*

I had to learn a bit about my money attitudes, too. Since I to some degree fall into the "amiable" financial personality group, I like Jacquie and our kids to have the things they want (okay, and I like to have the things I want, too), so I would frequently go along with purchases people didn't need or that we really couldn't afford at the time. But I also have a fair amount of the "analytical" personality in me as well, so this would generate all sorts of internal conflict.

So you can see the problem. If we fall into our normal behaviors, we can easily spend too much money. Jacquie has to practice self-control and not become manipulative, and I have to stand my ground and offer sound reasons why we can or cannot spend money on something. Once we realized this, we made a huge leap forward in managing our finances.

The issues of power and control can be even more critical when one partner in a relationship decides to stay at home with the children, thus bringing in no outside income—even if it's a joint decision. The situation is similar when, like Sarah, one of the partners earns less.

Most couples strive for the concept of shared finances, even if their actual methods of handling their incomes and expenses vary. In other words, most truly committed couples, whether married or unmarried, same-sex or heterosexual, first-time marrieds or second or third timers, operate under the "what's-mine-is-yours" philosophy to one extent or another.

But when one partner quits work to stay at home with the kids (or for any other reason), he or she often begins to feel not only dependent on the supporting partner but also as if he or she has less right to the partner's money. That, in turn, can lead to feelings of powerlessness, frustration, anger, and resentment, which threaten the relationship.

As one woman who has a full-time job caring for her and her husband's three-year-old twins told us: "I feel as if I have to ask my husband for permission to buy things I really need. It's like being a kid all over again."

There's another side to the control issue that can be equally problematic. Often one partner in the relationship "handles" the finances: keeps the accounts, pays the bills, invests the money, decides when the big purchases can be made, and so on. That person may not be a control freak, but may just have taken on the job by default. In fact, if the person who handles the family finances is married to an impulse spender who pays no attention to financial reality, that person may be frustrated because the spender is *not* an equal partner in their money management duties.

Mike: *This has always been one of our biggest problems. Jacquie has no interest in doing it, so I manage our money. Actually, the "analytical" part of me prefers it that way. I do our banking, pay our bills, prepare our taxes, keep an eye on our budget, and generally try to keep all our financial balls in the air at one time. These days that includes putting our daughter through college and preparing to send our son to college.*

In the bad old days, Jacquie took the old "It's easier to apologize than to ask for permission" approach to spending money. She'd come walking in the door with a bunch of shopping bags just as I was sitting there trying to figure out how to pay the VISA bill. I'd invariably flip out, and a huge scene would ensue.

The problem was solved with three easy changes: learning to communicate about spending, creating and sticking to a budget, and planning together for large purchases. I know it sounds simple, but, at least for us, it was a difficult transition. Part of the problem was that, as you learned a few moments ago, Jacquie hates dealing with money and also hates to be told what to do. So I was in a no-win situation. I was expected to be the financial decision maker yet my decision making frequently generated anger and arguments. Once we began to make decisions together, the arguments stopped (most of the time, anyway).

Jacquie: *Yeah, yeah, yeah. How little some men under-*

stand. I never wanted Mike to be the decision maker—that was his ego talking. I intended to make all the important decisions. I just wanted him to do the grunt work.

Okay, I admit it, that was pretty insensitive of me. I concede, too, that it was a good idea for Mike to do much of the paperwork because I'm not much of a detail person. I don't read to the end of documents because I get bored quickly. But our new approach is working well for me because I don't have to get bogged down in boring details but don't have to fight to the death for a share in the decision making. And I do mean share, too.

Most surprising, though, is that I've discovered a real pleasure in the kind of problem solving that comes with making and sticking to a budget and planning for big purchases. Miracles do happen.

Gender Differences Exacerbate the Problem

Surprisingly, in these days of hard-won gender equality, psychologists agree that men and women often have very different money management, spending, and investing styles. These gender-based differences have a huge impact on couples' financial compatibility.

A study conducted at the University of Maryland in 1990 confirmed that men and women handle risks—and money—differently. Men are more willing to take risks in investments and financial dealings, in part because they view money as a visible manifestation of their success. They also are more certain of their own financial expertise and prefer to handle their own investments.

Women, on the other hand, seek less risky, more stable investments. They prefer to nourish a nest egg and are more satisfied with slow, steady growth. They don't expect to get rich by investing, and many consider stocks too uncertain to gamble on. They also aren't secure in their financial know-how and instead look to outside experts for advice.

Men's and women's attitudes differ on spending, too. While the narrowing earnings gap between men and women has spurred women to purchase more high-tech and big-ticket items than ever before, women tend to be more practical than men in their spending habits. Women, psychologists say, will spend because they feel they've earned the right, they deserve it, or because it's on sale or practical. Men spend to indicate their level of success and earning power.

Yet it's women who have the reputation for being kamikaze shoppers, ready to shop 'til they drop. A 1991 study by Maritz Marketing Research showed that fewer than half of all men buy their own clothes and toiletries, compared with four out of five women. So women may shop more often, but that's because they're responsible for buying for the whole family, not just for themselves.

And, interestingly, a recent survey by Mediamark Research revealed that an equal number of men and women—33.6 percent compared with 34.2 percent, respectively—described themselves as impulse buyers.

Women also don't save as much as men. A 1993 study by Merrill Lynch showed that women generally save only half of what men save, and they start saving later than men do. According to the study, just under half of the women aged 45 to 65 started saving for retirement before age 40, while more than two-thirds of the men had.

Ruth Hayden, a money counselor and author of *How to Turn your Money Life Around*, believes men and women are conditioned almost from birth to view money differently. In fact, she says, they are taught their differing views.

While women now are earning more than ever before, they still by and large earn less than men, and that affects the way they handle money. Women now total almost half of the U.S. workforce, but they still earn just over a quarter of what their male coworkers earn. As a result, women are less confident about their future earnings potential, and that impacts their spending, saving, and investment habits.

Whatever the cause of these financial gender differences, marketing experts and financial services firms have realized they can cash in on them by targeting specific marketing efforts to a specific gender. Financial services firms, in particular, have discovered the huge untapped female investment market, and they are going after women by researching their needs and preferences.

And as more women succumb to the lure of the investment world, there is more basis for financial incompatibility in couples and more issues over which to fight.

Bringing Different Money Styles to a Marriage

Regardless of what the experts say about gender-based differences, you can throw out the stereotypes—women aren't always the practical ones or the savers, and vice versa.

Stephanie Van Hooser and her husband, Steve, have been married thirteen months and have very different money styles. Their styles are so different and so problematic, in fact, that Stephanie fears Steve's justifiable concerns over her bad financial track record and poor credit rating will prevent them from achieving a dream they both share of owning their own business.

Stephanie is 26, Steve is 28. They're both well-educated, career-driven, and share common goals. And unlike many couples, they've engaged in frequent discussions about spending habits, investing, and money management.

"Unfortunately," Stephanie says, "sometimes shared goals don't necessarily imply shared values. I grew up in a family where my parents came from modest upbringings and worked incredibly hard to obtain financial security for us. I think they wanted to give their children, and even themselves, everything they had historically been deprived of. They were exceedingly generous and I never wanted for anything. I never had an allowance or a savings account during my childhood; if I needed money my father simply handed it to me. I never learned the value of a dollar, or more importantly, how difficult it is to earn enough dollars to simply cover the basics—let alone the small luxuries I took for granted."

Steve, on the other hand, grew up in a financially comfortable, but conservative, family. He was given an allowance from age 5, started earning five dollars a week doing household chores, and was allowed to spend exactly half of all his earnings. The other half was promptly deposited in a savings account. All through high school he paid for his own clothes, lunches, gas, and other purchases. He's proud to say that while his parents paid for his college education, he provided all his own spending money.

By the end of her sophomore year in college, Stephanie says, she received two preapproved credit cards in the mail and "had an absolutely grand time foolishly wining and dining my friends. I thought it was free money. I proceeded to enter into years of revolving debt. I shudder now to think of the money I paid out in interest."

She says things came to a head right before graduation. "My parents disapproved of my spending habits and feared for my future credit. (I had been using my college allowance to make the minimum payments, and then kept right on charging.) They chose to let me sink or swim instead of helping. In retrospect I should thank them, but at the time I felt furiously helpless. When I graduated I had approximately $5,200 in debt and an incredibly low-paying job working in the publishing industry in Boston. Steve and I were dating at this time and I was very honest with him about my debt load."

Steve placed her on a budget and had her cash in a savings bond, and she slowly and painfully plowed her way out of debt, sticking to hiking and biking instead of wining and dining for entertainment. Several years later they married and combined their finances.

"I'm ashamed to admit that I had little to bring to the table. Steve, on the other hand, had twelve months' salary in liquid savings, an IRA, a healthy 401(k), and investments in several mutual funds."

They still argue over how, when, and on what to spend their money, since Stephanie isn't totally cured of her childhood spending habits. But what worries her more is their dream for the future of owning their own business.

"Steve and I want to own our own business but I'm afraid my credit will hurt our chances for getting a loan. Worse, Steve has expressed doubts about my ability to comanage a business. I know he loves me, but to have him not trust me is terribly hurtful.

"One thing's for certain though, I'm definitely much more educated than I used to be about finances and I do have Steve to thank for that. But as we continue to work towards owning our own business I'm afraid problems could be around the corner."

External Factors Also Play a Part

Personality, environment, childhood, and genetics all play a part in creating your personal money management style; that style, paired with your partner's, helps determine the degree to which couples fight about money. But ever-changing external factors and demographics also can be sources of money battles.

Couples are marrying later than ever before, after they have become used to managing their own money without interference. Combining different money styles after years of entrenched habits of your own can be more difficult than if you were starting your career and your relationship at the same time.

The downsizing trend that has swept corporate America also has played a role in many couples' money squabbles. If you've been enjoying a certain level of financial comfort derived from two incomes and one of you loses his job, an otherwise stable marriage can be rocked to its foundations. The stress over how to pay those suddenly enormous bills, combined with new feelings of failure, impotence, and self-castigation, can explode into major battles and destroy a marriage.

Baby boomers in particular find it difficult to adjust to reduced income and expectations. They grew up in times of plenty, when the expectation was that their lives would be as comfortable or better than those of their parents. Their needs and desires have driven the marketplace since they were born. They learned early and well how to live the good life, and when the party suddenly ends with the loss of a job or a missed promotion, they have trouble coping. They fight about money, and their marriages flounder as a result.

And now that women are moving further onto the fast track professionally, couples may find they have two overachieving partners engaged in career competition. That, too, can drive a financial wedge into their marriage. The "I-make-more-than-you-so-I'm-better-than-you," or "I-make-more-than-you-so-I-can-spend-more-than-you" kind of thinking can seep into a good marriage and poison it.

There's also the second-marriage syndrome. Of the 2.3 million marriages that will take place this year, 40 percent will involve a person tying the knot for the second or third time. And many of those marrying for the second time bring an entire family to the table, not just themselves.

Today, one in five American families—more than 5 million—is a "blended" family. And studies show that the majority of blended families have less wealth than other family types. That can spell financial distress. When a couple is disappointed with the amount of money they have, they find their whole relationship less satisfying, psychologists say.

Merging two families complicates the new couple's financial picture in myriad ways, and can lead to bitter disputes over how to handle assets and debts acquired during the previous marriage, how to combine family incomes and expenses, what to do about alimony and child support payments, and whose kids get what from whom both during the marriage and as future beneficiaries.

Same-sex couples and those who choose to live together—committed to the future, but for whatever reason unwilling to get married—also have unique financial pressures that can lead to deadly disputes. These couples are denied most of the financial arrangements and benefits that married couples enjoy. For example, same-sex couples routinely are unable to share medical coverage and pension benefits, are denied family status in caring for ill partners, cannot inherit automatically, and cannot protect their children from costly custody battles. Some progressive companies are slowly changing some of these policies, but they are the exception, not the rule.

Financing the Blended Family

Don and Sheila Tobin have been married since 1994. He had been widowed in 1992 after an eighteen-year marriage, and she was divorced in 1991 after five years of marriage. They each have two children. Sheila's two boys were 4 and 6 at the time of the marriage. Don, who is eleven years older than Sheila, has a daughter and son who were 19 and 16, respectively.

Don owns a real estate business, and Sheila is a sales associate for the firm. His income is considerably more than hers, and he also brought more assets to the marriage—a home and several investment and retirement accounts. Although his resources had been diminished somewhat by his wife's illness and several years of suffering through a depressed real estate market, he is still financially comfortable.

They both say that coming to terms over money matters was not an easy task. Entering the marriage, they agreed that they each would be responsible for the expenses of their own children. It soon became apparent, however, that doing so was easier said than done. While Don's finances have been strained by having two children in college at the same time, he frequently contributes to the needs of Sheila's kids if her cash is running a bit tight. He admits he sometimes gets resentful.

"I feel obligated to help out if she can't afford something," he says. "But when I'm already struggling to make tuition payments, the extra money is hard to part with."

The problem is exacerbated by the unreliability of Sheila's ex-husband in making child support payments. He misses some payments, and when he does make a payment, it's frequently less than he's supposed to pay.

"So Sheila has to pay for things that deadbeat should be paying for," Don says. "And if she can't, I try to. It definitely causes a few arguments."

They also had to merge very different money styles. Don had been used to spending freely and is still inclined to buy expensive items without much forethought. Sheila, already careful with money before her first marriage, became even more so when she became a single parent with two children to support.

"Our biggest arguments are about spending on entertainment or luxury items," Sheila says. "His tastes are definitely more extravagant than mine, so even going out to dinner can cause a problem. He'll want to go someplace fancy and I'll argue that we can't afford it. So he'll get stubborn and insist that we go and that he pay for the meal. Then I'll feel guilty about not contributing."

One way they've eased their money differences has been to let Sheila create a budget and take care of the day-to-day management of their expenses. They both agree she's better at it. Also, Don has learned to be more understanding of her feelings about money and to rein in his own spending habits.

"She must be doing something right, because we've even been able to put some money aside since she took over," he laughs.

SO WHAT'S THE CURE FOR ALL THIS MONEY MADNESS?

Now you know why many couples are financially incompatible and why couples fight about money. It's time to apply that knowledge to yourselves.

First, you need to decide to become full financial partners and begin investing in your joint future. To do that you must discover your individual money styles. Then you need to take specific steps to marry your money management styles. We'll tell you how to do that, step by step, in chapter 2.

It will take some self-analysis, some rethinking and discussion of joint values and goals. And it will mean making some tough personal choices and changes. But it will be well worth investing your time and effort. The investment will pay dividends in both your relationship and your bank account.

2

Marrying Your Money Styles

We've already figured out that couples fight about money because they're financially incompatible. And they're incompatible because, for a variety of reasons, they begin with, or develop, conflicting individual money styles.

For you and all the other financially challenged couples out there, the only cure to your financial conflicts is to marry your warring money styles and become full, comfortable financial partners. Only then can the two of you truly plan—financially—for the rest of your lives.

In order to successfully marry your money styles you need to do three things:

- determine your individual money habits
- reevaluate your lifestyle and financial goals and priorities
- take practical steps to change the way you handle money as a couple

In this chapter we'll take you through each of these steps, one by one, with detailed suggestions on what to do to reach your goal. It'll be like a workshop, with emphasis on the *work* portion of that word. And you two will be doing the work. You may want to grab pencils and notepads, or maybe your laptop computers. Whatever works for the two of you.

You'll be searching your souls, making lists, thinking out loud, and breaking down your future financial partnership into specific action steps. It'll be like negotiating a contract, of sorts. Let's get started.

DETERMINE YOUR INDIVIDUAL MONEY STYLES

Before you can marry your money styles and begin working together as full financial partners, you need to determine your individual styles. Think about it. You can't fit two disparate pieces into a single, smoothly working component until you understand fully how each of the separate pieces functions. So your first job is to analyze your individual attitudes and beliefs about money. Here's what you need to do.

Break That Last Taboo

Remember what Freud said about money being the last taboo? Remember how Mom and Dad frowned if, as children, we asked innocently about money matters? Well, ignore the taboo and forget those ingrained childhood habits. Money should be no more taboo a subject for couples than sex, education, careers, or children. In fact, it's essential that you break the bonds of the taboo and start talking openly about money: what it means to you, both as individuals and as a couple, and how you plan to handle it.

Now, grab your pencils and paper and start making lists. Ideally, you should do this exercise together, sharing and confiding along the way. If that makes you uncomfortable, you can do it separately and then share the results.

First, each of you needs to list what you consider to be your basic personality traits. Forget money for a minute, just think about who you are. Are you a perfectionist, a control freak, or hopelessly disorganized? Do you take charge or resist taking responsibility? Do you continually seek affection, or are you reserved and distant? When you've finished describing yourself, do the same thing again, only this time describing each other.

Next, you each should list your feelings about money. Close your eyes and make it a free-association game. What feelings come to mind when you utter the word *money?* Fear, anxiety, peace, joy, fun, pleasure? List those responses on your paper. Again, when you've finished describing *your* feelings, write down what you think your partner's feelings are.

Also under feelings, but in a different column, list how you, and then your partner, feel about specific kinds of money-related activities like saving, investing, gambling, assuming debt, purchasing big-ticket items like cars and houses, and paying for small purchases like books or compact discs.

Finally, make another couple of columns headed Habits. Describe how each of you responds—what your habits and actions, rather than your feelings are—to the above money-related activities such as saving, spending, investing, etc. Share your lists and talk honestly about them.

Jacquie: *Watch out for rose-colored glasses. Mike likes to think he's practical about money and that he's very careful not to overspend. He actually believes he's single-handedly saving us from my improvident spending. Baloney. Yes, he's good about not overspending when it's my idea to go out to dinner, or when I come home with an unexpected purchase. But two days later, when he's in the mood for a meal out, he's very capable of conveniently forgetting the dire straits he cited earlier in the week. Then, although nothing about our finances has changed— we haven't won the lottery, for example—he'll suggest that nice Mexican restaurant we like so much. That's infuriating, to say the least.*

Mike: *Okay, guilty as charged. I admitted in chapter 1* *that I can spend money as easily as the next person. And I am sometimes inconsistent in my financial decisions. Part of this has to do with the "amiable" part of my financial personality. If we haven't dined out for a while, or one of the kids really wants something, I'll have a change of heart and part with the dough. Jacquie has every right to be frustrated with my inconsistency.*

Take Mel Prince's Money Attitude Inventory Test

To further identify your individual money attitudes and habits, take the following test created by Mel Prince, an expert on consumer behavior and marketing. Prince, who studies money attitudes, has isolated what he calls the eight major money attitude traits: impulse spending, frugality, risk aversion, nest egg mentality, gambling, self-esteem, control over one's own money, and contempt for money.

In this test he doesn't try to squeeze you into one specific category. Rather, he has prepared questions that will help you determine how strongly you possess each trait. There's no correlation between the various traits, so don't worry about making your responses consistent.

The test probably will indicate that your money attitude is composed of varied, sometimes conflicting, traits. You may already know that. For example, perhaps you're very practical and cost-conscious in most of your spending habits but insist on the best at whatever price when buying clothes, haircuts, and other items that affect your personal appearance.

We think you'll find this test an excellent self-diagnostic tool, since you need to pinpoint your own financial foibles as accurately as you can before you can merge your money style with your partner's.

Money Attitude Inventory Test

Circle the appropriate number at the right of each statement. Be sure to circle only one number for each statement. After each three questions, total the numerical value of your responses.

1=agree strongly   4=disagree somewhat
2=agree somewhat   5=disagree strongly
3=neutral

I often buy items I don't really need because they're on sale.	1 2 3 4 5
I often get carried away when I shop.	1 2 3 4 5
I tend to make financial decisions based on how I feel at the moment.	1 2 3 4 5
Subtotal #1—Impulse Spending	_____

I feel guilty when I spend money, even when it's for necessities.	1 2 3 4 5
I tend to be very critical of the way I've handled my money matters.	1 2 3 4 5
It bothers me to have to buy something when it isn't on sale.	1 2 3 4 5
Subtotal #2—Frugality	_____

Negotiating the price of a new car is a frightening experience.	1 2 3 4 5
I don't like investments where there's a chance of losing money.	1 2 3 4 5
I don't feel like I'm in control of my financial security.	1 2 3 4 5
Subtotal #3—Risk Aversion	_____

I feel it's important to have a large savings fund for emergencies.	1 2 3 4 5
I often think about the investments I should have made.	1 2 3 4 5
My parents taught me the wisdom of saving for a rainy day.	1 2 3 4 5
Subtotal #4—Nest Egg Mentality	_____

I like to gamble, but I often get carried away.	1 2 3 4 5
If I had enough money, I'd quit work and live a life of leisure.	1 2 3 4 5
I often buy lottery tickets in the hope of striking it rich.	1 2 3 4 5
Subtotal #5—Gambling	_____

I feel if I had enough money people would give me the respect I deserve.	1 2 3 4 5
I tend to measure people's success by how much money they have.	1 2 3 4 5
I judge my own success by how much money I make relative to others.	1 2 3 4 5
Subtotal #6—Self-esteem	_____

I need to be actively involved in my money matters.	1 2 3 4 5
I always know how much money I have in my wallet.	1 2 3 4 5
I tend to be very assertive in my money dealings with others.	1 2 3 4 5
Subtotal #7—Control Over Own Money	_____

Most rich people are vulgar and disgusting.	1 2 3 4 5
I only want enough money to have the freedom to do what I really want.	1 2 3 4 5
I feel that fate plays a large part in how wealthy a person becomes.	1 2 3 4 5
Subtotal #8—Contempt for Money	_____

Scoring Your Results:
3–6 Indicates a strong tendency toward the trait
7–11 Indicates a medium tendency toward the trait
12–15 Indictates a weak tendency toward the trait

Check Your Lists and Test Results against Four Classic Personality Types

Remember what financial psychologist Ken Doyle said about people's behavior and money? Doyle wrote that fights about money stem from differences between the four classic personality types: the analytical person, for whom money means control; the driven person, for whom money means competence; the expressive person, for whom money means esteem; and the amiable person, for whom money means love.

Looking at the lists you just compiled, and your test results, identify which of the four personality types comes closest to describing you. To refresh your memory about how each type handles money, here's what Doyle wrote:

Analytical: ". . . gains confidence by experiencing order and suffers anxiety at the loss of control. He or she uses money as a talisman against the loss of control, saves money to protect against unnamed threats and engages in behaviors such as bargain hunting and hoarding and those that suggest indecisiveness, cautiousness, stubbornness, and unusual ability to defer gratification."

Driven: "gains confidence by demonstrating achievement and suffers anxiety at the possible loss of competence . . . uses money as a talisman against the fear of being found incompetent, spends money on things that will 'prove' his or her success to other people . . ."

Expressive: "learned to use appearances to avoid isolation . . . stresses appearances and self-expression to the extent that one suspects a deep anxiety about what other people think. He or she uses money as a talisman against loss of self-esteem, spends money to buy respect, and engages in behavior that indicates feelings of privilege and possessions."

Amiable: "learned to use relationships to counteract feelings of isolation . . . the amiable gains confidence by receiving affection and suffers anxiety at the thought of loss of relationship. He or she uses money as a talisman against the fear of losing affection, saves money to hold on to people and engages in behaviors that indicate feelings of low self-esteem and low potency, that money is evil and that center in excessive giving, sharing, and the inability to say no."

Another Way of Analyzing Your Money Style

Just in case no flashbulbs lit up when you reviewed your lists and test results against Doyle's personality types, here's another way of looking at yourself. Olivia Mellan, a Washington, D.C., psychotherapist who specializes in money conflicts, describes five basic money styles in her book, *Money Harmony: Resolving Basic Conflicts in Your Life and Relationships.* They are: the hoarder, the spender, the money monk, the avoider, and the amasser. She adds a spin-off, the binger, and defines them all this way:

Hoarder: Likes to save money and prioritize financial goals. "You probably have a budget and may enjoy the processes of making up a budget and reviewing it periodically. You most likely have a hard time spending money on yourself and your loved ones for luxury items or even practical gifts."

Spender: Enjoys using money to buy goods and services for immediate pleasure. "You probably get satisfaction from spending money on gifts for others. The odds are that you have a hard time saving money and prioritizing things you'd like in your life. As a result, it may be difficult for you to put aside enough money for future-oriented purchases and long-term financial goals. You may spend most or all of the money you earn, and you may even be in debt." Spenders hate making budgets and adhering to them.

Binger: A combination of the hoarder and the spender. "They tend to save and save, and then blow the money all at once, like a too-tight spring that pops under excessive tension. They often spend large amounts of money on one of their spending binges." The binges, which can hit at any time, can lead to serious overspending and debt.

Money Monk: You think that money is dirty, bad, and that if you have too much of it, it will corrupt you. "In general, you believe that money is the root of all evil. You identify with people of modest means rather than with those who amass wealth. If you happen to come into a windfall . . . you would tend to be uneasy. . . . You would probably avoid investing your money, for fear that it might grow and make you even wealthier."

Avoider: You probably have a hard time balancing your checkbook and paying bills promptly. "You may avoid making a budget or keeping any kind of financial record. You won't know how much money you have, how much you owe, how much you spend." This may be because you feel incompetent about your money life or because of a "kind of aristocratic disdain toward the boring, seemingly unimportant details" of your money life.

Amasser: You are happiest when you have large amounts of money to spend, to save, or to invest. "If you are not actually spending, saving, or investing, you may feel empty or not fully alive. You tend to equate money with self-worth and power, so a lack of money may lead to feelings of failure and even depression."

Armed with your test and lists, and checking them against Doyle's and Mellan's different—but potentially complementary—approaches to financial self-analysis, your personal money styles and motivations should begin to become clear. Moreover, the reasons for the arguments you have as a couple over finances should begin to make sense. That, in itself, won't make them disappear. But only by understanding your individual attitudes toward money can you begin to marry your money styles and form a viable financial partnership.

REEVALUATE YOUR LIFESTYLE AND FINANCIAL GOALS AND PRIORITIES

Now that you each have a better understanding of your individual money styles and how they work—or *don't* work—together, it's time to figure out just where you want to go as a couple. We're talking the broad vision here, not just specific financial goals. We'll get to those in subsequent chapters. Right now, let's explore overall lifestyle goals and pinpoint what kind of life you want to lead.

You need to decide whether career is of primary importance in your life, or if family and leisure time take precedence. A recent survey of 1,000 people by Yankelovich Partners revealed that half have a lot more to do at work than they did several years ago. Almost as many reported having less time to spend with their spouses.

How important is wealth in your personal life-scheme? Do you want to lead a simplified lifestyle in which you have enough wealth to support your basic needs and family, or do you aspire to a BMW and vacation homes in Vail and Cancun?

Determine Your General Lifestyle Goals

It's not always a simple matter to figure out what kind of life you want to lead and how to get there. Many of us live day to day, paycheck to paycheck, activity to activity, without really mapping out a life path or overall goal for our lives. Such plans don't have to be restrictive—they can change as you do. But it's important for the two of you to understand as you start out what kind of lifestyle you want to lead in order to ensure you get there—together. And only by understanding your lifestyle goals can you plan your financial goals, priorities, and action plans.

In order to help you determine your lifestyle goals and priorities, you should answer the following questions together. Your answers will begin to build the foundation for your future *and* your future financial plans. You need to be honest here, because in order to manage your finances properly and ensure sufficient financial resources for the kind of future lifestyle you desire, you need to be certain about what kind of life you want to be living in five years, ten years, twenty years, and even further down the road.

So, sharpen your pencils again and take the following lifestyle attitudinal survey.

Lifestyle Attitudinal Self-Survey

What are your career interests?
- Do you enjoy your work and career?
- Would you prefer to change your job or career?
- Would you like to have the financial resources to start your own business?
- Would you prefer not to have to work at all?

What are your financial priorities?
- Do you want to be wealthy enough to live a luxurious lifestyle?
- Do you want to have just enough money to live a simple lifestyle with minimal possessions and expenses?
- Do you want to save money to provide your children with a good college education?
- Do you want to leave your children a substantial inheritance or spend what you earn?

What kind of retirement life do you want?
- Do you want a luxurious, or at least comfortable, retirement life in which you can travel and enjoy leisure time activities that cost money?
- Do you prefer a spare, simple retirement lifestyle without costly possessions and activities?
- Do you want to continue to work part-time during retirement, to remain productive or for financial reasons?

Answer these questions honestly and be sure you're on the same wavelength in terms of overall lifestyle goals. You'd be surprised how many couples neglect this simple step and then, down the road, find they're unhappy with the quality and direction of their life. They discover they can't afford to do the things they want to do, or that one partner wants fur while the other is quite happy wearing denim.

By that time it's often too late to make significant adjustments in your financial planning and management in order to support a different lifestyle. But if you can determine early in your relationship what kind of life you want to lead, you can take the appropriate steps, financially and otherwise, to get there.

A True Confession

Jacquie: *It's clear to me now that I'd deceived myself pretty well over the years about my attitude about money and how I wanted to live my life. Before Mike and I got married, I was married to a medical student who is now a wealthy heart specialist. When I learned (after marriage) that he was serious about wanting his wife to be a stay-at-home, child-raising ornament who would primarily be a testament to his wealth, I bailed out.*

A few years later I married Mike, then a struggling artist with little discernible economic potential. I was earning good money so it didn't matter. Besides, I was convinced that money wasn't important and didn't want to think about it. I assumed, of course, that it would always magically be there, ready to be spent, as it had been when I was growing up. Mike and I both made career and life choices based on the assumption that money meant little to us.

A few years ago—thankfully in time to make some changes—reality bit. Several things actually happened to open my eyes. First, I realized that I wasn't going to be promoted any higher in the hierarchy of the newspaper business, in which

I had worked nearly twenty years, and therefore couldn't antici-pate making really big bucks in my career. Then I watched my two brothers, both younger, become wealthy in the stock options business. The kind of money they were making meant they and their families were able to do things that Mike and I simply could not afford to do.

I didn't resent their financial success, and didn't want to live a totally different lifestyle. We like our lives. We're both writers and editors at an Ivy League university and we write books and freelance articles as well. The academic world we work in enhances the writing we do for ourselves, and our jobs allow us the freedom and time to travel around and watch our son play ice hockey.

But I realized and regretted the limitations we had unwit-tingly placed on our lives by the unconscious choice we made to ignore financial planning. There were things we wanted to do and places we wanted to go that we could not manage financially because we hadn't planned and invested properly. And there was also the slowly emerging specter of retirement. Those realizations propelled us to get our financial act together—finally.

Mike: *I think there are two reasons for the somewhat lack-adaisical attitude I had toward money for so many years. One was growing up in an upper-middle-class home where money was never an issue. My father had a successful career as a chemical engineer and entrepreneur, and my mother was a housewife. They put three kids through college with no financial difficulty that I was aware of, and we always had pretty much whatever we wanted. Of course, since money wasn't really talked about at home, I'm not sure I'd have been aware if there had been hard times.*

The other reason was the counterculture movement that was so pervasive in the late 60s and early 70s, which coincided with my college years and our early years together. The simple life-style was seen as noble, and the pursuit of money was considered almost immoral. This attitude certainly defined our lifestyle and those of many of our friends for quite a few years. Twenty years ago, one of Jacquie's now-wealthy, captain-of-industry brothers was living on 10 acres in rural Vermont, scratching out a living making furniture, tending bar, doing construction, and whatever else would earn him a buck.

But, like tens of thousands of other baby boomers, Jacquie and I, her brother, and most of our friends eventually discovered that children and houses and college tuition and the hope of retirement tend to make a person a bit more realistic about money. As she said, reality bit.

Recognize the Importance of Compromise and Respect

By now you've determined your individual money styles and understand why you've spent so much time fighting about money. Hopefully, you have a better understanding of what makes each of you tick, financially. With that knowledge you're on your way to marrying your money styles and becoming financial partners.

You also just performed a reality check on your respective dreams for your future. If you've discovered you're worlds apart on where you want to be headed, you have a major problem—one beyond the scope of this book. We suggest you seek professional counseling and concentrate on your nonfinancial problems. But if, by and large, you share the same goals and want to live the same kind of lifestyle, you can take some simple steps to becoming full financial partners, ready to invest in your shared future.

First, though, you need to remember a very important word: *compromise.* Among the definitions of *compromise* are "a settlement in which each side gives up some demands or makes concessions"; and "to settle or adjust by concessions on both sides."

The ability to compromise will be critical in allowing the two of you to marry your money styles. Each of you will have to change and make concessions, and those concessions must flow from mutual respect. That means you each will have to learn how to modify your behavior to adjust to one another's needs and idiosyncrasies.

For example, let's say you have an absolute compulsion to pay your credit card bills the day they arrive. You're a fanatic for order, and that seems to you the only responsible thing to do. But it happens to drive your husband crazy. First, he points out, by paying before the due date you lose the interest you can earn on the money. Furthermore, he adds, in your haste you may overlook other, more pressing debts that need to be paid or expenses that are coming up.

But he may have habits that make you crazy. For example, he may drive you up the wall by habitually overtipping waiters in restaurants. To you that seems needlessly extravagant when you need to save money for other things. Besides, you point out, it makes him look like he's trying to act like a big shot.

So, you compromise. Maybe he can agree to leave a 15 percent tip for good service, rather than 20 to 25 percent, if you agree to organize the credit card bills as they come in but defer payment until the end of the month. It's a win-win situation as the result of discussion, compromise, and respect.

Set Your Financial Goals

Together, you need to set some financial goals and develop a general plan to meet those goals. Again, we're not talking about a detailed financial plan; we'll get to that later. Right now you just need to determine short-term, mid-term, and long-term financial goals. Put these down on paper, or in your computer.

In fact, if you haven't already started a joint financial notebook, do it now. Use a three-ring binder so you can add the tests and questions and answers you did earlier, as well as information you begin to gather from other sources on financial topics.

Your short-term goals should be for three months to three years. For example, if your credit cards are maxed out, one goal should be to pay off that high-interest debt. You should plan to immediately take out a lower-interest loan, pay off the various credit cards, and then pay off the new loan as quickly as possible, but within three years at most.

Another short-term goal might be to save for holiday shopping or for a first-ever Caribbean vacation. A traditional short-term goal is to save the down payment for a house. Don't think just in terms of spending, however. One short-term goal should be to establish a savings account, however small at the start.

Mid-term goals should be from three to five years. You might want to have built up a $10,000 nest egg in your savings account. Or enough for an addition to your house in preparation for the arrival of your first child. Or for a new car or boat.

Long-term goals should include your lifetime concerns: saving for your children's college education; investing for your retirement; maybe buying a vacation home.

Whatever your goals, be sure to put several deadlines and price tags beside them in your notebook so each of you knows exactly what you're working toward. It will be much easier to forgo a new suit or gourmet dinner at a fancy new restaurant if you know that money instead will go into the savings account that in six months will buy you that Caribbean vacation.

TAKE THESE STEPS TO START YOUR NEW FINANCIAL PARTNERSHIP

Marrying your individual money styles and beginning a full financial partnership is one of the biggest challenges you will face as a couple. By now you have a better understanding of your individual money styles and how to work with them as a couple. And you've defined some lifestyle and financial goals. Now, you're probably scratching your heads and saying: "Fine, but how do we actually carry out this new financial partnership? What do we do next?"

Not to worry—we've got some simple steps to start you on your way. And if you're still fighting about money after taking these steps, we've got some remedial exercises you can do to correct the problems. But first, try the approach mapped out below.

Organize Your "Operating Committee"

Your home—and your relationship—is as much a financial institution as any business. So the first thing you need to do is organize it and run it like a business. Think of yourself and your partner as members of your corporate finance committee, and set a regular weekly meeting day, time, and place to sit and discuss financial management issues, including both short- and longer-term decisions that need to be made. You may even want to set aside time at your operating committee meeting once a month to share the actual process of paying the bills and keeping the accounts up to date.

This structure forces both of you to keep abreast of your financial situation and to participate fully in financial decisions as partners and members of the finance committee. It will also cut down on the heat-of-the-moment kinds of quarrels about money that arise when you're not talking about your finances regularly and when one of you is not fully aware of your financial circumstances.

This finance committee meeting should be conducive to work, not play. In other words, don't hold this meeting in the bedroom. And if there's a TV in the room, be sure it's turned off, not just down low. An office or den with good lighting, two comfortable, though not too cushy chairs, and a table big enough to spread out your work materials, including calculator and computer, would be ideal. Barring that, a well-lit kitchen that's off limits to the rest of the family during your committee meetings will work just fine.

You need to have an agenda for these financial pow-wows. At your first meeting, your main agenda item will be to determine your current financial status, including your assets and liabilities. More about that later. Eventually your meeting agendas will flow naturally and logically from the previous meeting, from weekly events, and from your agreed-upon goals. But it's important, especially at first, that each of you jot down agenda items as they occur to you during the week. Ideally this should be done on a computer both of you can access. If that's not possible, keep a large notepad in a regular spot at home and add to it as items occur to you.

It's best to set your meetings for the same day and time each week, otherwise they may slip away from you in the press of daily events. But that may not always be possible, so be sure to confirm your next meeting time at the end of each meeting. Make these meeting dates a serious business and don't cancel them for frivolous reasons. Remember, your future financial well-being depends on them.

Decide How to Set Up Your Accounts

There are a million ways you can set up your financial systems. Many young people just starting out immediately pool all their money in joint checking and savings accounts. They consider it a sign of their infinite love and trust. Others choose to maintain separate checking accounts but contribute to a joint savings account and joint household account. Some of these people insist on contributing equally regardless of income, while others scale their contributions to joint accounts to their earnings.

Only you can decide what works for you as a couple. Just be sure neither partner feels exploited or patronized.

Those marrying for the second or third time may be slow to merge their finances and often choose to keep at least some separate accounts. That's because their finances are usually more complex, with alimony, support payments, and expenses for the children of the various unions. Their personal holdings and investments also may be more extensive, as they usually are older and further along in their careers when they become a couple.

They may live in the house that's hers from a divorce settlement and that's to become the property of her children by her ex-husband upon her death. They may vacation at the beach house he bought with his business partner as an investment years earlier. They may have each brought their own cars to the marriage and have separate IRAs that were set up before their marriage. Her children may get ample monthly support payments from her ex while they both may share the burden of supporting his two older children who live with them. But he also sends regular support checks to his two youngest, who live with their mother.

You get the picture. Sorting all that out while avoiding hurt feelings and building trust in a new relationship may require the tact of a diplomat and the financial skills of a CPA.

Lisa Bennett and Kate Frankfurt, Brooklynites who work hard to manage their money, have separate checking accounts for personal expenses. But they share all expenses they have in common—rent, utilities, and food—by each putting the same amount into a third account each month. "But we don't get anal about every penny," Lisa says.

She points out that finances can get complicated for gay couples. Lisa and Kate are "out"—they live openly together as a gay couple and do share a joint savings account. But they have to maintain separate medical insurance policies, meeting separate deductibles. That gets costly.

Mark Levine and Deirdre Martin, on the other hand, merge all their money into one checking account. They also maintain joint investment accounts. Freelance writers who live in upstate New York, they don't have the financial predictability of regular paychecks. Their income arrives sporadically in large chunks, so they are both very careful about budgeting and keeping track of expenditures. In fact, as we'll see in a minute, they share just about every aspect of their financial situation.

Divide Financial Tasks

If you're really going to be full financial partners, it's important that you share the daily, weekly, and monthly financial tasks your partnership requires. Determine who will sort the bills, pay the bills, track expenses and income, track the budget, write the checks, stuff and mail the envelopes, decide on the investments, and deposit the savings. You can divide these tasks according to your individual interests and skills, and they don't necessarily have to be divided equally.

Some couples, like writers Mark and Deirdre, handle *all* their financial activities together, even to the point of taking turns paying the bills each month.

"We're both terribly neurotic about money," says Mark. "And since our cash flow comes in spurts rather than in a steady stream, it makes us both feel more at ease if we play as active a role as possible in managing our finances."

But not every couple needs to be so precise. The idea isn't necessarily to accomplish an exact 50/50 split of duties, but the active engagement, physically as well as mentally, of both partners in the process. Even if you're just licking stamps for envelopes in which to pay the bills, chances are you'll feel you have a higher stake in your family's finances than you would if all the financial activities took place in a vacuum, somewhere out of your sight.

Jacquie: *For years I let Mike handle all our finances, including the monthly drudgery of paying bills, setting aside savings for big items, and overseeing our retirement plans and investments. My lack of participation related to my former inability to deal with money. And frankly, he liked the work— sort of. He has a streak of the accountant in him, thank goodness. But it was a big burden as well, especially when times were tight and I was an ostrich, hiding my head in financial oblivion.*

Over the years Mike would sometimes try to wash his hands of these chores, particularly when I was more unreasonable than usual about money, but I always knew in the end he'd prefer to do the job his way to be sure of the end result. His willingness to go it alone only served to perpetuate my financial recalcitrance.

Mike: *I do have a bit of accountant in me, and one reason I liked to take care of our finances myself was the sense that in doing so I was keeping things under control. But eventually I realized that I was kidding myself. We were totally out of control. And the cause of our financial free fall was our inability to make decisions together.*

We weren't teetering on the edge of bankruptcy or anything. But we had a lot of credit card debt, and when we did manage to put money aside we usually ended up pulling it out and spending it later. We learned the hard way that having just one person involved in the finances doesn't work, particularly when the other person has an extreme aversion to the topic. It can only lead to anger and even worse communication.

Determine Your Net Worth

The first agenda item at your first finance committee meeting will be a discussion of your current financial situation. To put that into perspective, you need to determine your net worth, including your assets and liabilities. One of you can do the legwork on this before the meeting, and then discuss the report together, or you can work together to compile and analyze the information. We recommend the latter, as a way of really digging in and getting started together, right from the get-go. Here's what you need to do:

First, do an inventory of everything you own that has financial value. (Use the worksheet on page 46 as a guide.) List tangible assets such as your home, vacation or rental property, investment-quality art or jewelry, collectibles, and antiques. If you aren't sure, estimate conservatively.

Next, itemize investments such as checking and savings accounts, cash-value life insurance policies, certificates of deposit, Individual Retirement Accounts, stocks, bonds, and mutual funds. Check last year's tax return for investments you may have overlooked. Also check through your safety deposit box for forgotten assets like savings bonds. And don't forget pension funds. If you have a guaranteed pension, your employer's benefits department can tell you its current value. Once you've listed all your assets, compute the current value.

Next, figure out your liabilities. List all your debts, including mortgages, loans, credit card balances, and any other outstanding bills. (Speaking of bills, this is also a good time to check your credit rating. Contact one of the following credit rating agencies and order a copy of your credit report: Trans-Union, 800-916-8800; TRW, 800-682-7654; or Equifax, 800-685-1111. Credit, and how you use or abuse it, can have a major impact on your relationship. For a full explanation of the credit conundrum, see chapter 4.) Add up your liabilities, then subtract them from your assets. The result is your current overall net worth. If the bottom line strikes fear in your heart, don't panic. This is a critical first pit stop on the road to financial security. Later, in chapter 3, you'll use this information to help you draw up a new, realistic, yet ambitious household budget.

Use this tally sheet to compute your household's net worth:

ASSETS

Cash/equivalents

    Cash on hand, checking account(s)   _____

    Savings accounts   _____

    Money-market accounts   _____

    Certificates of deposit   _____

Securities

    Stocks   _____

    Bonds   _____

    Mutual funds   _____

    Limited partnerships   _____

    Other   _____

Retirement plans

    IRAs   _____

    401(k)s   _____

    Profit sharing   _____

    Pension   _____

Insurance

    Cash-value life   _____

    Annuities   _____

Real estate

    Residence   _____

    Vacation property   _____

    Rental property   _____

    Land   _____

Antiques/collectibles/jewelry/art   _____

Business equity   _____

Personal property   _____

Automobiles   _____

Other vehicles (boats, motorcycles, RVs, etc.)   _____

Other property   _____

                         Total Assets   _____

LIABILITIES

Real estate loans

  Primary home mortgage   _____

  Second mortgage/home equity loan   _____

  Home equity line of credit   _____

  Vacation home mortgage   _____

  Rental property loan   _____

Installment loans

  Auto   _____

  Education   _____

  Other   _____

Credit card balances   _____

Brokerage account loans   _____

Insurance policy loans   _____

401(k) loans   _____

Other   _____

                                    _____

Total Liabilities   _____

TOTAL ASSETS   _____

LESS TOTAL LIABILITIES   _____

NET WORTH   _____

TEN TIPS FOR COPING WITH SETBACKS IN YOUR BUDDING FINANCIAL PARTNERSHIP

So far in this chapter you've determined your individual money styles and gained insight into how to marry those disparate styles. You've reevaluated your overall lifestyle priorities and set short-, mid-, and long-term financial goals. Then, you took some practical steps to start on the road to financial union. It's now clear sailing toward financial security.

Well, maybe not. There's probably still a cloud or two in the sky. Even an occasional downpour. Don't worry, that's to be expected. No couple can cure their financial disorders overnight. You'll experience setbacks where your different money styles once again clash. If that happens, call an emergency meeting of your finance committee and consider the following coping strategies:

Tip #1—Pay Yourself Before Paying Your Bills

It's hard to find money for a savings account, particularly if you first plow through your routine expenses and pile of bills, then try to find whatever's left over. Usually you'll come up empty-handed. So try making a savings deposit on the first of each month, before you start paying any bills. You may need to start small, but at least you'll establish the habit of saving, and in time the savings amount will grow.

Tip #2—Set Individual "Safe-Spending" Levels

If you don't like the idea of separate checking accounts but don't want the threat of potential arguments over every "unnecessary" purchase, set aside a specific amount (don't call it a limit) that each of you can spend for nonessentials on a weekly or monthly basis. This is not an allowance for daily living expenses, like bus or taxi fare, gas, lunch money, and the like. Rather, this should be for real "extras," self-indulgences like clothes and accessories, recreation equipment, or even an unbudgeted trip to the ballet or a morning at a spa.

Tip #3—Set a "Red Alert" Level

This is the flip side of the previous tip. Agree that neither of you will make any purchase above a certain dollar amount—say $25 or $50, depending on your circumstances—without consulting the other. This gives each of you some flexibility and autonomy but places realistic limits on your spending.

Tip #4—Try the Combination Approach to Spending

If you just can't agree on what type of purchases to make, let the spender pick out the top-of-the-line VCR, while the hoarder gets to choose the competitively priced, reliable TV set. You both get to make a choice, to satisfy your deeper, talismanic money needs, and maybe you can even learn something from each other.

Tip #5—Try Role-Reversal

Have the spender agree to refrain from making one impulse purchase a week for a month, while the hoarder makes one impulse purchase each week. This reversal will help you better understand your partner's money style and should help you both moderate your habits.

Tip #6—Make Deals

If one partner is dying to make some big purchases while the other is frantic to save for a rainy day, make a deal to defer the purchase of costly items until you've saved a decent emergency fund. Then, the spender gets a chance to splurge, within reasonable, agreed-upon limits.

Tip #7—Alternate Goals

If you really have trouble agreeing over short-term goals, try taking the "your-turn-my-turn approach." If you take turns setting and reaching short-term goals, you may be able to come to agreement on longer-term goals.

Tip #8—Try "Single Item Deprivation"

If you need to cut costs to meet your financial goals, try eliminating one or two items completely instead of reducing expenses across the board. Trying to cut back on everything at once can lead to frustration and instant couples combustion. Maybe clean your own house for a while instead of paying a cleaning service. Or wash your own car, or take your lunch instead of eating out. Most of us can find some "sacrifice" we can make, if we have a specific goal in mind.

Tip #9—Revamp Your Reward System

Too many of us buy things we don't need as a reward: we're feeling down and need cheering up, or we've had a tough week, or we've been good for awhile about watching what we spend. Try rewarding yourself in other ways that don't mean additional expense, like going for a walk with the dog, or spending an extra hour or two reading a trashy novel instead of cleaning the house. Or, reward yourself with smaller, less expensive purchases like a book, dessert out, or Saturday breakfast at a diner instead of more clothes, jewelry, or dinner at a gourmet restaurant.

Tip #10—Dump and Run

If all else fails to cure a chronic overspender or a partner who simply can't get it together to pay attention to finances, dump all your family's financial responsibilities on them for a month or two. Hand them the checkbook and the bills, and refuse to participate. The shock of seeing the numbers in black and white, or maybe red, might sober your partner and bring him or her into the partnership as a full participant. Of course, it could also lead to bankruptcy, so think twice before trying this strategy.

There's no magic formula for maintaining a successful financial partnership. In the end it comes down to mutual understanding, respect, goal-setting, compromise, organization, and hard work. In the months ahead when you get stressed out over trying to put together a complete financial plan for a lifetime together, read back over this chapter for insight, inspiration, and practical advice. Use the strategies outlined above. You'll be amazed at how well they work.

By now you should have held your first finance committee meeting. You should have calculated and discussed your net worth. It's time to move on to the next step: to figure out how to live within a weekly and monthly budget that will allow you to increase that net worth and set you on the road to financial security. In chapter 3 we'll do just that.

3

Establishing a Household Budget

Budget. The very word sends shivers down many spines. For those who fear or hate the word, it translates to "budge," as in "No power on earth can make me budge. Or follow a budget."

The word *budget* actually does derive from the French word *bouge*, which means a leather bag or purse. But for our purposes we'll go with Webster's definition: "a plan or schedule adjusting expenses during a certain period to the estimated or fixed income for that period."

For those of you with orderly tendencies, that concept can bring the same feeling of comfort as grandma's goose down quilt. And the bottom line is, even if it hurts a little bit at first, a household budget is essential to sound financial planning. The preparation and execution of a good budget will help you gain control over your finances by helping you determine exactly what you're spending and why you're spending it. Once you know what you're spending in a given category, and what you actually need to spend, you will be able to make any adjustments necessary to achieve your financial goals.

Jacquie: *By now you've probably guessed, I'm one of those who always hated the word* budget. *For me it conjures a very specific image from early childhood. When I was very young my father worked as a carpenter while putting himself through* *architecture school. My mother was a homemaker and money was, to say the least, tight.*

In those days they had a very strict household budget and it worked very simply. Each week my father doled out to my mother her household cash, in crisp green bills, which she slipped into neatly categorized sections of a dark brown cardboard accordion folder. The folder was then tied around the middle with an attached string, and hidden in the linen closet.

My father was, and still is, a kind, generous man. He would give me the world if he had it to give. But in those days he seemed to me an enormous giant, a very strong man and an immutable authority figure. By contrast my mother seemed weak and powerless, and that accordion file, that budget, was to me a symbol of her lack of power. The symbol oppressed me and today I still find the word "budget" abhorrent.

So we don't call ours a budget. It's a "financial plan," and I'm happy to say it works for both of us.

Mike: *Budget, schmudget. I don't care what she calls it as long as she sticks to it. The lesson to be learned here is if you've historically had a problem managing your income and expenses, play whatever little game you need to get your spending under control. If you need to call it a "financial plan," call it a financial plan. If you're more comfortable with "fiscal accountability report," use that. Names don't matter. It's the results that count.*

ANALYZING YOUR CASH FLOW

In chapter 2 you determined your net worth and outlined your financial goals. Now you need to complete your financial self-analysis by analyzing your cash flow—your expenses and sources of income. This is important for four reasons:

- It will show you whether you are living within or beyond your income.

- It will give you a firm idea of your standard of living.
- It will indicate your savings potential.
- It will pinpoint financial problem areas.

In doing your cash flow analysis you'll list all the expenditures you make on a regular or occasional basis and compare those with your income (there's a worksheet on page 55 to help with this exercise). This will define your current standard of living, help you later in determining what adjustments you need to make to change that standard of living, and prepare for the future, including retirement.

Keep two things in mind as you do your cash flow analysis: be complete and honest, and don't underestimate your expenses. Your budget and financial success will only be as successful as your numbers are real. If you fudge, you're only cheating yourself and your long-term financial success.

You can assemble your cash flow worksheet either by winging it—guess-timating your expense numbers—or by actually tracking those numbers. If you decide to track, you can do it historically, with records and receipts from the past six months, assuming you have them, or by carefully keeping such records for the next three months. Either way will work if you're honest and if you have an honest interest in sticking to a budget.

Jacquie: *Just wing it. A budget is only an experiment anyway, and you're going to have to be somewhat flexible the first year or two until you get the hang of it. Don't get overly anal before you even get started or you'll kill each other just over the budget preparation process.*

Mike: *Wrong. You need to be as precise as possible. (Can you see where we still have a few financial differences?) A budget is only as good as the numbers that go into it. If you don't* *have records, start tomorrow by tracking every single expense. Being thorough is the key.*

CASH FLOW WORKSHEET

INCOME

	Monthly	Annual
Salary	_____	_____
Bonuses	_____	_____
Self-employment income	_____	_____
Rental income	_____	_____
Dividends	_____	_____
Interest	_____	_____
Capital gains	_____	_____
Royalties	_____	_____
Social Security	_____	_____
Pension income	_____	_____
Other income	_____	_____
Total Cash Available	$_____	$_____

EXPENSES

Mortgage/rent	_____	_____
Utilities	_____	_____
Gas/oil	_____	_____
Electric	_____	_____
Water	_____	_____
Sewer	_____	_____
Property taxes	_____	_____
Home maintenance	_____	_____
Car payments	_____	_____
Car/commuting expenses	_____	_____
Maintenance/repairs	_____	_____
Gas	_____	_____
Commuting fees/tolls	_____	_____
Credit card/loan payments	_____	_____
Insurance premiums	_____	_____

Life	_____	_____
Health	_____	_____
Disability	_____	_____
Home	_____	_____
Car	_____	_____
Liability	_____	_____
Other	_____	_____
Income taxes	_____	_____
Employment taxes	_____	_____
Food	_____	_____
Clothing	_____	_____
Medical expenses	_____	_____
Child care	_____	_____
Education	_____	_____
Entertainment	_____	_____
Vacations	_____	_____
Alimony	_____	_____
Gifts	_____	_____
Personal needs	_____	_____
Charitable contributions	_____	_____
Savings/investments	_____	_____
Emergency fund	_____	_____
Vacation fund	_____	_____
Investment fund	_____	_____
Other	_____	_____
Other payments	_____	_____
Total Expenses	($_____)	($_____)
Net Cash Flow	$_____	$_____

Obviously, you may need to adapt this worksheet to suit your own particular circumstances. Be sure you include all regular expenditures, but don't forget to include infrequent or one-of-a-kind expenses like new brakes for the car, a new hot water heater, a new garage roof, or your best friend's daughter's baby gift. You don't want to have to steal from your food fund to pay for baby booties. This requires a little foresight. You can't predict all your expenses, but if you know something is going to need repair or replacing, factor it into your expenses.

Analyze your completed worksheet carefully to understand exactly where your money is coming from and where it's going. Are you saving what you need and spending on what's most important to you? Are there some surprises? Are you spending a lot more in certain areas than you thought? Are there places you can trim and reallocate, perhaps putting more in savings or a vacation fund? If you want to make some changes in your spending and saving habits, now's the time to do it.

As a reality check, you may want to compare each category of expenditure to those of other Americans. According to a 1992 survey published in *Consumer Reports*, readers reported spending 26 percent of their annual income on state, federal, and local taxes and Social Security; 21 percent on housing costs, including rent or mortgage; 14 percent on food; 9 percent on transportation; 8 percent on savings and investments; 5 percent on vacations; 4 percent on health care and health insurance; 3 percent on clothing; and 10 percent on other things.

Alarmed that expenditure profile is a bit different than your own? Don't be. Just remember that the average *Consumer Reports* reader is a bit more financially responsible than most people. After all, that's why they read the magazine in the first place.

You Need to Be Flexible

Remember, any household budget should be flexible enough to adapt to your own changing needs and priorities. You don't want to feel imprisoned by your own budget, or you'll soon find at least one of you making a break for freedom—maybe in the form of a shopping spree not soon forgotten, as the bills keep pouring in.

And priorities do change. An April 14, 1997 article by Christina Duff in the *Wall Street Journal* reported that an analysis of consumer spending since 1989 showed major shifts in priorities. According to Duff, American families "have grown less house-proud and car crazy during the 1990s, and are plowing more of their income into goods or services that they think will help them stay healthy, on the go and in the know: mountain bikes, educational toys, museum memberships, chiropractic sessions, computers and home-entertainment centers."

Key Commerce Department statistics were cited in the article:

- Total U.S. spending rose 15 percent to almost $5 trillion since 1989, while spending on new cars and trucks dropped 28 percent, to $73.65 billion.
- Spending on home computers is a 12 times bigger portion of total spending than seven years ago.
- In 1996 Americans spent $22.05 billion at casinos, more than twice what they gambled away in 1989.
- Spending on alternative medicine jumped 69 percent.
- Overall sporting goods spending rose 53 percent to $17.36 billion.

The article concluded that "essentials—food, shelter, clothing and medical care—still eat up about half of the average household budget, just as they did in 1989. But even within these stable categories, tastes are changing and expenses are being reallocated—particularly by those with the most disposable income to play with."

Easy Credit May Be a Problem

You may find that easy credit is wreaking havoc on your spending habits. Experts say about 10 percent of Americans overextend on credit routinely, and they offer this guideline: If you find you're spending more than 20 percent of your salary, not including mortgages, on credit purchases even before your paycheck arrives, you're overextended and won't have any discretionary income to budget. If you're in that category, a carefully structured budget—and one you can live with—can help you out of your credit hole. (We'll look at the advantages and pitfalls of credit in detail in chapter 4.)

Keep Simple—But Accurate—Records

While it might be okay to wing it when you fill out your cash flow worksheet, it's now time to end any flights of fantasy and start keeping good, detailed records of your income and expenditures. This will help your financial management in two ways.

First, it will simplify that most onerous of jobs, the tracking of business and living expenses for tax purposes. Imagine, if you will, an April 14 in which you *aren't* tearing out each other's hair, screaming, and hunting madly for receipts and check stubs under the bed and in the back of desk drawers.

Second, once you have your budget set, if you keep accurate and up-to-date records you can compare your actual spending in specific categories with your budget and spot problem spending areas before they get out of hand. In fact, you'll know exactly where you are and how well you're doing in adhering to your spending plan, while it's not too late to make changes.

Some couples get overwrought about the best way to go about their record keeping and accounting. It seems like a major undertaking and far too complicated to deal with. It's easier, in fact, to just stuff those receipts into any old drawer, along with bobby pins and parking tickets and the kids' report cards.

But the great thing is you can tailor your record keeping to your personal style, or to the style of whichever partner is going to keep the records. And it can be as simple as a shoe box, or set of shoe boxes, or as high-tech as a sophisticated computer software program for household financial management. There are many such programs on the market, and most are quite affordable.

A compromise between the two is an old-fashioned, handwritten ledger book or spiral notebook, in which you log all your expenditures as you go. That's just a step away from a budget book, where you can tally the month's expenditures in a given category and record it next to the budgeted amount. In fact, any combination of the above will work just fine, provided you both know how the system works, agree to make it work, and can relieve each other as needed in maintaining the records.

Jacquie: *Record keeping has been a real problem for me, and of course that means it's a nightmare for Mike, our accountant, at the end of the month. I'm usually in such a rush I can't always remember or find the time to write down the check number or amount of a check when making a purchase. My intentions are good, but sometimes I remember one, and not the other. I don't intend to make his life miserable in quite this way, but it happens.*

I remember as far back as college days when the bank would send me an overdraft statement. I'd call my mother frantically and insist she march up to the bank to tell them they were wrong, they'd made a mistake. And I had my checkbook record to prove it. Of course the bank was never wrong. I'd simply forgotten to write down one critical check, written on the fly.

I'm really making an effort now and have improved. And guess what. Last weekend Mr. Perfect Financial Wizard borrowed my checkbook at the mall, and I discovered an hour later he'd neglected to write down the check and the amount for our Eddie Bauer spring fling.

Mike: *Oh, yeah?! Well, why don't you mention the time you forgot to give me the ATM receipt for a $300 withdrawal* *from our checking account? That little debit went unrecorded for a couple of weeks until I got a call from a local merchant (fortunately it was a friend) to tell me I'd bounced a check.*

Seriously, though, record keeping is difficult even for the most organized of people. We operate with two separate checkbooks drawn on one checking account (hey, whatever works, right?), so I try to enter any checks that have been written or ATM withdrawals made in a master ledger every evening when I get home. I've found that the system works fine—IF I keep it up to date. As soon as I fall behind, we lose track of what we're spending, and things get all out of whack. Whatever system you choose, the key to making it work is keeping it current.

PREPARING YOUR BUDGET

Okay. You're holding regular weekly finance committee meetings. You've analyzed your net worth and your cash flow, you've set financial goals and priorities, and you've started keeping detailed records of your income and expenditures. You're on your way to gaining control over your finances. You're taking charge. The next step is to actually prepare (and then follow) your budget.

Before you put your budget on paper (or in the computer), do a reality check on the foundation on which your budget will be based: your income. Just how secure is each partner's income? Could an unplanned pregnancy, business downsizing, or buyout alter that income stream, and with it your financial stability? If there is any insecurity in your job or income, be very conservative in your spending plan. In fact, budget for a bigger emergency fund right from the start, if a suddenly reduced income is at all likely.

You can use your cash flow worksheet as the basis for your budget document. Remember, though, that there's one key difference between the two: the cash flow analysis was a historical record of what your expenditures have been. Your new budget document will be a road map detailing what you *plan* to spend. This is where you need to start making changes in your spending habits in order to achieve your new goals.

So simply take another blank copy of that cash flow worksheet and revise it as necessary to turn it into a spending plan tailored to achieving your goals. Under "Monthly," add a column labeled "Amount Budgeted" and one labeled "Amount Spent." Do the same for "Annual."

Your budget will take the guesswork out of your finances. No more figuring "Hey, sure, what's one more dinner and movie out? We can probably afford it." Maybe you can afford it in the sense that there's money in your checking account. But maybe that money should be allocated for something else: winter boots for the kids, a tune-up for the car, or the electric bill.

Without a written budget, you wouldn't know exactly where your finances stand at any given moment. You might know how much money is in your checking account, but you wouldn't know exactly what that money was needed for. But if you're operating your household on a budget, and keep your expenditure records up-to-date, you can check to see if you've spent all the recreation/entertainment money budgeted for the current month, or whether there's enough left over for another dinner out.

Two reminders here: be realistic and be flexible. In drawing up your budget do not underestimate your expenses just so you can build in a regular weekly dinner out. That's a recipe for red ink. If you honestly want to create a solid financial partnership and real financial security, you have to be honest about expenses and income.

On the other hand, it may take you some months to

fine-tune your budget, so don't get frustrated if a couple of unexpected expenses throw a kink in your spending plan in the beginning. Just be flexible and accommodate those expenses by cutting down elsewhere without cutting into savings.

And be flexible enough to accommodate occasionally changing priorities. If you've spent the monthly entertainment budget but really crave a night out at dinner and a movie, decide what you can do without until next month. Some things can wait, after all. Just make sure you're spending money that was to be used for another discretionary purchase like a new sport coat and not money that was designated for the utility bill.

Look on it as a challenge, maybe even a jigsaw puzzle. You'll be surprised, once you get into it, how much satisfaction you can find in making a budget work.

USING YOUR BUDGET

Your budget may be a masterpiece of documentation, compromise, and planning, but it's worthless unless you actually put it to use. You may revise it, alter it, and curse at it, but whatever you do, don't ignore it. Drawing up the budget is not enough. That's just the starting point.

Whether you use the high-tech computer method of tracking your budget or the low-tech, handwritten method, post a copy of your budget someplace obvious and convenient—the refrigerator, a bulletin board, the hall table, or a desk in the study. Then, update the budget daily, recording all expenses in each expense category on the budget itself, in the appropriate expense category.

Or, if you're maintaining a separate ledger for all daily expenses, keep that right with your budget document. Both partners should record daily expenses in the ledger. Then, at or before your weekly finance meeting, the designated "accountant" in the relationship can transfer the week's expenses, by category, to the budget. And budget review should always be an item on your weekly meeting agenda.

The key to a successful household budget is simple:

• Be consistent in your budgeting effort. One month on and three off will get you nowhere but more frustrated.

• Keep detailed, accurate records, according to a system that works well for both of you. If you need a combination shoe box and ledger approach because one partner can't operate without that shoe box, so be it. The more organized or patient partner can gather the shoe box receipts weekly and update the ledger and budget.

• Be disciplined about limiting expenditures. If you don't have to curb expenditures, you don't need a budget. But if you had unlimited resources, not only would you not need a budget but you also wouldn't be reading this book. Budgeting means predetermining your expenditures according to your income and personal plan—a plan designed to achieve a specific set of goals. If you blow off the budget and refuse to limit your expenditures according to your plan, you might as well forget your goals. You'll never get there.

If you follow your plan, on the other hand, you can't miss. Financial success, as you've defined it in your goals and budget plan, is sure to follow.

A Helpful Hint for Compulsive Spenders

If either partner still has a serious problem with compulsive spending and runaway debt, review chapters 1 and 2. If that doesn't suggest sufficient ways to cure the problem, try Debtors Anonymous. The program is modeled after the 12-step Alcoholics Anonymous program, and has had much success with people from all walks of life and all socioeconomic backgrounds. For information, check your telephone book, or write to the group's national headquarters at Debtors Anonymous, P.O. Box 400, Grand Central Station, New York, NY 10163-0400.

WHAT'S NEXT?

If you've followed our advice and done your homework, you're off and running now as financial partners heading for financial success. Of course, in addition to establishing goals and preparing a budget, you'll need some other help to create a complete financial partnership and ensure financial success. The next step is to establish joint and separate credit. Read on.

4

The Credit Conundrum

This chapter focuses on one of the most necessary—and vexing—aspects of dealing with money: the use of credit. Handled wisely, credit can make your life together easier and more pleasant. Handled poorly, it can bring the two of you to your knees under the weight of excessive debt and unmanageable monthly payments. In the worst of cases, it can cause you to lose valued possessions, including even your home. Learning to use credit wisely is critical to both your financial health and the health of your relationship.

THE PROS AND CONS OF CREDIT

Unless one or both of you are independently wealthy, you're going to need credit at various times during your life together. Let's look at the pros and cons of borrowing.

The Advantages of Credit

Used correctly, credit is a wonderful financial tool. It has three main advantages.

Credit allows you to make major purchases. While the two of you undoubtedly have no problems buying the weekly groceries, putting gas in the car, paying the utility bills, and managing life's other day-to-day expenses, you more than likely don't have the cash needed for more expensive purchases like automobiles and houses. Credit allows you to borrow the money needed to buy them.

Credit provides convenience. Before the first credit cards were issued back in the 1950s, people had three ways of making purchases: they could pay with cash, pay with a check, or establish an account with a merchant and charge their purchases by signing a copy of the receipt. The disadvantage was that most such arrangements were possible only with local merchants. When people traveled, they needed to carry a lot of money with them. This was inconvenient and risky.

Today, however, all our purchases can be handled with a little plastic card. We can travel around the world and charge just about anything to our credit cards. It eliminates the need to carry a great deal of cash or even a checkbook. We just sign our names to the purchase slips and then pay for everything when the monthly bill arrives. Plus we get a neat, itemized accounting of where we made purchases that helps us monitor our spending.

Credit provides access to money for emergencies. Credit also allows us to get the money we need to deal with personal or financial crises.

The Disadvantages of Credit

Used unwisely, credit can drag consumers into perilous financial waters. Here are the main reasons why.

Credit is too easily available. If you're like us, not a week goes by without several credit card offers arriving in the mail. Most of them are "pre-approved," a fact that screams out at us in large letters right on the envelope. All we have to do is answer a few questions, sign the agreement, send it back to the bank that's issuing the card, and bingo, we have another $5,000 worth of credit. Even our daughter, a 19-year-old college student with sporadic and low-paying employment, has a credit card (which she has handled very responsibly, thank goodness). If she wanted to, she could probably have three or four.

For too many consumers, the lure of all these offers is impossible to ignore, and they end up with five, six, or seven or more cards. (There are currently nearly 900 million credit cards in the wallets and purses of Americans with a cumulative $3 *trillion* in buying power.) However, that in itself is not the problem. Here's the problem.

Credit makes overspending too easy. People get into trouble with credit cards because they treat them as loans rather than as a convenient way to purchase goods and services. People realize they have an enormous amount of purchasing power with that little piece of plastic. When they see something they want—and may even need—but don't have the cash to purchase the item, they charge it to their credit card. In 1996, Americans purchased nearly $450 billion worth of goods and services with their cards.

The problem is this behavior can become a pattern that can go on for some time until one day the person suddenly comes to the realization that their monthly credit card payments have begun to take up an enormous part of their net income. By the time the payments are made, there's barely enough money left over for the mortgage, the groceries, the car payment, and the other monthly bills. If the situation becomes bad enough, it can lead to the next problem.

Credit can result in financial ruin. If you've been paying attention to reports in the media over the last couple of years, you'll know that personal bankruptcies are at an all-time high. Thousands of people, saddled with debts that cumulatively far exceed their assets, are filing for bankruptcy and simply walking away from their creditors to start their financial lives all over again.

Some of these people are the victims of job losses or other unfortunate occurrences. But many got themselves in over their heads by accumulating huge credit card debts. Some of them are compulsive spenders. One of the network news shows did a piece a few years ago on a woman who had accrued tens of thousands of dollars worth of credit card debt from clothing purchases. The clothes literally filled a bedroom, and the stack of unpaid bills was nearly a foot thick. But the most ridiculous aspect of the situation was that none of the clothing had ever been worn. It was still in bags and on hangers with the tags attached.

Mike: *Here's another confession. We were once very careless with credit cards and found ourselves with a fairly hefty debt load. We had several VISA and MasterCard accounts, and at one point had pretty much reached our credit limit on each of them.*

Of course, the banks loved us. They were earning 18 and 19 percent on their money while we slowly whittled away at our balances. Because we always made our monthly payments and were usually able to pay at least twice the minimum payment, they saw us as ideal customers. They would increase our credit limits and send us more checks to use for cash advances. Other banks, smelling blood, would deluge us with offers of their own for yet more cards.

Somewhere deep within our troubled financial souls, we knew we were being idiots. But we sort of became accustomed to factoring those card payments into our budget. They became as much a part of our lives as the mortgage and the car payment and the utility bill. So for a long time we just kept writing checks (and charging purchases).

The light bulb finally went off when our daughter was about 10 years old and I started worrying about paying for college. At that point, we had very little money put aside, and I began to panic. This led me to the first serious, in-depth assessment of our finances. That's when the reality of just how much money we were throwing away on interest finally hit me. Paying down that debt became our first priority. We took out a home equity loan (at a lower interest rate than the cards), paid all the banks, and turned in all but one credit card. Two years later we had paid off the loan. Since then, we've used credit cards the way they're supposed to be used, as a convenience. And although I can't honestly say we never carry a balance, we rarely owe more than a few hundred dollars.

Jacquie: *My money myopia really was evident in my credit card use. I never saw the statements and really didn't pay attention to how much I was spending. If I wanted it, I charged it. Mike would periodically complain, and that would curtail my spending for a bit. But eventually I would return to my old ways.*

Again, as in changing many of our other habits, the key for getting our credit card spending under control was communication. When Mike finally freaked out over our credit card debt, he gave me a list showing who we owed money to and how much we owed. Then he showed me how much of our monthly payments were going toward interest. I'll have to admit I was shocked. That finally made it real for me.

Paying off those debts was a very liberating experience. It also made us feel more like partners.

ESTABLISHING CREDIT

We've learned that credit is a two-edged sword that can cut deeply when misused. But the fact remains that credit is a virtual necessity in our society. Getting it, and maintaining it, takes a bit of effort.

The Equal Credit Opportunity Act

As a consumer, it's important that you know that your right to credit is protected by the Equal Opportunity Credit Act. This piece of legislation was designed to eliminate the lending discrimination against minorities and women that plagued the financial industry for decades. The act states that lenders cannot consider sex, race, religion, marital status, or national origin when considering an applicant's creditworthiness. Age is treated a little differently, and can be considered in a few very special instances. For applicants over age 62, however, age cannot be considered.

The act also requires lenders to respond to credit applicants within thirty days of the application date. This prevents them from resorting to the old trick of not responding at all. If you are turned down, or offered less credit than you wanted, the lender must either inform you as to the exact reason or tell you that you have a right to know the reason. If you choose to find out, you can file a request for the information within sixty days. The lender then has thirty days to respond to your request.

Obtaining a Credit Card

The best way to begin to establish credit is to get a credit card. These days, it's quite easy (easier than it should be, in fact) to get one. As we mentioned earlier, even our daughter, a college student with little income, was solicited by a bank and given a card.

Actually, college students, particularly seniors who are about to graduate and enter the job market, are a common target of most credit card companies. The companies reason, quite rightly, that parents sleep a little easier knowing that with the card tucked away in their pockets their son or daughter can deal with a sudden financial emergency. (Of course, if the card is filled up with purchases from the Gap and the local beer emporium, it won't do much good.) Some companies will allow a student to open an account in their own name. Others might require that a parent also be listed on the account.

Mike: *I got my first credit card, a MasterCard that I still have today, more than twenty years ago when I was in college. I received a call from the bank with whom I had a checking account telling me I'd been preapproved for a card with a $500 credit limit. All I had to do was sign the application form they would send me.*

Of course, I was dumbfounded. Here I was in school, without a regular job, and a bank wanted to give me a credit card. I looked around at the hovel of an apartment I shared with two other guys and thought, "If they could see this place, they'd never do this." At the same time, I was somewhat flattered. It almost made me feel like a real adult. So I said sure, send me the form. I signed it, sent it back, and a week later, the card arrived in the mail.

I'll have to admit that in accepting their offer, establishing credit was the furthest thing from my mind. Nonetheless, I did find myself very careful with the card and was quite prudent in using it. And I always paid the bills in full. So, in spite of my naiveté, I was in fact getting my credit record off to a good start.

Jacquie: *I had a credit card in college that my father had given me for emergencies. The account was in his name, though, so the bills went directly to him. Of course, his idea of an emergency and my idea of an emergency didn't always mesh. To him, an emergency was getting stranded somewhere with a broken-down car. To me, an emergency was not having the cash I needed for a pair of shoes or a sweater that I desperately wanted. So out came the card.*

Needless to say, this often resulted in exasperated phone calls from home telling me to stop. But it was only when my father started deducting such expenditures from my monthly allowance that I was able to keep the card in my wallet.

For those who aren't so fortunate to have the banks knocking on their door, getting credit can be a vicious circle: You can't get a credit card without having established credit, and you can't establish credit without a credit card. It is something of a catch-22, but there are ways to deal with the problem.

Start Small

The best way to start establishing credit is to apply for a gasoline company or department store card. These are the two easiest types of credit card to obtain because these companies use them as marketing tools to entice people to spend their money with them. In effect, by granting credit, they're creating customers. Your credit line will no doubt be quite modest, maybe $500, but that's not a problem. You're not interested in buying a house, you're interested in demonstrating your fiscal responsibility.

You can accomplish this by using these cards for small purchases. Fill up the tank a couple of times or go to the department store and buy some socks. When the bills come, pay them off immediately. Then repeat the process. Each charge and payment will appear on your credit report, and over time you'll begin to paint a portrait of two responsible citizens who pay their bills promptly.

If you find that your circumstances make getting even a gasoline company card impossible, you can establish credit by borrowing someone else's credit. If you know someone who has established credit (such as a parent or sibling) and is willing to sign as a guarantor of your credit application, most banks and companies will be happy to issue you a card. Since the credit card will still be in your name, the credit bureau will never know that you needed a cosigner to get the card.

Another good way to start establishing credit is to take out a loan from a bank with whom you have a savings account. Let's say you have $1,000 in a passbook account. You can borrow $500 from the bank, which will then freeze $500 of the money in your account to secure the loan. Pay the money back as quickly as possible, and you've taken the first step toward establishing a healthy credit rating.

Getting Other Cards

Once you've established a good track record with your gasoline card or department store card, you might want to start shopping around for a VISA or MasterCard. The best way is to deal with a local bank that offers one or both of these cards rather than a huge national banking conglomerate. Using a local bank lets you deal face-to-face with bank officers and puts a more personal spin on things. You can explain your needs, and they can get a better picture of your financial situation. Opening a checking account and a savings account with the bank can't hurt, either. You'll find most local banks are more willing to issue a card to someone who's a regular customer.

Joint or Separate Credit?

The bottom line with credit cards is that the person or persons whose name(s) are on the account are responsible for payment. If you're a married couple and you both work, you may choose to have separate cards and assume full responsibility for your individual debts. But if one of you does not work, both names should be on the account. If they're not, the one whose name is not on the account could have his or her cards recalled if the spouse should die or leave the marriage.

If you're an unmarried couple, you can frequently obtain a joint credit card if one of you cosigns the other's application and agrees to be equally responsible for any debt. The decision to do this, however, is totally up to the two of you and will be dictated by your own financial attitudes. But keep in mind that, as with a married couple, if one of you doesn't work, the death or departure of the other could result in no credit at all for the person whose name is not on the account.

Types of Credit Cards

Credit cards are issued by banks, gasoline companies, retailers, and travel and entertainment companies like American Express. There are a number of important differences between them.

Bank Cards

Banks and other organizations, including securities brokerage firms, typically issue VISA and MasterCard credit cards. These are the two most common forms of credit card and can be used at hundreds of thousands of establishments around the world. Users usually pay an annual fee (although many banks are now dropping the fee in an effort to entice new customers) and begin to incur interest on their account balances twenty to thirty days after their bills arrive in the mail. Interest rates can range anywhere from 9 percent to 22 percent depending on the state in which the issuing institution is located. Some cards may also charge transaction fees or other fees.

Many bank cards offer a cash advance option. The issuing institution will send you checks that can be used to make purchases or to obtain cash at a bank. You can also obtain cash advances by using your card at an ATM. But these are really just extremely expensive loans and should be avoided except in emergencies. Interest on cash advances usually begins to accrue the moment the money changes hands. In addition, many banks will charge a fee for the transaction.

Bank cards also issue what are known as "premium" cards such as a VISA Gold Card or a Platinum MasterCard. These cards play to people's vanities and egos by making them feel special, a "cut above" the standard cardholder. Aside from higher credit limits and cash advances and a few minor perks like free traveler's checks and free credit life insurance, these cards aren't worth the inflated fees they carry. Some banks charge more than twice their regular card fee. Our advice? Save your money and hobnob with the common people.

Travel and Entertainment Cards

These cards (American Express, Diner's Club, and Carte Blanche are the most common) operate like bank cards, with a couple of major exceptions. They generally don't have preset limits, and the entire balance is due each month. Also unlike bank cards, they don't charge interest after thirty days, they charge a late fee. They're also quick to cancel your account should you become unacceptably delinquent with your payments.

In some ways, travel and entertainment cards make a lot more sense than bank cards because you have to pay your bill each month. Armed with that knowledge, most people are more likely to pay attention to what they're spending. If you have had, or are likely to have, trouble controlling your spending impulses, one of these may be just the card for you.

There is one catch, however. Because they want their money every month, travel and entertainment companies are a bit more picky than banks about who they issue cards to. An adequate income and solid credit record are critical if you hope to get one.

Travel and entertainment cards also offer the gamut of vanity cards with gold and platinum labels. Like bank cards, they're not worth the extra fee unless they really provide a useful service or some other advantage.

Debit Cards

Banks that issue these cards debit a designated account for your purchases as soon as the charge arrives, rather than billing you. Because the money is removed from your account almost immediately, using a debit card is similar to using a checkbook and requires the same attention. Like travel and entertainment cards, debit cards can be a good choice for those who are too easily tempted by the lure of easy purchases offered by bank cards.

Finding Low-Interest Credit Cards

Credit cards' annual fees and interest rates vary greatly. For information and advice on obtaining low-interest credit cards, you should join the Bankcard Holders of America. This nonprofit organization charges $18 for a membership, an amount that can pay for itself with the savings on just a purchase or two. Write or call Bankcard Holders of America, 560 Herndon Parkway, Suite 120, Herndon, VA 22070, (703) 481-1110. Another good source for information is *Barron's*, which provides a list of lower-interest rate cards each week.

Using Credit Cards Responsibly

Credit cards were created to allow consumers to avoid the hassle of carrying a great deal of cash or to have to write checks. They were not designed to be loans. If the two of you are using them to purchase things you otherwise couldn't afford, you're making a serious mistake.

Having said that, I'll also be the first to admit that banks love people who carry enormous credit card debt, as long as they make their minimum payment each month. Who wouldn't love to have a customer like that? The 18 or 19 percent or more in interest the banks earn with credit card debt would make anyone quite happy.

The problem with credit cards, and the reason so many people get in trouble with them, is they remove the pain from the purchasing process. If you have to pay cash or write a check for something, you're much more likely to pause and ask yourself, "Now, wait a minute. Do we really need this?" This is because by paying real money, you experience the immediate reduction in your checking account balance or in the amount of money you have in your wallet. Paying for the groceries might finally become an issue.

If you're using plastic, on the other hand, it's not like real money. You happily waltz out of the store with your purchase and defer the issue of payment until the bill comes. And then you can decide whether to pay the entire amount or pay it off over a series of months. But soon, too many purchases, too many monthly payments, and too much interest can put you under an unbearable financial burden.

The only way to use credit cards responsibly is to pay off your card balances every month. To do that, you must carefully monitor your purchases and make sure the money to pay for them will be there when the bills arrive. If you're using your credit cards for purchases you can't afford, you're on a road that can only lead to financial disaster.

The answer to the problem? Put your credit cards away in a drawer and pay cash for everything. If you have a financial emergency in which you truly have nowhere else to turn, get them out of the drawer and use them. But for furniture? Televisions? Stereos? Clothing? Dinners out? Save your money and then make these purchases when you've put enough money aside. Your days of instant gratification are over.

Weaning Yourselves of the Credit Card Habit

The first step in weaning yourself of the credit card habit is to pay off all your credit card debt. The least painful method to accomplish this is to consolidate all your card balances into one large sum and make monthly payments until the debt is paid off.

There are several ways to accomplish this. Some banks will offer you a debt consolidation loan at a much lower interest rate than you're paying on your credit card balances. You also can consider a home equity loan, which will give you the advantage of tax-deductible interest.

You can even pay off credit cards with other credit cards. Lately, many banks have been offering low-interest rates on new credit cards for a period of time. For example, we just received an offer for a "Platinum" VISA card with a 3.9 percent interest rate for the first year and a balance transfer option. Using such a card, you could pay off your other card balances and enjoy the low interest rate for a year. If you still have a balance at the end of that time, you can take another bank up on their low-interest offer. As long as banks keep offering short-term, low-interest cards, you can repeat the process indefinitely until your balance is paid off.

Avoiding Credit Card Fraud

Once you have a credit card, you can fall prey to all sorts of scams. That short series of numbers on your card has quite a bit of monetary value, and there are lots of crooks out there who would like to use them for their own gain. Here are some tips for avoiding credit card problems and scams.

• Never give your credit card number to someone over the telephone unless you initiated the call and the other party is well-known and reputable. If someone finds out your credit card number and expiration date, and they know your address and telephone number, they can go on a telephone shopping spree.

• Tear up the carbon paper from credit card receipts. By looking through trash bins and copying valid credit card numbers from these carbons, thieves can charge purchases to your account.

• Keep all your credit card receipts and check them against your monthly billing statement. If you find you're being billed for a purchase you didn't make, or the amount is incorrect, contact the credit card company immediately and contest the charge. If the problem continues, cancel the card.

• Report the loss or theft of a credit card immediately. In theory your liability for charges made to lost or stolen cards is limited. But it's still important to report the situation as quickly as possible.

• Carefully dispose of any preapproved credit card offers you receive in the mail. If these should fall into the wrong hands, they can be used to fraudulently open credit card accounts in your name.

• Cut old credit cards into pieces before throwing them away. Not all retail clerks bother to check the expiration date on a card, so an old card in the wrong hands can cause the real cardholder a great deal of trouble.

• Don't apply for affinity credit cards. These are cards that bear the logo or emblem of an organization and donate a certain percentage of your purchase dollars to the organization. Such cards are becoming very popular with colleges and universities to raise funds. The problem is they charge you very high interest rates and annual fees while actually contributing very little to the organization. If you want to help out your alma mater, do it the old-fashioned way and send them a check.

• Beware of secured credit cards. These cards require you to make a minimum deposit with a bank, which then issues you a credit line equal to the amount you deposit. So you don't really have credit, you have a debit card. And you're also losing interest on the money you've deposited with the bank. (As we'll see later in the chapter, the only time to consider a secured card is when your credit rating is in the tank.)

LOANS

While the two of you can use credit cards—responsibly, we hope—for the day-to-day purchases of relatively inexpensive items, the time will come when you'll be going hat in hand to a lending institution for a car loan, home mortgage, or other substantial chunk of money. It's important to know the various types of loan options and which ones are best for your particular need.

Types of Loans

There are two main types of loans—secured and unsecured. Both can be repaid over a period of years in monthly payments. They may also be single-payment loans, which are repaid in one lump sum at the end of an agreed-upon period of time.

Secured Loans

A secured loan is backed by some property or asset owned by the borrower. For example, the two most common types of consumer loans, home mortgages and car loans, are secured loans. The lending institution loans you the money based on the fact that if you default on the loan, they can legally seize your car or house and sell it to get their money back.

In this case, the car and the house are considered collateral. Other forms of collateral include savings accounts, Treasury bills, and stocks and bonds.

Unsecured Loans

These loans are just what their name implies. The lender is loaning money without requiring that the borrower have collateral to back it up. If the borrower defaults, the lender has no choice but to resort to legal action to get the money back. Lenders typically will only make these types of loans to people in whom they have the utmost faith. If your credit history is a little rocky, your chances of getting an unsecured loan are very slim.

Mike: *We took out our first loan in 1976 to buy one of the legendary jokes in American automotive history—a brand-new American Motors Pacer (as you can see, we still had a lot to learn about cars). We got the loan from the credit union at the newspaper where Jacquie was an editor. I can still remember the terms: $166.26 a month for three years, which we paid like clockwork.*

When we had six months or so left on the first loan, we applied for a second loan to buy a used Dodge pickup truck. The credit union consolidated the two loans, and our monthly payment grew to around $200 and added another two years to the repayment schedule.

We were religious about making the payments and paid off the loan right on time. It was the first step in demonstrating our ability and willingness to pay off a significant debt. This track record was important when we applied for our first mortgage a few years later.

Jacquie: *It's telling that I have no recollection of those loans or how much they were for, even though my signature was obviously on the applications. It shows you just how one-sided our money management was. Today I know exactly what we owe money for and how much our payments are.*

The Loan Application

When you first approach a lending institution for a loan, they may or may not know anything about you. If you're dealing with a bank where you have a long-term relationship, you'll have passed the first hurdle (assuming your financial history is sound, that is). If it's one that you've never dealt with before, you need to put your best foot forward. That means being prepared.

Have Complete Records

A lending institution's main concern is that you'll be able to make the payments on your loan, so the first thing they'll want to see is information on your financial situation. This can include W-2 forms, your most recent income tax return, investment account statements, and credit card account information. They will probably also order a copy of your credit report. If there are problems on your report, you'll have to iron them out with the lender and demonstrate that you've turned over a new leaf. *Helpful hint: If you're planning on applying for a large loan, get a copy of your credit report well beforehand. You don't need any surprises at the last minute. (Refer to page 88 to learn how to order a copy of your credit report.)*

Prepare Written Documents

It can't hurt to show the lender you've already thought about paying back the loan. You can do this by preparing several documents. The first should be a statement showing how much you want to borrow, what you're borrowing the money for, and how you expect to pay back the loan. The second should be a statement of financial assets and liabilities. The last should be a budget detailing all your expenses and demonstrating how your loan payments fit into your budget.

Call Beforehand

Bankers and other financial service professionals are busy people, and applying for a loan can be time-consuming. Don't just waltz in the door unannounced and expect them to drop whatever they're doing to take care of you. Call beforehand to make an appointment and explain briefly why you're interested in borrowing money. When you show up with your carefully prepared materials, it will demonstrate your thoroughness and foresight.

Where to Get a Loan

There are numerous sources of loans, some of which might surprise you. But regardless of the source of the loan, you'll have two objectives when applying. One, you'll want to be accepted, and two, you'll want the best interest rate and repayment terms you can find. Here are some conventional—and unconventional—loan sources.

Credit Unions

Credit unions are "owned" by their depositors, so they usually offer them the best interest rates. Most credit unions require that you be a member to apply for a loan.

Banks and Savings and Loans

All banks and savings and loan companies provide loans for all sorts of things. The rates will vary from institution to institution. For example, you may find that you generally get better rates from savings and loans than from banks. You may also find that you get better rates from an institution with which you've conducted business for a long time.

Finance Companies

These are the sharks of the loan world and should only be used after you've exhausted all your other resources. They're generally a bit quicker to approve a loan than a bank or a savings and loan, but they also charge much higher interest.

Retirement Plans

One of the advantages of Keoghs, 401(k)s, pension plans, and IRAs is that their owners can borrow money from them. The downside is that there are usually restrictions that limit the conditions under which you can borrow, how much you can borrow, and how long you have to pay the money back. For example, you usually can only borrow from the funds that you contributed and not those your employer contributed. There are also varying tax ramifications. It's not always the best move, so you should check with your accountant before you make a decision. But when you do borrow from these accounts, the great thing is that you're borrowing money from yourself, so the interest you pay on the loans goes back into your account and not to a lender.

Life Insurance Policies

If you have a cash value life insurance policy that has been building equity over the years, you can borrow up to the full amount of the cash value at interest rates as low as 5 percent. You can usually get the money quickly with little red tape.

The only problem with borrowing against a life insurance policy is that the insurance company will often reduce the death benefits of the policy by the amount of the loan that's outstanding at the time of death. This might reduce the interest rate earned by the cash value remaining in the policy. An outstanding loan balance also may cause your premiums to rise as the policy ages.

Brokerage Accounts

Most securities brokerage firms will let their customers make what are called "margin loans." These loans allow a person to borrow up to 50 percent of the value of the stocks and 80 percent of the value of the bonds in their accounts. The interest rate paid on margin loans will fluctuate along with market rates.

Margin loans are not for people with small brokerage accounts. The brokerage firm will usually require a minimum balance in the account. It also will require a pledge of more securities or a partial repayment of the loan should the value of the securities in the margin account begin to fall. A rapid decline in the price of the stock in a margin account can wipe an investor out, so this form of borrowing must be used with great caution.

YOUR CREDIT RATING

As you use your credit card or repay a small loan, you'll begin to create a personal credit rating—a record of your reliability (or unreliability) in paying your debts. As you make purchases and receive bills, your payment record is recorded by the lender. Over time, a sort of fiscal biography of you is compiled by credit bureaus from information provided by your creditors. If you're conscientious in paying your bills, your credit rating remains in good standing. If you miss payments or end up having a debt turned over to a collection agency, your credit rating can go in the tank.

Why is your credit rating so important? Because it determines whether or not you'll qualify for critical loans in the future. For example, many young people have a lot of trouble managing credit responsibly. When they first get a credit card, they may go on spending sprees and suddenly find themselves up to their limit with enormous monthly payments. If they can't meet their payments, they begin to paint a rather unpleasant picture of themselves. Down the road, if they haven't been able to improve their credit habits, they may find themselves turned down for the important loans needed to buy their first car or to get a mortgage for a home.

So good credit habits need to start early. If you and your partner are young, perhaps just starting out your life together, you need to carefully monitor the use of credit cards and make sure you can repay any loans you take out. Otherwise, you'll find yourself in trouble when you *really* need credit.

How Your Credit Rating Is Compiled

When you and/or your partner apply for a credit card or a loan, the lender relies on your credit rating to ascertain the likelihood that you'll be able (and willing) to pay your debt. To do this, the lender will send your name to one of the major credit bureaus in the country to get a copy of your credit report. Today, some even have electronic links to credit bureaus and are able to get the information they need in just a few seconds.

What's in the report? It begins with your demographic characteristics. The basic information in your file will include your name, address, birthdate, and Social Security number. Some credit bureaus may also have additional information such as education, employment record, and marital status.

The rest of the report is the history of you as a borrower. Banks, department stores, and other creditors provide the credit bureau with information on how timely you have been in paying your bills and how much debt you're currently carrying. Lenders then use this information to decide whether or not to give you a credit card or loan.

Most reports include information on credit cards like VISA and MasterCard and charge accounts with large retailers like Sears and J. C. Penney. Home mortgage records are also being reported to credit bureaus more and more often. Any indebtedness from a court action may also appear.

There are some debts that won't appear on your credit report. Your utility bill, telephone bill, cable bill, rent payments, and dental and medical bills will not be included and therefore will not affect your credit rating. *(Helpful hint: When money is tight, pay the minimum payments on your credit card and store bills first to protect your credit rating. You can worry about the phone and utility bills later.)*

Some creditors use scoring systems to evaluate your creditworthiness. In fact, many spend a lot of money to have scoring systems custom designed for their businesses. These systems assign positive or negative values to various characteristics. For example, different age groups receive different point values, with the over-50 crowd usually receiving the highest number of points. Personal income is usually highest in this age range, and many of them are no longer burdened with the expenses associated with raising and educating children. Conversely, people under 30, those with young children and fledgling careers, usually receive the fewest points.

Occupations are also rated. Not surprisingly, professionals and administrators usually score highest. Farmworkers and small business owners frequently score lowest. Number of years on the job is also considered. The longer you've been in your current position, the more points you receive.

Obtaining and Checking Your Credit Report

People whose credit reports are in error usually don't discover this fact until they're turned down for a loan. It's not a pleasant way to find out. Checking your credit report in advance will allow you to avoid such a predicament.

Getting a copy of your credit report is simple. The first step is to locate the credit bureaus in your area. There are hundreds of such small firms that specialize in regional markets. You also can contact one of the following large nationwide credit bureaus:

- Equifax Information Services
  P.O. Box 4091
  Atlanta, GA 30302
  (404) 885-8000

- TRW Information Services
  Customer Assistance
  P.O. Box 749029
  Dallas, TX 74374-9029
  (214) 235-1200

- Trans-Union Credit Information Company
  Eastern Region
  P.O. Box 360
  Philadelphia, PA 19105
  (215) 569-4582

- Midwestern Region
  222 South First Street, Suite 201
  Louisville, KY 40202
  (502) 584-0121

- Western Region
  P.O. Box 3110
  Fullerton, CA 92634
  (714) 738-3800

Credit bureaus are required by law only to let you *see* a copy of your credit report, not send you a copy. This means you may have to pay a visit to the credit bureau office. Fortunately, however, most credit bureaus are a bit more user friendly these days and will provide you with a copy (for a fee, of course, usually around $25). You can obtain a copy of your report by writing a letter to the credit bureau, containing your name, Social Security number, and addresses you have used during the previous five years. If you've been turned down for credit recently, you can obtain a copy free of charge.

Once you have the report in hand, you'll probably find it a bit difficult to decipher. There are lots of codes and symbols that can only be interpreted by reading the fine print. Once you've figured out the language, you'll see that the report contains the credit limit for each of your accounts, your account balances, any late payments or current payments past due, the date the information was last updated, and so on. Some credit reports are updated once a month, others every two or three months.

Credit Checking Clubs

Some of the larger credit bureaus have created credit checking clubs. For an annual fee, they'll provide periodic updates and notify you when someone has checked your file. Although it's a tempting service (we all like to know who's checking us out, after all), it's hardly worth the money. There's really no reason you need to know every time someone checks your credit. It's cheaper just to pay for a copy of your report once a year, or when you're anticipating a major purchase, to make sure it's accurate.

If Your Credit Report Contains Errors

Just like other large bureaucratic organizations, credit bureaus are quite prone to making mistakes, so there's a good chance your credit report may not be accurate. A 1991 Consumers Union report found that 48 percent of the reports it evaluated contained at least one error. These mistakes can be caused by something as simple as someone hitting the wrong number on a keyboard. They can also result from a situation in which you returned a purchase that was unsatisfactory but the charge remained reported on your credit report as an unpaid bill.

Correcting an inaccurate credit report can be time-consuming and aggravating. You do have some clout on your side, however. The Fair Credit Reporting Act requires that any incorrect information in a credit report be corrected. The problem lies in the fact that credit bureaus can only correct mistakes for which they are responsible. If the problem is incorrect information supplied by a creditor, then the creditor is responsible for correcting the information.

Let's say you discover that your credit report indicates you haven't been making payments to a department store charge account, even though you've been quite diligent in getting those payments off to the store each month. You may only discover this problem when you're turned down for a loan. To correct the report, you need to deal directly with the store itself. This usually requires a letter or two to the company's credit manager pointing out the mistake and asking that it be rectified. Mention in your letters that you are writing under the provisions of the Fair Credit Reporting Act (or the Fair Credit Billing Act if it's a billing issue). That will get their attention. If the store fails to respond within ninety days, it's in violation of the law.

Special Problems for Women

For years, women were treated unfairly by most credit-issuing institutions. There were concerns that a woman's employment might be interrupted by pregnancy, that her employment might be sporadic, or that her income would be reduced should she become widowed or divorced.

This all changed with the passage of the Equal Credit Opportunity Act. Among its provisions, the act required lenders to take into account alimony, child support, income from part-time employment, and pensions when considering women for loans. It also made discrimination on the basis of age illegal. This is especially important to older women whose husbands may have passed away.

Nevertheless, there are still problems. Some institutions will discourage a woman to whom they don't want to extend credit by using the rationale that a rejection of her credit application will mar her credit record. In their eyes, discouraging her from applying means they won't have a loan rejection included in the statistics that are monitored by federal agencies looking for discriminatory practices.

Another problem revolves around the issue of whether credit records are reported for both husbands and wives. Many women who were married before the Equal Credit Opportunity Act went into effect would find that even though they may have had a credit card or some other charge account jointly with their husbands, credit bureau records of the account's activities existed only in their husbands' names. When these women would apply for credit of their own, they would find that no records existed in their own names. Under the Equal Credit Opportunity Act, if two parties are jointly responsible for an account, records must exist in both their names.

Today, most lending institutions follow this practice. But there are still some that will maintain records in the husband's name alone. For this reason, it's a good idea for most women to get a copy of their credit report and make sure their names are included on any joint account activity. If it's not, the situation can be rectified by writing creditors and asking them to report all account activity in both names as required by the Equal Credit Opportunity Act. Again, invoking the law should get their attention. A second check of the credit report will then be needed to make sure the information is now included.

There are also provisions whereby one spouse can be given the status of "user." In other words, even if a credit card account is in a husband's name, his wife will receive credit for the manner in which the account is handled. User status is usually denoted in a special column on a credit report or is indicated by a code.

Special Problems for Couples

When two people come together in a relationship, they each bring their own credit history with them. Can this cause problems? You bet, particularly if one partner has been rather cavalier with credit and the other has operated with penny-pinching discipline.

What should be done? Well, the obvious answer is that any bad credit records should be straightened out as quickly as possible. They're facing a future together—one that we'll assume involves buying a house and possibly raising children. As we learned earlier in the chapter, it's hard to accomplish these things without credit. A poor credit record on the part of one person in a couple can result in real difficulty getting loans for major items like cars and houses if both partners are going to be applying for the loan.

Repairing a bad credit history will take time and discipline. It might even require the services of a financial counselor. The good thing is that the credit of the partner with the good record will not be damaged by the poor credit of the other partner.

GETTING TURNED DOWN FOR CREDIT

We mentioned earlier in the chapter that one of the downsides of credit is its easily availability, but that doesn't mean that the two of you will automatically qualify for every loan you apply for. This is particularly true if either of you has had trouble with credit in the past. Just as the law protects consumers by prohibiting lenders from discriminating, it also protects lenders by spelling out the conditions under which they have the right to turn down an applicant for credit. The Federal Reserve Board lists the following conditions under which you can be denied credit:

- Incomplete credit application
- Insufficient credit references
- Inability to verify credit references
- Temporary or irregular employment
- Inability to verify employment
- Length of employment
- Insufficient income
- Excessive obligations
- Inability to verify income
- Inadequate collateral
- Too short a period of residence

- Temporary residence
- Inability to verify residence
- No credit file
- Delinquent credit obligations
- Garnishment, attachment, foreclosure, repossession, or suit
- Bankruptcy
- Unacceptable terms or conditions requested by the applicant

As you can see from this list, even people with squeaky clean financial histories may have trouble getting credit. For example, people who have moved a lot may be turned down, even if their frequent moves were the result of getting better jobs with higher salaries. And their job hopping, too, can be held against them, regardless of the nature of the position or their income.

If either of you finds yourself in such a situation, don't give up. There are two ways to approach lending institutions. The first is to allow the bureaucratic wheels to turn and let the pencil pushers use their formulas and charts and point systems to evaluate you. If you should get turned down, you can then figuratively whack them on the forehead a few times to get their attention and request a personal, face-to-face evaluation. Make an appointment with a loan officer and explain your situation by laying your financial cards right on the table. They generally are reasonable people and will more than likely grant you your loan once you've presented your case.

You can also look for trouble spots while filling out the application. Suppose you've only had your job for six months and your two previous jobs for a year each. You know that's likely to raise a red flag with the lender's scoring system. So next to the line on time of employment you write, "See supplement A." Then on a separate sheet of paper you explain that it's normal in your industry to move from job to job and that each move has been accompanied by increased responsibilities and increased income.

You can follow this procedure for any question that might cause a problem, in the process turning negatives into positives. There are several advantages to doing this. One, it shows the lender that you're well acquainted with the lending process and sophisticated enough to know how it works. You're also more likely to get the loan application out of the hands of a clerk and into the hands of someone with the experience to understand your situation.

Don't Panic

Have you ever seen those ads in the backs of magazines or on television that promise credit to anyone, no matter how wretched their credit history may be? These companies feed on people who are desperate for a loan. If the two of you are in properly dire straits, you might be tempted to take one of them up on their offer.

There's just one problem. What these companies are offering isn't credit. If they promise you a credit card, what they're really going to give you is a "secured" card. To minimize their risk (the truth is they're really not as enamored of you as they make you think), they'll require you to make a sizable cash deposit as collateral against any charges you make with the card. If you fail to pay your bills, they're safe because they already have your money. Another thing to keep in mind is that more than one person who has done business with these companies has had their deposit disappear.

Another promise these companies will make is to clean up your credit history for a fee. Often the fee can be quite exorbitant. But the service they're offering is almost impossible to provide. If your record of paying your debts is lousy, they can't rewrite history.

What these companies are more likely to do is deluge

the credit bureau with claims (false, by the way) that their records are in error. This serves to have the negative entries in your file removed for review and provides a window of opportunity for you to obtain a credit card or a loan. But when the files are checked and proven correct, you may have opened yourself up to fraud charges.

A more reasonable strategy is to obtain a secured credit card from a reputable bank. You'll still have to provide a cash deposit as collateral, but you won't have to worry about your money disappearing.

SOLVING DEBT PROBLEMS

If either or both of you have amassed too much debt, it's important to realize that you *can* climb out of the hole you've dug yourself into. The degree of difficulty of your ascent will be determined by the severity of your problem.

It won't be easy. Getting out from under a debt load takes time and discipline and is always accompanied by a great deal of psychological and financial stress. It will test both the strength of your relationship and your individual strengths. But you can take heart from the fact that the successful confrontation of a debt problem often strengthens relationships and improves communication over money issues.

Watch for the Warning Signs

It's not difficult to determine if you have debt problems. There are a number of warning signs.

- **Cash advances**—You find yourself taking out cash advances on your credit cards just to meet normal, day-to-day expenses.
- **The bills are backing up**—Before you've paid last

month's bills, you find that this month's bills are already arriving.

- **Minimum payments**—You're only able to make the minimum payments on your various monthly bills.
- **Playing payment games**—You send the phone payment to the bank and the VISA payment to the phone company to buy time. Or you "forget" to sign your checks.
- **Increasing balances**—Despite the fact that you make your monthly payments, your account balances continue to climb.
- **Transferring debt**—You're using cash advances from one credit card to meet the payments on another.
- **Excessive cash outlay**—You find that you're spending more than 25 percent of your net monthly income on installment payments, other than your mortgage.
- **Dipping into savings**—You begin to take money out of savings accounts to meet your monthly payments.
- **Obtaining additional credit**—You find yourself accepting offers for additional credit cards because you've reached the credit limits on your existing cards.
- **Delinquency**—You start to fall behind on your mortgage, rent, utility bills, and other regular monthly expenses.

If you find that you or your partner fall into one or more of these situations, you must act immediately to begin to get your debt problems under control.

Analyze the Problem

Confronting a debt problem is kind of like confronting a drinking problem. You have to admit that the problem exists. Only then can you begin to take the steps necessary to solve it.

The first step in dealing with excessive debt is to tally up the damage. Just how much money *do* you owe? People who are careful with credit can usually tell you who their creditors are and exactly how much they owe each one. People with debt problems, on the other hand, are often unable to tell you how much they owe. When they find out, they're stunned.

Create a Budget

Once you've determined how much you owe, you need to begin to pay off as much of your debt as possible each month. This requires creating a very strict budget and sticking to it. After you pay your fixed costs like the rent or mortgage, utility bills, and car payment, direct as much money as you can toward paying down your bills.

This will no doubt require some serious behavior modification. If you have debt problems, they more than likely came from overspending on things you can't afford. That's going to have to stop. No more meals out, no more impulse purchases, no more weekend trips, *no more debt!*

Cut Up Your Credit Cards

This solves the problem of accruing any further debt. If you don't have credit cards, you don't have the means to charge purchases. Leave yourselves one card so you have something to use in a legitimate emergency. The best approach is to make that one card a travel and entertainment card like American Express. That way, you'll have no choice but to pay off the entire bill when it arrives.

Also, tear up any cash advance checks you receive in the mail. These are extremely dangerous to the compulsive shopper. If you throw them away, they can't hurt you.

Prioritize Your Payments

Make a list of the debt amounts for your individual accounts and the interest rates on each. Then target those with the highest interest rates for immediate payment. For example, let's say you have three credit card debts. One carries an interest rate of 14 percent, another is 16 percent, and the third is 20 percent. Pay the minimum amounts for the two lower-interest cards and direct all your remaining cash toward the 20 percent card. When that one is paid off, focus on the 16 percent card.

Negotiate with Your Creditors

Creditors would rather have you repay your debts at a snail's pace than have to seize your assets, take you to court, or have you declare bankruptcy and not repay them at all. If you find you just can't meet all your obligations in a timely manner, contact your creditors, explain your situation, and ask for a special payment plan. Most creditors will reduce your minimum payments, grant you a temporary delay in payments, or agree not to tack on late charges to your balance.

Explore Debt Consolidation

A debt consolidation loan allows you to pay off all your individual creditors and make one monthly payment to a single creditor. It can be a great strategy—*if* you are able to obtain a loan at a reasonable interest rate. But if you have to take out a debt consolidation loan at 21 or 22 percent to pay off debts with lower interest rates, you're not helping yourself over the long run. While the new single minimum payments may be lower than the cumulative minimum payments you were making, they will be spread out over a longer period of time. Thus, your total cash outlay to pay off the loan will be much higher.

The best strategy for debt consolidation is a home

equity loan. They're available at much lower interest rates than what you're paying on your credit card balances, and the interest you pay on the loans is generally tax deductible. Of course, the two of you must ask yourselves if you're willing to put your house on the line. If you can't make the payments on the loan, you're not only in debt up to your ears, you're also without a home.

Consult a Credit Counselor

If you find yourselves so overwhelmed by debt problems that you can't come up with your own debt reduction strategies, you may need to see a credit counselor. Most banks and credit unions offer credit counseling services to their account holders. They also may support nonprofit credit counseling agencies. Family service agencies are another source of assistance.

These organizations offer a variety of services. They can help you set up a budget and a monthly repayment plan. Some will take money from you and distribute it to your various creditors, which prevents you from spending it on something else. They'll also frequently act as a liaison between you and your creditors to help create a repayment plan that both sides can live with.

If you decide you need a credit counselor, make sure you use one who's affiliated with a reputable financial institution or service agency. There are plenty of unqualified, self-proclaimed counselors out there who will be happy to help you—for an exorbitant fee. All too often, they'll just make your situation worse.

Here are two places to contact for credit counseling. They each have affiliates all over the country.

- National Foundation for Consumer Credit
  8701 Georgia Avenue
  Silver Spring, MD 20910

- Family Service America
  11700 West Lake Park Drive
  Milwaukee, WI 53224

BANKRUPTCY—NAVIGATING THE ULTIMATE DISASTER

Some people develop debt problems so severe that no amount of planning or negotiation can help them. For these people, declaring personal bankruptcy is the final resort.

What Is Bankruptcy?

Bankruptcy is kind of like financial surrender. You're hanging out the white flag and, in effect, admitting defeat by petitioning the court for legal protection from your creditors. Your liabilities far outweigh your assets, and there's no way to pay them off.

Bankruptcy is not an easy way out of debt and is not a pleasant situation. It's almost always a source of incredible personal and family stress. However, it does serve to buy you time to reorganize your finances and develop a repayment plan. It can also completely free you of your financial obligations—at a cost.

Before you decide to file for bankruptcy, you should consult with a credit counselor and an attorney. And don't use a bankruptcy attorney. They're ready and waiting to take you by the hand and lead you through the bankruptcy process. Use another attorney who can help you look at your circumstances more objectively.

Forms of Bankruptcy

There are two main forms of personal bankruptcy: Chapter 7 and Chapter 13. A third form, Chapter 11, also exists but is almost always used by businesses. However, for individuals with significant assets and the money to pay the legal bills, Chapter 11 is sometimes a better route.

Chapter 7 Bankruptcy

This is the most severe of the three forms and is often called "straight bankruptcy." It offers you the least amount of protection of your personal property, most of which will have to be liquidated to pay off your debts.

You can either file for Chapter 7 of your own accord or be forced into it by creditors. Once the proper legal papers are filed, the court issues an injunction forbidding creditors from further harassing you. (Chapter 7 will *not* protect any cosigners on your accounts, however, and creditors can immediately demand they repay any of your outstanding loans they agreed to guarantee.) The court also assigns a trustee to oversee the liquidation of your assets. Once all your assets have been sold and the proceeds distributed to your creditors (who receive only a portion of what they are owed), the court grants you a discharge that voids any judgments previously made against you. However, you'll be prohibited from filing for bankruptcy again for six years.

Chapter 7 is quite harsh, but it doesn't leave you completely destitute. You're allowed to keep up to $7,500 of your equity over and above mortgages and liens on your real estate; up to $4,000 worth of personal property such as clothing and appliances; $500 worth of jewelry; $750 in professional items such as tools or books; up to $4,000 in cash value life insurance; and income from benefits like Social Security, unemployment, alimony, welfare, and pensions. *If you're a married couple filing jointly for bankruptcy, these figures will double.*

What Chapter 7 doesn't do is let you off the hook for certain debts. These include a variety of taxes, including unpaid withholding and Social Security taxes; debts incurred from embezzlement, fraud, or larceny; financial liabilities incurred because of willful or reckless acts against another person or property; and student loans less than five years old.

Chapter 13 Bankruptcy

Rather than forcing you to sell off most of your assets to pay off your creditors, Chapter 13 bankruptcy buys you time to reorganize your financial life and get back on your feet. The idea behind it is that, given time, you do have the financial wherewithal to pay some or all of your debts. Chapter 13 allows you to restructure your finances so that you can do just that. In fact, the full legal term for Chapter 13 is "Adjustments of Debts of an Individual with Regular Income."

As with Chapter 7, once you file for Chapter 13 protection, your creditors are forbidden from harassing you, and your property receives the same amount of minimal protection. It also protects cosigners of your loans, at least for a while. Your creditors can only go after any cosigners after the court-approved plan makes it clear that your creditors will not be paid in full. Then the cosigners will be responsible for any amounts you were not able to pay.

After you file for Chapter 13, you must present the court with a monthly budget that shows how much money you'll have left over after your minimal living expenses are covered. The court will then approve or modify your plan. After that, you can begin to whittle away at your debts over three years, repaying anywhere from 10 percent to the entire amount. At the end of that period, the court will discharge you from all further indebtedness.

RESTORING CREDIT

No matter which form of bankruptcy you choose, it will absolutely destroy your credit rating. Of the two, Chapter

13 shows that you at least made an honest effort to repay your debts, so creditors may be more willing to take a chance on you. But it will still be years before you are free and clear of the huge blemish on your financial history.

The only way to restore your credit is to begin all over again. For most people, the first step is to obtain a secured credit card from a bank. With your deposit safely tucked away in their bosoms, most banks will be willing to grant you a modest line of credit. Use it for small purchases and pay the bills in full as soon as they arrive. Over time, as you accumulate some savings, you can use them as collateral to take out a secured loan. Again, stick to the repayment schedule and pay off the loan on time.

Only by operating in this manner can you restore your credit rating. And it won't happen quickly. Most people take four or five years to restore themselves to full credit-worthiness. And a bankruptcy won't disappear from your credit report for ten years. (Check to make sure it does. It doesn't always happen automatically.) Bankruptcy is a hard lesson, but for most people it's a lesson they only have to suffer through once.

TEN TIPS TO MINIMIZE CREDIT COSTS

The manner in which the two of you handle credit will have an enormous effect on your life together. Here are ten tips to help you keep your credit costs to a minimum.

1. Find credit cards with the lowest annual fees. Some banks these days charge no fees whatsoever. Another good rule of thumb: the bigger the bank, the more expensive its credit cards. You'll usually be better off with a card from Mayberry Savings & Loan than with one from Citibank.

2. Always pay off your entire monthly credit card bill.

You can't even deduct the interest charges from your taxes anymore.

3. If you must carry balances on your credit cards, find cards with the lowest interest rates.

4. Don't use premium credit cards. The extra fees are seldom worth it.

5. Check your credit card bills carefully. Mistakes often happen, and they're rarely in your favor.

6. Only borrow money for things you really need, such as automobiles, houses, home improvements, and your children's education. Pay cash for everything else.

7. Shop around for the cheapest loans. Banks are very competitive and are eager to get your business.

8. Pay off your highest interest rate loans first.

9. Arrange to have loan payments deducted directly from your savings or checking accounts. Some banks will lower your interest rate a bit if you agree to this arrangement.

10. If you're deeply in debt, use a home equity loan to consolidate your loans. You'll pay a lower interest rate than your credit card rates and the interest on home equity loans is usually tax-deductible.

5

Drafting a Life Plan:
Serial, Life-Stage Financial Planning

There are numerous ways to look at long-term financial planning. In chapter 2, to get you started on your financial partnership, we suggested you set some general financial goals: short-term, mid-term, and long-term. Many couples manage their finances quite satisfactorily all their lives on just the basis of those general goals, or with the simple additional aid of a carefully constructed budget. That can work, to be sure. But we don't recommend it.

We call what results the "pop-up method of financial planning." That's the method whereby whatever pops up on your financial horizon at a given moment—either a goal or an expense—you deal with in whatever way seems appropriate at the time and then move on. It's history, forgotten. That method is reactive, not proactive. It's hardly financial planning at all, in fact. It's more like a shooting gallery. Envision this: targets appear regularly in a row, say flying ducks, and you take random shots at them. You hit some, miss a lot. No problem, it's just a game.

Maybe you're sailing along at age 34, both of you with well-paying, professional jobs. You each have a nice car, spend a lot on rent in the big city, entertain yourselves and your friends well, and haven't saved much, if anything.

One of you gets an itch to buy a boat big enough to spend weekends on and you figure, why not? You can kind of afford the payments if you tighten your belts a bit. Kind of.

Four months later, when summer's waned and the boat's in dry dock, you discover you're about to become parents. It's something you always wanted, but right now you're not ready financially. Not even close. No home, no life insurance, no savings, and an expensive lifestyle into which it would be difficult, if not impossible, to insert a child. Of course, you can always take the kid for a ride on your boat—next summer.

We'll call that scenario a miss. And it happened because you followed the pop-up method of financial planning instead of the life-stage method of financial planning that we recommend.

The life-stage method of financial planning is something of a compromise between the pop-up method outlined above and the "do-it-all-at-once method" which some experts recommend. That's when you approach financial planning as a huge, complex, total mass. In that method you try to wrestle with all your financial issues at the same time. It's great for overly obsessive control freaks, but most of us simply can't focus and concentrate on all aspects of our finances at once. And we don't have to. At age 20, for example, most of us don't care about retirement, and don't have the basic tools to plan for it. Many of us hardly even have a career from which we can think about retiring.

So we recommend the life-stage method of financial planning, which basically approaches financial planning serially, based on life's natural stages and the events that take place during those stages. It's a very practical, easy-to-handle, commonsense approach, and one we've found works well for just about all couples. As long as you're talking and communicating well, share common goals, and agree on how you want to live your life together, the life-stage method will work almost effortlessly.

In this chapter we'll give you a general outline of the financial decisions you will make and steps you will need to take as a couple throughout your life. Financial planning for couples is really just a constant shifting of your disposable income from your very short-term needs to mid-term needs to long-term needs and very long-term needs. For example, you'll always have current pressing needs and priorities, like paying for your wedding, or furnishing your apartment. You'll appropriately attend to those first.

But later you may decide that buying a house is your biggest priority, so you sacrifice some current spending to save for a house. And always looming in the background is your need to save for your longest-term need, retirement.

We'll take you through the five stages of life that we've found most appropriate for financial planning, and give you a checklist of what you need to accomplish at each particular stage. In Part 2 of this book we'll discuss in more detail specific major life-stage financial events, like planning for college and planning for retirement, among others. But for now we'll discuss the major events that are likely to take place in each stage of your life and draft a life plan for successfully accommodating and profiting by those events.

The five major life stages we'll discuss are:

- Stage 1—Joining Forces
- Stage 2—Preparing to Nest
- Stage 3—Achieving Midlife
- Stage 4—Getting Ready to Retire
- Stage 5—Starting Over

Jacquie: *Thank heavens this last one's not necessary for everyone. But you never know. Just when you may be ready to* *cash in and enjoy the fruits of your well-earned financial success, you may find yourself facing the future alone again after many comfortable years as a couple. Unfortunately, many do, so you'd better be prepared.*

What you're going to do under the life-stage method of planning is construct a financial plan that will last a lifetime. When you join forces, you have to decide who owns what, who makes what, how you'll handle your finances, and how you'll start saving and investing as a couple. When you get ready to nest, or start a family, you'll be concerned with buying a house, protecting your partner and children financially, and building assets to safeguard their future. At midlife, you'll want to maximize your earned income and begin to prepare for retirement.

When you get ready to retire you'll need to be sure that your retirement income will meet your needs and expectations and that there will be no unpleasant financial surprises after the champagne corks have popped at your retirement party. And finally, if you're going to have to start over as a single you may need to rethink some financial strategies in order to ensure that you can provide adequately for a different kind of future than you're envisioning right now. Here's how to plan serially, by life stages:

STAGE 1—JOINING FORCES

When you join forces, either through marriage or as an unmarried couple, you're forming a financial partnership. How much of a partnership is for you to decide, but for our purposes we'll assume you've made a deep and abiding commitment that you expect will last forever. That means as soon as you join forces you need to make changes in your financial arrangements to reflect your new until-death-do-you-part partnership.

Your income probably won't be great at this time in your lives, and you're likely to have some immediate expenses: paying for a wedding, a honeymoon, deposit on an apartment, furnishings, maybe purchase of a car. It's important to put a little bit into a savings fund, if only to establish the habit, but don't worry about how much. And don't worry yet about starting a retirement fund. Your immediate needs come first right now. Here's your checklist for Stage 1.

Merge Your Finances

You're beginning your life together as financial partners. You need to be sure you merge your finances in a way that works for you. We talked quite a bit in chapters 2 and 3 about how to merge your finances and begin managing your money as partners, so we'll just review those steps for you here.

Organize your finance committee. Your home is a financial institution, just like any business, so you need to organize it and run it like a business. You and your partner will be members of the family finance committee, so set a regular weekly meeting day, time, and place to sit and discuss financial management issues. You may want to set aside time at your finance committee meeting once a month to share the actual process of paying the bills and maintaining the accounts.

Be sure to prepare an agenda for these meetings. For the first meeting you need to determine your current financial status, including your joint assets and liabilities. Also set general short-term, mid-term, and long-term financial goals. Eventually meeting agendas will flow from the previous meeting, from weekly events and from your agreed-upon goals. It's important, though, that each of you jot down agenda items as they occur to you during the week. Consider these meeting dates as sacrosanct, and don't cancel them for frivolous reasons.

Decide how to set up your accounts. We advise setting up joint savings and checking accounts. It's clean and simple that way. We've never had a problem with this method, and we think it shows a level of trust and commitment that can strengthen your relationship. But if you feel it could be unduly awkward, either in terms of record keeping or personal expenditures, try establishing a joint household account, joint savings account, and separate personal checking accounts. You can decide who contributes what to which account.

If you are marrying for a second time or are a same-sex couple you may, because your finances are more complex, prefer to keep at least some separate accounts. The key here is not to get hung up on *which* system you choose. Just decide on whatever system works best for you, then be sure to clearly define and stick to your system.

Divide financial tasks. To ensure that you start your partnership off on the right, cooperative step, share the regular, recurring financial tasks your partnership requires. Determine who will pay the bills, keep track of the budget, write the checks, decide on the investments, deposit the savings. You can divide these tasks according to your interests and skills. Don't worry about splitting tasks 50/50; just be sure you're both engaged in the process.

Determine your net worth and prepare a budget. We said the first agenda item at your first finance committee meeting will be a discussion of your current financial situation. You need to determine your net worth, including your assets and liabilities. First, do an inventory of everything you own that has financial value (see worksheet in chapter 2). List real assets such as your home, vacation or rental property, investment-quality art or jewelry, collectibles, and antiques. Next, itemize liquid assets such as checking and savings accounts, life insurance, certificates of deposit, Individual Retirement Accounts, stocks, bonds, securities, mutual funds, and pension funds. When you have listed all your assets, compute the current value.

Now, determine your liabilities. List all your debts, including mortgages, loans, credit card balances, outstanding bills. Add up your liabilities, then subtract them from your assets. The result is your current overall net worth. Now, use this information to draw up a household budget. You should have done this when you read chapter 3, so just pull it out of your financial notebook. If you didn't quite get to it then, do it now. Then, stick to it.

Review Your Tax Situation

You won't need to make changes in your taxes at every stage in your life, but you definitely will want to make adjustments when you join forces as a married couple. There's no question that getting married affects the amount of income tax you have to pay. If you're merging two incomes, you may be hit with the "marriage tax penalty."

There are two key questions to ask with regard to taxes: Will you have one income or two, and what's your situation regarding tax losses?

The answer to the first question will partly determine whether you pay more in taxes as a married couple than you did as separate singles. If you're marrying someone who earns a hefty income, getting married could cost you in terms of taxes. In fact, the closer your incomes, the more likely it is that your tax bill as a married couple will be higher.

As a married couple you have only two options for how to file your income tax returns: you can file "married-filing-jointly" or "married-filing-separately." Generally, filing separately will result in your paying more than filing jointly. However, the total amount of tax you pay as a couple filing jointly is usually higher than if you had remained single and filed separately. Rethinking those marriage plans? Believe us, some do, especially older folks on fixed incomes.

The other side of the coin, so to speak, is that if one of you doesn't plan on producing any income once you're married, your tax situation will actually improve with marriage. That's because while you won't add a second income to your tax return, you can still benefit from a second personal exemption deduction. Also, you'll be using different tax tables to compute your tax, and the married-filing-jointly tax tables are more advantageous than the single tax tables. Together, these changes may reduce your tax bill quite a bit.

Then there's the question of tax losses. If your spouse brings a tax loss to the marriage it will affect your tax situation—either negatively or positively, depending on your overall tax situation and the nature of the loss. In this case it might be a good idea to consult a tax expert before tying the knot with the tax loss still on the books, or before deciding how to file.

Start Saving

When you're young and just starting out, with two incomes and no major expenses like mortgages or college payments, you should save as much as you can. Once your initial spending needs—the wedding, honeymoon, and furnishings—are accomplished, you should live simply and start saving, as your life is only going to get more costly and more complicated as you progress through life's stages.

The first savings fund to tackle is a contingency fund, designed to cushion you through hard times. A contingency fund is extremely critical for the self-employed, but it is also essential for those with jobs. In today's business climate no jobs are secure, and it's unwise to assume anything else.

Your contingency fund should contain enough to cover three to six months' worth of living expenses, and possibly more, if you are in a low-demand field or self-employed.

Once your contingency fund is set, your saving and investing plans should be guided by the short-, mid-, and long-term goals you mapped out earlier. Is the purchase of a house your biggest mid-term goal? Start that savings fund now. We'll address this in more detail in the next stage, but for now it's important to start building a savings account. If a short-term goal is a vacation trip abroad, start saving for that now, too.

At minimum, 10 to 15 percent of your income should go toward savings. It'll only get harder from here on.

Some experts will advise you to start investing immediately in a tax-deferred retirement plan, such as a 401(k) plan. That's not a bad idea, as the plans in which employers provide matching funds can build quickly and steadily. Check the plans each of you is offered through your employer and choose the one that provides the best matching arrangement.

Different plans also offer different investment options, and you should examine the plans closely to see which investment option has a better track record on rate of return. There's no guarantee that a great track record will continue into the future, of course, but it's a place to start.

There's a downside to investing in a tax-deferred retirement plan, however. Such plans are aimed at forcing you to save to finance your retirement, and therefore you must commit your funds for a long time. Some plans, although not all, have loan provisions, but most penalize you if you try to access your money before you reach retirement age.

So if you will need to use these funds for a down payment on a home or to pay college tuition down the road, look closely at the plan's loan provisions and think twice about how much of your savings you commit to the retirement plan.

Instead, you may want to consider holding off on the tax-deferred retirement plan and invest your savings in a combination of a safe and accessible money-market fund and a riskier, growth-stock mutual fund. That's a real smart strategy for this stage of your life, because not only will you be able to get at some of your money when you need it for a down payment on a home or business but the rest of your money will also be growing for the long term.

Let's look at it another way: Generally speaking, for short-term goals of three months to three years, including your contingency fund, you should invest in a cash-type account—for example, a passbook bank savings account, short-term certificate of deposit, or a money-market fund. What you're looking for here is quick, easy access, safety of principal, and rate of return.

For mid-term goals of three to five years, most experts suggest investing in a dedicated bond, or certificate of deposit, that matures about the time you expect to make your planned expenditure. Dedicated bonds and longer term CDs usually pay higher rates of interest than money-market funds and passbook accounts; but they are less liquid, so you really need to time your expenditure accurately. If you end up needing the money before the bond or CD matures, you risk incurring a penalty for cashing in. An exception is the U.S. Series EE bonds, which can be redeemed any time after you've held them for six months with no loss of principal.

For longer-term goals of more than five years, you'll want to look at a wide range of options, including pension investment options and tax-deferred retirement plans. You don't want to invest in riskier, but potentially higher-return, instruments at this stage in your life unless you have excess money to play with and can tolerate a high level of risk.

Jacquie: *If there's one thing I hope you take from this book, and take to heart, it's the concept of saving. Do it any way that works for you, but do it now. In our life, it's the one thing I wish I could reach back into the past, over the long spendthrift years, and change. Mike and I finally came to realize the importance of saving, as many come to a spiritual awakening, way too late in our lives as a couple. Okay, it's never too late. But on the other hand, if we'd started saving when we joined forces, who knows how different our lives might be right now.*

The ugly truth is we always lived right up to and, I admit, exceeding our income. Thank God for Mike's grandmother's regular annual gifts. And gifts from my parents and Mike's, as well, gifts that bought summer camp stays for our children and refrigerators and other necessities of life.

Somehow it seemed, from the privileged perspective of our upper-middle-class, spoiled lives, that we made so little and deserved so much. We just never had enough left over to save. And somehow, I'm embarrassed to report, it never occurred to either of us bright, reasonably high-IQ kids to adjust our spending to accommodate both essentials and savings. Oh, to do it all over again.

Mike: *Oh, the sad confessions of the reformed. Okay, we weren't exactly great about saving, but she forgets that we managed to scrape up enough dough for a down payment for our first house and to buy a number of cars over the years. Plus we have pension plans and 401(k) plans through our employers. So there is some money put aside, and it's growing.*

On the other hand, that's forced savings—money that gets put aside automatically. It's easy when someone does it for you. Saving on your own requires greater self-control, and that's where we fell short for years and years. We eventually turned the corner, and it wasn't too late. But still, Jacquie's right. If we had started sooner, we would be better off today.

Check Insurance and Benefits

The first thing both of you need to do is change your beneficiary from your parents or whomever to each other.

Do this for your pension plans, as well as for your life insurance policies if you already have them.

Be sure to address the question of health insurance immediately. If you both have coverage through your employers, examine the plans thoroughly to determine which provides the best range of benefits. Health insurance plans vary greatly both in cost and in benefits offered. Usually you can save money by dropping separate coverage and using spousal benefits from one of your employers. Generally you have thirty days from the date of the marriage to add your spouse to your policy without a medical examination being required.

And while many employers' health coverage does not extend coverage to same-sex partners, more companies are moving in that direction every year, so it doesn't hurt to check.

One warning on dropping separate coverage and switching one partner to a spousal plan. If you decide to drop your own employer's health insurance and switch to coverage under your spouse's plan, you may have trouble resuming coverage under your employer's plan if your spouse is fired and loses coverage. Before you can switch back and regain the coverage you had initially you may have to take a medical exam. You should check on requirements for resumption of coverage before you make the final decision to switch.

Consider Your "Estate"

The idea may seem a bit silly, but no matter how insignificant your assets are now it's not too soon to begin planning for your estate. Estate planning involves consideration of wills, ownership of assets, beneficiary designations, powers of attorney, and living wills. In effect, it's planning for the management and eventual disbursement of your assets.

Don't neglect a will. Don't put off writing a will, no

matter how immortal you feel right now. If you die intestate—without a will—it can cost your spouse a considerable portion of your estate, and a major migraine as well. Of course there may be days when you not only want to ensure that your partner has a migraine when you're gone but you may also swear to return to haunt him or her.

Plan to haunt your partner if you must, but you'll want to do your haunting in familiar surroundings at your convenience, so meanwhile call your lawyer and have him draft a simple, straightforward will. Usually it's much less hassle and expense than you think—a couple of hundred dollars at most.

Jacquie: *Mike and I put off writing our wills for a number of years. For a long time, we felt we didn't own enough to warrant wills, but that was a mistake. Our children were four and eight at the time, and we were very alarmed to learn that if we had died intestate the children would have become wards of the state, even though our families would have been happy to raise them. The state, of course, had no way of knowing that we wanted my brother to raise our children if we could not. We called a lawyer immediately and got the job done.*

Mike: *It's an extremely important consideration and should be taken care of as soon as you commit to a life together. Without wills, you have no control over the disposal of your assets or the futures of your children. You also should sit down with your attorney periodically to make sure your wills are still reflective of your needs and desires. As our life circumstances have changed, our wills have changed as well.*

Start with joint ownership. We suggest that at this stage of your life you plan for joint ownership with rights of survivorship. In that way, you acquire all your assets—such as cars, home, and bank accounts—as joint owners, and when one spouse dies the survivor becomes the sole owner. Joint ownership can help you avoid delays in transferring assets after death. Later, as your estate grows, you may want to consider owning some property individually or with your children.

The marital estate tax deduction provides an unlimited deduction for the value of property transferred to your spouse during life or at death. The payment of estate tax is postponed until the second spouse dies. If you own too much jointly, you could end up with an unnecessarily large estate tax upon the death of the second spouse. Obviously, everyone's situation is different, so speak with your accountant and attorney about your own circumstances.

A prenuptial agreement may be appropriate. If either spouse brings substantial assets to the marriage, or if you have children from a prior marriage, or if one of your families owns a business, you may want to consider a prenuptial agreement before tying the knot. A prenuptial agreement is a legal document that typically defines who will get which assets in the event the marriage dissolves. It's wise to consult two separate lawyers if you decide to go this route.

Consider a domestic partner agreement. For same-sex couples and those who choose not to marry but are committed to the relationship, you may want to consider a domestic partner agreement. A domestic partner agreement, which would work much the same way as a prenuptial agreement, will help you formalize—and legalize—your financial partnership. Remember, many laws that pertain to married couples simply do not extend to unmarried partners, so extra precautions are needed to protect your joint financial assets.

Again, you will need to consult your attorney in this matter, as each state's laws regarding such agreements are different. You also may want to consult a professional estate planner to help you negotiate the unique tax and inheritance considerations you will face as domestic partners.

Think about durable powers of attorney and living wills. Like a will, these aren't things we like to think about when we're young, but to be sure that your wishes are carried out in the event that you become incapacitated you really need three documents: a durable power of attorney, a durable power of attorney for health care, and a living will. So think ahead and get this done.

A durable power of attorney allows your partner to act on your behalf if you're unable to because you're incapacitated. It can ease the burden your partner will face during such crises when your financial and legal affairs otherwise would be frozen.

A durable power of attorney for health care specifies who you want to make medical decisions for you if you cannot. A living will allows you to specify exactly what life-sustaining medical treatments you do and do not want undertaken on your behalf. To be sure your wishes are followed when you are no longer able to make such decisions, have all these documents drafted. The attorney who prepares your wills can draft these as well, usually for a small additional fee.

STAGE 2—PREPARING TO NEST

Picture this: You've been together five blissful years, have been working hard, moving ahead in your careers, managing your finances, and socking away a healthy savings fund. You look around, take a deep breath, and decide it's time to start a family. Or maybe not. Maybe you decide a family's not right for you, but you want to continue building a better life for yourselves. You figure it's time to purchase a home of your own.

These are probably the two biggest events that will mark the second stage of your life as a couple. And regardless of which scenario fits, you'll need to make some changes in your financial planning as you prepare to nest. Here's your checklist for this stage.

Having a Family? Decide on One Income or Two

If you decide it's time to start a family, you have to decide whether to continue earning two salaries or cut back to one. Obviously, if you both decide to keep working, you'll have more money to spend on your growing family's new needs, and hopefully enough left over to invest and save. On the other hand, you'll find that the complexities of life as a two-income couple with children are enormous, even daunting. Just getting the laundry done can be a major hurdle. Will the additional income offset the inconvenience or the cost of child care? That's a quality of life decision, but a financial one as well.

If you decide it's really important for your emotional well-being for one partner to stop working and care for your child, you need to be sure you can afford to do that. Don't make such a decision off the top of your heads— sit down and work the numbers. What are your expenses? What is the net income of the partner who will continue to work? What new expenses will you accrue with your new family? Don't forget to factor day-care expenses into the dual-income-plus-baby equation. Then decide if you really can afford to cut back to one income.

Determine How Much House You Can Afford

Before you go looking for a house you need to determine how much house you can afford. Start by assuming you want to put down as little as possible in order to be able to purchase your home sooner and not decimate your cash reserves. In most cases, that means you'll need at least 20 percent of the purchase price of the house. Very few lending institutions will consider you for a mortgage unless you have at least that much.

Most realtors recommend one formula or another for

determining home affordability. Forget the formulas. We suggest using a different, more personal approach. First, you need to decide exactly how much you can afford to spend per month on shelter. Start from what you're spending on rent. If you're currently spending $1,000 a month on rent, you know you can afford to spend that much on a monthly mortgage payment.

Next, consider what you're willing or able to give up in terms of monthly discretionary spending. Can you live without that health club membership or skip two dinners out a month for a savings, say, of $200 a month? Okay, now you can afford $1,200 a month on shelter. But because the interest on a mortgage payment, unlike rent, is tax deductible, you can actually go a bit higher, say another $100 a month. That brings you to $1,300 a month without a real pinch in the pocketbook.

Now, what exactly does that $1,300 mean? Go to the real estate section of your bookstore or the library and pick up a copy of what's known as the little blue book of interest amortization charts. Several are published in paperback each year, including *McGraw-Hill's Interest Amortization Tables* and *Mortgage Payments (Barron's Financial Tables for Better Money Management)*. These books have page after page of charts with various kinds of interest rates, including all possible mortgage rates—fixed-rate, 30-year loans at 8 percent, 9.75 percent, 10 percent, etc. There are variable rates, 15-year rates, and on and on.

Check your local newspaper to see what the average mortgage rate is currently for a 30-year, fixed-rate loan. If it's 8 percent, check that line on the chart in the interest book. You'll find a list of payments. Since you determined you can spend $1,300 a month, check that amount for an 8 percent, 30-year mortgage. Let's say you discover that amount will get you a $150,000 mortgage.

If you're planning on taking out a $150,000 mortgage, you're going to need a minimum of $37,500 in cash for a down payment. (Since you have to put down at least 20 percent of the purchase price, your minimum down payment will be 25 percent of the mortgage.) This means you can afford a $187,500 house. But don't start looking in that price range. Houses are always listed for a higher price than the seller will accept. Start looking at houses priced in the $200,000 to $225,000 range. If you find one you love, with any luck you'll be able to negotiate the price down to the amount you can afford.

Remember—those formulas we rejected all come from real estate brokers and bankers who don't have your best interests at heart. Our approach is based entirely on what you as a couple can afford to spend on shelter.

Redo Your Household Budget

Your household budget has gotten you this far, so don't let it slide now. You need to redo your budget to reflect this new stage of your life so you can continue to use it as a tool to manage your financial partnership. Don't forget to include all of your new baby- and house-related expenses, including children's health care costs and house repairs, utilities, insurance, and taxes. And, don't forget to claim an extra dependent on your taxes.

Continue Saving As Best You Can

Most of us simply don't have the resources at this stage to begin an aggressive new saving and investing strategy, or to maintain one, so don't let it bother you. But don't forget the concept altogether, either. For now, despite those new expenses, keep socking away at least a few dollars a month. Your savings may grow very slowly for a few years, but they will grow, and you'll retain the habit of saving, which is most important.

However, if you've decided to start a family it's also time to start your child's college fund. We'll cover this in detail in chapter 9, but for now be aware that tax considerations will be a factor in your decision on the best savings vehicle to use for this.

With a custodial account you put funds in your child's name, and until age 14 the first $650 of the child's interest income is tax-free. The next $650 is taxed at 15 percent, and anything over $1,300 is taxed at your rate. Other investment tools may allow you to keep control of those assets and give you a tax break as well. Consider tax-exempt bonds or growth-oriented mutual funds. More on all this in chapter 9.

Buy Life Insurance

We'll talk about the safety net of insurance in detail in chapter 6, but a few words of advice now for planning purposes: If you haven't already done it, now is the time to buy life insurance. Now that you own a house and perhaps have a family, you want to ensure that a surviving spouse can continue to meet mortgage payments or pay off the loan, as well as meet other household expenses and your financial obligations to your child.

Check Your Disability, Property, and Health Insurance

Check your coverage—or purchase such insurance if you haven't already—to be sure you have adequate coverage for both your growing family and your new home. You may need to augment or increase your disability insurance coverage to reflect your increased living expenses.

Don't forget to add your new family member to your health insurance policy, and be sure the policy adequately covers all the needs of your family.

Update Your Wills

If you haven't gotten around to it yet, be sure you finally write your wills. If they're written, update them and name a guardian for your child. The guardian is the person responsible for your child's day-to-day care and welfare after both your deaths, and that's something you don't want to leave to chance or to the will of the courts.

STAGE 3—ACHIEVING MIDLIFE

So you've hit your forties and your family's maturing right along with you. You've hit your stride career-wise and even can find time to work on your golf swing at the country club. Right now life is good, finances are good, and hopefully you've been following our advice and laying the groundwork for the financial adventures that aren't far off on the horizon: paying for college and boosting your retirement fund. For most of us, those are the major financial events that mark this third stage of our lives.

Here's what you need to be thinking about:

Do a Mid-term Assessment of Your Money Management Skills

It's not too late to do a careful, honest assessment of your money management skills and habits. Ask yourself these questions and answer them honestly: Are you living within your income and within your budget? Do you even have a budget, or did you let that concept slide down the drain as you tried to pay for travel hockey, braces (not necessarily connected to the hockey), dance lessons, and recitals.

What's the status of your savings? Are you up to your ears in credit card debt, living off a new card every six months? Or are you socking money away?

If you're doing everything right, communicating well about money, and happy about your financial health, keep it up. But if you've let your financial partnership fall apart and your money management skills get rusty, reread the first couple of chapters of this book and get back on track.

It's not too late. Draft a new budget, reinstitute those weekly finance committee meetings, dust off the deposit slips, and start planning for the future. You'll need it.

Check the Progress of Your Retirement and College Funds

This is the time when your retirement savings plan must swing into full gear. Unfortunately, recent statistics show that too many Americans—particularly the baby boomers—aren't saving adequately for retirement. In fact, many aren't saving at all. They assume, wrongly, that retirement will take care of itself. So if you haven't already, take charge now of your retirement planning and savings.

We'll cover retirement planning in detail in chapter 10, but for now, be sure you're taking full advantage of tax-favored investment plans such as IRAs, your employer's 401(k), and Keoghs.

You also need to do a reality check on your children's college funds, which we'll cover in detail in chapter 9. Have you saved what you'll need to pay out? If you've been focusing on growth-oriented investments for this, you may want to switch to something safer, like Series EE savings bonds. And be sure to consider what options are out there for financial aid or unusual college financing options. You'll find that even if your income and assets are comfortable, there may be ways to ease the burden.

For example, depending on your income (and this changes yearly with inflation), the interest on U.S. savings bonds and on Series EE bonds can be tax-free if the bonds are bought in your name but used for your child's tuition.

Or, if you plan to sell real estate, stocks, or bonds to pay those college costs, you may want to give those assets to your child and thereby shift the tax bill on the profits to your child. A couple can give each child up to $20,000 a year without incurring federal gift taxes. And if your child is age 14 or older, she pays no tax on the first $650 of interest income, 15 percent tax on the next $23,350, and 28 percent on the next $33,200. That can add up to significant savings indeed. For children under 14, unearned income in excess of $1,300 is taxed at their parents' tax rate.

However, if you can't afford to shift those assets, or if there are none to shift, you may want to borrow against your house with a home equity line of credit. The interest payments will be deductible.

Reassess Your Insurance Needs

As the value of your assets increases over the years, you may need to increase your coverage. Check to ensure that your homeowner's policy fully covers your house and possessions, and make sure your home is insured for the full amount it would cost to replace it.

This is also the stage of your life during which you may become a director of various community organizations. If that's the case, check with the organization on liability coverage; if you don't consider it to be adequate and the organization is unwilling to make a change, you should consider an umbrella policy of your own.

Also review your life insurance coverage. After age 40, the premiums on term life insurance begin to rise dramatically. Depending on the age of your children, you may be able to cut back on coverage.

Consider Reorganizing Your Estate

Your estate is the assets you leave to someone else when you die. If you leave your estate to your spouse, there's no such thing as estate tax. Your spouse inherits everything tax-free, whether you leave $50,000 in assets or $50 million.

The estate is taxed only when it passes from one generation to the next, and even then current tax law provides that an individual's estate—what he or she owns solely— is tax-exempt up to $600,000.

By this stage of your life, however, your assets may be near or have exceeded that $600,000 mark, so check it out. If you want to avoid having your children hit with a huge tax bill on your demise, you might consider starting to gift them with up to $10,000 a year each, shifting some of your assets into their name, or making them part owner of your assets.

STAGE 4—GETTING READY TO RETIRE

Retirement isn't something you start thinking about at age 55. We've touched on retirement planning at earlier life stages, and for the full story you'll want to read chapter 10. But now it's getting down to the wire. You're ready, psychologically, to step back from the world of work and try on a more relaxed lifestyle. Here's what you need to think about:

Check the Status of Your Retirement Fund

The key question is, Will you have enough saved when the blissful day arrives to retire comfortably? The general rule is that to maintain your standard of living in retirement, your retirement income should equal 75 percent of your preretirement take-home pay. Of course, you can retire comfortably on less, and many do, but to ensure that you're able to maintain your current lifestyle use the 75 percent rule.

Another way of estimating whether you're ready to retire comfortably is to determine exactly what you are currently spending. Then, using that as a base, estimate your expenses, modifying them upwards and downwards as appropriate, for your first actual retirement year. For example, you'll be spending less on lunches out, parking and commuting, business clothes, and other business-related expenses. And with the children gone, family expenses will be cut way back. But what about the extra greens fees for golf at area clubs other than your own, and travel expenses for all those day and week-long trips to friends and relatives you haven't had time to visit in recent years? You'll need to add those in.

One reminder: Many couples choose to move to another state or region when they retire, or even maintain residency in two states. That can affect your expenses in ways you haven't—but should—consider. For example, will the climate and environment affect your health and health insurance? What about safety, transportation costs, state and local taxes? All of these factors need to be calculated into your retirement expenses and lifestyle.

Once you've estimated those expenses, you need to determine whether you'll be able to pay them. To do that, analyze the sources and amount of after-tax income you'd have if you were to retire immediately. That will include Social Security, pension funds, 401(k) funds, and any other income you might have. Use the worksheet in chapter 10 to calculate in detail if your income will be sufficient to retire. If the bottom line says "go," you're on the right track.

Reassess Your Insurance Needs

Once again, you should rethink your insurance coverage at this stage of your life. You may decide you no longer need life insurance. On the other hand, your life insurance policy may be needed to provide adequate income for the surviving spouse.

At this stage you also should consider long-term care insurance, which is similar to disability insurance and will protect you against the debilitating cost of long-term health care. You can get a policy that covers both custodial and at-home care in the event of a protracted illness. At age 50, premiums are substantially cheaper than they are for those age 60 and over. And if you wait too long you may not be healthy enough to get coverage.

You need to be sure you have health coverage, as well, during retirement. If you're age 65 or older, you're eligible for Medicare, the federal health insurance program, which offers both hospital and medical insurance. The Social Security Administration can provide you with information about the program. It also handles enrollment.

If you don't stop working after age 65, your employer must provide coverage. Federal law also requires that you be allowed to continue in the company's group plan for 18 months following retirement. After that, you may have the option of reverting to an individual policy under the company plan.

Be aware, too, that Medicare isn't perfect and leaves you unprotected in several ways, including deductibles, coinsurance amounts, and some coverage gaps. For example, Medicare doesn't pay for medical tests for, or the cost of, eyeglasses and hearing aids, out-of-pocket hospital prescription drugs, care received outside the United States, and custodial care, among others. To fill these gaps you may want to consider buying Medigap insurance, which is private health insurance designed specifically to fill the gaps between Medicare and your insurance needs.

Decide How You Want to Receive Your Retirement Income

Once you decide you're ready, psychologically and financially, to retire, you need to set up the distribution of your retirement income. And with that decision you have new tax issues to consider, for the way in which your retirement benefits are distributed can affect the amount and timing of taxes you pay on those benefits. In order to choose the best retirement payment option you need to consider not only the tax implications but also your personal needs for use of the funds.

Generally speaking, a lump-sum distribution may give you more flexibility in using the money. If you choose a lump-sum distribution, your best option probably is to roll it over into an IRA, where you will continue to earn tax-deferred interest. If you are over age 59½, you can begin to take money out of the account as you need to.

If, on the other hand, you take the lump sum in cash, you'll owe income tax on the whole amount. However, you may be able to use five- or ten-year forward averaging to soften the tax bite. That's a one-time tax on the distribution that reduces your total tax by treating it as if it were received in smaller amounts over a five-year or ten-year period. You should check to see if you qualify.

STAGE 5—STARTING OVER

You may have planned for your joint retirement from the day you became a couple. You probably envisioned yourselves sailing off on a Caribbean cruise, or slipping off to your cottage by the lake, ready to relish your well-earned leisure time together. And it's a beautiful dream. But sometimes dreams turn into nightmares, and instead of sailing into retirement together you may need to start over again—alone. Death or divorce may strike when you least expect it and shatter your dreams of shared retirement. For that matter, you may end up having to start over well before the retirement stage. No matter what your age, you'll never be prepared psychologically for such a tragedy, but you *can* be prepared to deal with it financially. Here's how:

Take Your Time and Reassess Your Finances

This is *most* important: Don't make any hasty decisions about your finances. Take your time—as much as six months—and carefully reassess where you stand financially. This is the time when your long-established, active participation in the family finances, as a member of your finance committee, will serve you well. As a result of this involvement your family finances won't be a mystery to you and you'll be able to begin your financial reassessment with a sense of power and self-confidence.

However hard to come to grips with, and whatever your age and life stage, the reality is that now you must manage your finances and your financial future alone. If your financial partnership hasn't worked the way we hope it has, that will take significant adjustment. And you may need professional help to get started. If that's the case, don't hesitate. But on the other hand, if you've followed the advice in this book from chapter 1, you should be able to take over your family's financial management as a single person without too much problem in the end.

However, you may have to handle a big settlement from a divorce or from your deceased spouse's estate. That could boost your estate considerably, and you will have to decide how best to invest those assets. You may want to follow the guidelines you and your spouse have followed over the years you invested together, or you may decide you want to alter that investment course. That's a decision for you to make.

You will, however, need to be certain you're planning for a financially secure future, whether you're immediately facing retirement or whether retirement is still far down the road. If you're uncertain of the best course to follow, seek expert advice from a financial or estate planner.

Check All Your Important Documents

First, redo your will and your durable powers of attorney. Next, check your insurance policies to determine whether the beneficiaries should be changed. Chances are they should be. If you have young children you may want to review their designated guardians and decide if you want to set up trusts in their names.

In terms of taxes, you don't owe income tax on life insurance benefits. And you can take a break on appreciation. The tax on any appreciation in the value of property owned by your spouse is forgiven when he or she dies. If you owned property together, there is no tax on half the profit. Remember, too, you can file a joint return for the year of your spouse's death; if you have a dependent child you can use joint return rates for two years after death.

Rethink Your Insurance Coverage

You may no longer have a need for life insurance coverage. But if you still have young children, you may need to increase your life insurance and disability coverage.

Don't tamper with your long-term care coverage if you have it. It's even more necessary now than before, when you had a partner to share in your future care. If you don't have long-term care insurance and are over age 45, purchase it now. Remember, after age 60 it's harder and more costly to obtain coverage.

If your health insurance has been covered by your spouse's policy through an employer, that coverage must continue for thirty-six months. However, you may be required to pay as much as 102 percent of the premium. After that it may be possible to convert from the employer's group plan to an individual policy. Or, you may have to seek coverage elsewhere.

Starting over alone is never easy, but if you have participated as a full partner in your family's financial affairs you will find the transition much less traumatic than it would be otherwise.

GIVE THE LIFE-STAGE METHOD A TRY

So that's the life-stage method of financial planning. Okay, it's not rocket science. Yes, it's pretty much a function of logic. But that's just the point. Most of us live very much in the thick of small financial skirmishes day-to-day, and can easily lose sight of the overall battle plan we set out with. You know—our financial goals and priorities. We end up deciding to buy that boat on a whim, and BOOM—we're reeling from the effects of the pop-up method of financial planning. In effect, no effective financial planning at all.

So give this method a try. Correlate it with your own unique goals and priorities. Set it out in as much detail as possible in your financial planning notebook. Set up a chapter for each of the five life stages, or add a couple more stages if that seems to apply better to you as a couple. The point is to plan, and plan together, for the various stages of your lives. If you do that, each stage will end up richer, in terms of both life experience and wealth, than you ever believed possible. And you'll have more fun watching your plan unfold. Trust us.

PART TWO

LAYING THE
GROUNDWORK

6

Weaving Your Safety Net: Insurance Protection

As you go through life together, the two of you will acquire possessions, make binding financial commitments, possibly have children, and may suffer through serious illnesses and other catastrophes. You'll also more than likely become financially interdependent. Most couples today both work—you may even own a business together—and rely on both incomes to make ends meet.

This complex life you'll create will require protection in the form of various types of insurance. Your home and its furnishings, your cars, your businesses, and even your lives are vulnerable and need to be protected against the unforeseen. That's what insurance does.

HOW DOES INSURANCE WORK?

Insurance is a simple arrangement between you and your insurer. In return for a certain amount of money called a premium, the insurer agrees to compensate you for loss. You can insure your home, your possessions, your cars, your life, and just about anything else. People who organize golf tournaments and offer cars and other prizes for a hole in one can purchase insurance that covers their cost should a player actually get a hole in one and they have to pay off. Hollywood legend has it that the legs of 40s screen star Betty Grable were insured.

Not surprisingly, insurance is one of the most maligned segments of the financial services industry. To most of us, insurance seems little more than a void into which we pour money for a benefit we may never need. When we do need it, it's almost always in the midst of a traumatic financial or health crisis. And, ironically, although many of us own the one type of insurance all policyholders collect on eventually—life insurance—we're not around to enjoy the big payoff.

But like it or not, insurance is a necessity. It protects our property and our businesses, helps us withstand the financial stress of serious illnesses, and provides money for the people who depend on us when we die. In short, it provides stability, predictability, and security.

WHAT KINDS OF INSURANCE DO YOU NEED?

This is a decision the two of you need to make together. People's insurance needs vary greatly and are determined by many, many factors—whether you own or rent your home, the value of your home, whether or not you have children, your age, your income, whether or not you both work, and the amount of money you've set aside for retirement, to name just a few.

If you listen to insurance agents, you should insure everything you own. And why shouldn't they tell you that? When insurers pay you after a claim, the money comes from a huge pool of invested funds created from the premiums of all their customers. The money that's left over after they pay all their claims is profit. So the more premiums they can attract, the more money they make.

In fact, however, most people need less insurance than

the industry claims they do. For instance, when it comes to insuring your possessions, you only need to insure things that have a real cash value and that you would replace if they were lost or destroyed. This certainly includes your house, your furniture, and your car. But does it include your aunt Minnie's antique necklace? Even though it may be quite valuable, you couldn't replace it if you lost it, so why bother to insure it? If you were planning on selling it down the road to help finance a child's education, it might be worth insuring. But otherwise, don't waste your money.

Life insurance, too, is often oversold. First of all, not everyone needs it. Single people with no dependents certainly don't need it. Neither do older people whose children are grown and whose income from savings, pensions, and Social Security are adequate to get them through the rest of their lives.

You only need life insurance if you have dependents and a small estate. You should have enough insurance to pay off your mortgage, any outstanding short-term debts like car payments and credit cards, your kids' college tuition, and to keep your dependents on their feet for three or four years. You don't need to support them for the rest of their lives.

One important form of insurance that most people don't think about is disability insurance. You're much more likely to become disabled from an accident or illness than you are to die at an early age. And if you do, the disability insurance provided by your employer will pay you just a portion of your income over a fairly short term. Yet, most people fail to supplement their employer-provided disability insurance with private policies. They're worth the money.

Depending on your circumstances, one or both of you will probably need several if not all of the following types of insurance.

LIFE INSURANCE

Do either of you need life insurance? If others are financially dependent on you, yes. If you have children, a mortgage, car payments, and other short- and long-term financial obligations, you both may need life insurance. Your family depends on your income and will need to replace it, at least temporarily, should you pass away.

But if no one would suffer financially if either of you suddenly moved on to the great beyond, then you're wasting your money. If you have no children and your individual incomes are enough to meet all financial needs, then why buy insurance? Granted, it will provide a nice payoff in the unlikely event that one of you should die unexpectedly, but is it worth the years and years of premiums? Of course not. You'd be much better off putting that money in an investment account.

How Much Life Insurance Do You Need?

Again, this depends on your individual circumstances. The insurance industry has any number of complex forms that it uses to help people answer this question. Most will put you to sleep.

The best way to determine your life insurance needs is to simply ask yourself the following question: How many years of my current after-tax income would our family need to continue its current lifestyle and meet future needs? The answer is usually less than you would think. You'll need to pay off the mortgage and any other outstanding loans, of course, which for many people might take as little as two or three years of income. Then you may or may not have children to educate. But beyond that, assuming the surviving spouse or partner is currently working or is able to enter the workforce, other future needs should be covered.

You should also find out how much in Social Security *survivors'* benefits your minor children would qualify for if you should pass away. You can contact the Social Security Administration at 800-772-1213 for information on survivors' benefits.

What Kind of Life Insurance Should You Buy?

You have two basic choices, *cash value* life insurance (whole life insurance, universal life insurance, and variable life insurance are the most common) or *term* life insurance. Cash value insurance invests a portion of your premiums and slowly builds equity. Once you purchase a policy it stays in effect until you act to cancel it. If you should eventually cancel the policy, you'll receive the money the policy has accrued over the years. You may also be able to borrow from the equity to pay for college costs or other expenses.

Term insurance, on the other hand, is strictly pay-as-you-go. You write a check for your premium every year and that's it. At the end of each subsequent year you can renew the coverage for what will probably be steadily increasing premiums. If you pass away while a term policy is in effect, it pays off. But there's no equity or any other sort of financial benefit involved.

So which should you buy? "Well, gee," you might say. "It sounds like a no-brainer. We should buy the one that earns us money."

Well, guess again.

Buy Term Insurance Only

Let's put this in the simplest manner possible: Life insurance is a lousy investment, no matter how you look at it. That means you should pay as little as possible for it. And that means you should buy term insurance.

"But what about the money we'd earn with a cash value policy?" you might wonder.

It's peanuts, especially compared with what your money could earn in a mutual fund or some other investment product. The insurance industry, on the other hand, would have you believe that cash value life insurance is the greatest investment you can make. They'll point out that not only are you guaranteeing that there will be money for your family if you should pass away but you're also building equity you can borrow against down the road to help pay for college or meet other expenses.

Technically, this is true. You do build equity that you can use later on. The problem is you're paying many times what a term policy would cost, and very little of the difference between the two is actually being invested. Most of it ends up in the coffers of the insurance company and the pocket of the salesperson who sold you the policy (an insurance salesperson will make about ten times more commission when selling you a cash value policy than when selling a term policy). What that money should be doing is sitting in a retirement fund or a mutual fund with your names on it.

One of the arguments made in favor of cash value policies is that their premiums are "paid up" after a certain number of years. In other words, the policy continues to be in effect but you won't be shelling out any more money. Meanwhile, a term policy's premiums have to be paid like clockwork as long as you own the policy.

Again, technically, this is true. But since the premiums for a cash value policy are so much higher than those for a term policy, the total outlay for the cash value policy will be much higher. All you're really doing is paying the premiums in advance (and look who ends up with the money). It would take another twenty to thirty years of term premiums to match what you'd pay for a cash value policy that's considered "paid up" after fifteen or twenty years. And don't be fooled by the concept of your policy being "paid up." If you live long enough, there's a good chance you'll eventually exhaust those prepaid premiums and suddenly get a letter from the insurance company saying you need to put more money into the policy if you want it to stay in effect.

Another argument for cash value policies is that term insurance premiums keep increasing as you age. Again, true. But very few people need life insurance after a certain point in their lives. Once the kids are educated and on their own, the house is paid off, and pensions, Social Security, and retirement account income all kick in, life insurance becomes a big waste of money.

But perhaps the biggest problem with cash value life insurance is its cost. Because it's so expensive, most people are unable to afford the coverage they need. Nevertheless, buffaloed by the pitch of the salesperson and convinced they're doing the best thing for their children's future, they buy it anyway. So there they are, underinsured, paying huge premiums, and building equity at a snail's pace. If they took the same amount of money, bought a term policy, and invested the difference in a selection of mutual funds, they'd have the same amount of insurance coverage and a heck of a lot more money.

Despite all this, at least 75 percent of the life insurance policies sold today are cash value policies. It just goes to show you how effective the industry's marketing efforts are. Don't be lured in. Term policies are the only way to go.

Where Can You Buy Life Insurance?

Life insurance is an annoying fact of life. But the good news is there are many companies and organizations competing for your business. This means that with a little comparison shopping you can get adequate coverage at a reasonable price. Here are the most common sources of life insurance.

Brokers and Agents

For many people, the logical place to start is an insurance agent or an insurance broker. The two operate identically except for one important difference: an agent represents the insurance products of a single company, while a broker represents many companies. Which is best? Often it's the broker. By not being tied to a single company, he can scour the market for policies that best meet your needs.

This is not to say an agent can't get you an equally good product. Many big insurance companies have a wide variety of coverages and can keep many insurance shoppers happy.

Whichever you choose, check their reputations carefully. A reputable insurance professional will act in your best interests. Unfortunately, however, not all of them are reputable. Some will be more interested in making as much money off the sale of a policy than finding you the best coverage.

How can you tell the difference between the two? The best way is to ask friends and business associates for references. Almost everyone has had some experience with insurance agents and brokers, and those with good reputations quickly stand out from the crowd.

Beyond that, you need to rely on your own ability to ask questions and not accept everything you're told as gospel. If a salesperson seems to be pushing one policy over several others, don't be shy about asking what the commission is. You may find that the one he likes best for *you* just happens to put the most money in *his* pocket. Some salespeople will encourage you to cash in a policy you already have for a new one, arguing that the new one offers a better return and better coverage. Keep in mind that it earns him a new commission as well.

Your Employer

Many people are provided some amount of life insurance as part of their employment compensation. They're also frequently able to purchase additional coverage at very reasonable rates through their employers. Keep in mind, however, that if you leave your job you may not be able to continue coverage.

Low-Load Life Insurance Companies

It's becoming more and more common these days for insurance companies to sell life insurance directly to their customers at lower than average premiums. The reason? Because they sell directly to the consumer, they don't have the commission costs that they'd have if they went through an agent. They keep a little bit of the resulting profit and pass the rest on to you. Here are a few companies to consider.

- USAA Life
  San Antonio, Texas
  (800)531-8000

- Ameritas Low-Load
  Houston, Texas
  (800)552-3553

- American Life of New York
  New York, New York
  (212)399-5555

Savings Banks

Savings banks in Connecticut, New York, and Massachusetts are authorized to sell both cash value and term life insurance to people who work or live in the state. The amount you can purchase is limited, but the premiums are excellent.

Mike: *I've had several life insurance policies over the years. The first was a whole life policy that was sold to me in 1977 by a bug-eyed, bulldog-jowled, hyperactive ex-marine turned insurance salesman named Fran who came after me like he was assaulting the beaches of Iwo Jima. I was 25, our daughter was on the way, and I didn't know beans about insurance, so I immediately withered under Fran's aggressive sales pitches (actually, I was kind of afraid to not buy a policy from him). The next thing I knew my life was worth $100,000.*

Over time, and with a little research, I came to realize that I was throwing money down the drain. After five or six years, I canceled the policy, collected its meager proceeds (around $800, if I remember correctly), bought a term policy, and started investing the difference between the two premiums.

I still have that term policy today. In addition, the university where I work provides me, at no cost, with a policy that pays one-and-a-half times my salary, and I pay affordable premiums for a second term policy through the Teachers Insurance and Annuity Association/College Retirement Equities Fund (TIAA/CREF). Our kids are 19 and 16, and I figure I'll need life insurance for another ten years at most. Could I afford the same amount of coverage if I was buying whole life or some other form of cash value insurance? Possibly, but it would be painful.

Jacquie: *I have the same employer-provided coverage that Mike has plus a big term policy through TIAA/CREF. I only know I have them because Mike tells me I have them. This brings up an important point: Despite everything we say in this book, there will probably be one or two areas of personal finance that, no matter how much you try, you just can't make yourself take an interest in. For me, it's insurance. That's why Mike wrote this chapter by himself.*

HEALTH INSURANCE

Health insurance is one of the biggest crises facing the United States today. Our population is aging, which is putting increasing pressure on health care providers. The cost of care is increasing while its quality is decreasing. And the portion of the bill that insurance covers is going down.

The most fortunate of us have employer-provided health care plans. But for the millions of Americans whose employers don't provide coverage, or who are self-employed or unemployed, the cost of health insurance is an enormous burden. Many simply can't afford it. As a result, more than 30 million people in this country have no health care coverage. Most are just a serious illness away from financial ruin.

Employer-Provided Insurance

The best way to get health insurance today is to be an employee of a mid- to large-size company. If either of you works for a large corporation, consider yourselves lucky. You probably have about as good an employer-provided health care plan as is available. The company foots the bill for a good portion of the premium and withholds your contribution from your paycheck.

But if you work for a smaller company, your coverage is probably less comprehensive. If the firm is small enough, you may not be offered any coverage at all. Health insurance is becoming more and more expensive for everyone, corporate America included. Some companies find they simply can't afford it anymore.

When you become a couple, if you both have employer-provided health care you need to analyze each plan carefully before deciding what to do. Usually, you can opt for either individual or family coverage through your employer. If you're a couple with no children, you need to weigh the cost of having two individual plans against the cost of one family plan. You need to compare premiums, deductibles, and other costs to see which option offers the better deal.

If you have children, you need to compare the same costs for family coverage to see which employer's plan has the best coverage and costs.

If both of you choose family coverage in order to maximize your coverage, companies use the "birthday rule" to decide which company has the primary responsibility for a claim. This means the policy of the spouse whose birthday comes earlier in the year has to cover the claim. After the claim is settled, you can then submit the claim to the second company to cover some or all of the costs the first policy didn't cover (after the deductible is met).

Jacquie: *For a time after I started working at Cornell University, where Mike also is employed, we each purchased family health coverage. We work in different branches of the university, and they have totally different health plans. We thought we were buying more comprehensive coverage that way, that one would cover what the other didn't. That was a mistake.*

Mike: *In this Jacquie and I agree, and we reached agreement without too much debate, after looking more closely at the numbers and the coverage. Jacquie's is a managed care plan and is clearly superior for our needs, in terms of cost and coverage. Having two plans does give you better coverage in that the second plan will usually pick up a good portion of what the first plan doesn't cover. But unless you have an inordinate amount of medical costs—the kinds you'd be hit with in the event of a major illness or accident—it's unlikely the amount of money you'd recover through the second plan would approach the premiums you'd pay. We rarely have medical costs. So we dropped my family plan, which was costing us $1,000 a year in premiums.*

If You Lose Your Job

In 1986, the federal Consolidated Omnibus Budget Reconciliation Act (COBRA) was passed to make sure that people who have health care benefits through their employer can continue them if they should lose their jobs. The act states that any employer with more than nineteen employees must give their employees and their family members the opportunity to continue coverage for up to eighteen months if they are laid off (or retire). The cost can be expensive; a company can charge up to 102 percent of what it costs the company to provide the coverage (the extra 2 percent is for handling charges), but it's certainly better than having no coverage at all.

Another provision in the law protects people who have coverage through a spouse or other person. If the covered employee should die or a divorce occurs, the dependent person can purchase coverage through the employee's group plan for up to three years.

Buying Your Own Health Insurance

If you're self-employed or have lost your job, you face a severe financial challenge. The hunt for health insurance can be frustrating and confusing. Finding a policy that meets both your needs and your budget sometimes seems impossible. If you can spend some time searching, however, there's a good chance you can find coverage that fits.

Before you begin your search, however, you need to decide what sort of coverage you need. Everyone should have a plan that covers the big expenses—hospitalization, surgical bills, and associated costs such as X rays and laboratory work. If you're a young couple and just entering childbearing years, a good maternity and pediatric plan will also be a big priority.

Deductibles and Co-payments

A deductible is an amount of money that you agree to pay toward your annual health care costs before your benefits kick in. A co-payment is the percentage of the balance that you agree to pay. Let's say you have a $500 deductible and a 20 percent co-payment, and your only health care costs for the year are a couple of $75 visits to the doctor. In this case, you'd pay the $150, and your insurer would pay nothing.

The following year, however, you develop a serious condition that requires some minor surgery and a number of visits to the doctor. The total bill comes to $5,000. Of this, you'd pay the first $500. Of the $4,500 balance, the insurer would pay $3,600 and you'd pay $900. Most plans with co-payments have an annual maximum amount—usually $1,000—for which you're responsible. Once that amount is met, they pick up the entire tab.

Keep this in mind when looking at various health insurance plans: The higher the deductible and co-payments you're willing to take on, the cheaper the premiums will be.

Group Coverage

Group coverage is one good source of health insurance. If either of you belongs to a trade association or professional association, it may sponsor a group health care plan for its members. Or you may be able to find an organization with this benefit that you can join.

Group plans aren't perfect. For one thing, an insurance company can cancel a group plan at any time, leaving you high and dry. Also, state regulatory agencies usually pay less attention to group plans than individual plans. The coverage itself is also not always as comprehensive as you might want. Still, a good group plan can provide you with enough coverage to make your health care costs manageable.

Individual Coverage

This is the last resort for most people simply because of the cost. But there are some ways to minimize the financial pain. The simplest is to keep your deductibles as high as possible, assuming that your health has been good. If you have a history of illness, however, a high deductible might not be such a good idea.

HMOs

HMOs (Health Maintenance Organizations) are another option for people shopping for their own health insurance. HMOs provide comprehensive health care needs, from doctor visits (including routine physicals) to hospitalization and sometimes even prescription drugs and eyeglasses.

The problem with HMOs is that you can only use physicians who are part of the organization. For a long time, most HMOs would not reimburse members who went to physicians outside their network. Most have changed, though, and today a few will cover as much as 80 percent of the costs of an outside physician.

PPOs

PPOs (Preferred Provider Organizations) are virtually identical to HMOs. The main differences are cost (most PPOs have slightly higher premiums) and reimbursement for the costs of visiting providers outside the network (PPOs are more generous).

Maximum Lifetime Benefits

Health insurance plans guarantee coverage only up to a certain dollar amount over each individual's lifetime. Many plans provide a maximum of $1 million. At first that may seem quite adequate. But, in fact, a serious, long-term illness can eat through that figure in a surprisingly short time. You're better off with $2 million or $3 million in maximum benefits.

Guaranteed Renewal

Once they have health insurance, most people start worrying about losing it. For peace of mind, only buy a policy that guarantees annual renewal without a physical or any other strings attached.

Coverage for Unmarried and Same-sex Couples

If you're an unmarried couple or same-sex couple, and one of you is employed by a company that provides health insurance to its employees, things are starting to brighten. For years, most companies refused to acknowledge such nontraditional unions and wouldn't extend health care benefits to the partners of their employees.

This is finally starting to change. One by one, the nation's corporations are beginning to come out of the dark ages and opening up coverage to these new family units. As they do, thanks to the lockstep character of American business, more and more are following suit. It's not yet a universal change of policy, but it's heading in that direction.

HOMEOWNER'S AND RENTER'S INSURANCE

Whether the two of you own a home or just rent, you need insurance to protect your possessions. If you own your home you'll need homeowner's insurance. In fact, if you have a mortgage, you won't have a choice. All lending institutions require that their mortgagees have homeowner's insurance as a condition of their loans. After all, your house is the collateral for the money they're lending you. If it burns down, they want to make sure the money will be there to pay them back.

Renters, too, need insurance, not for the dwelling they live in but for all their possessions. Yet the majority of people who rent, especially young people early in their careers, fail to purchase this most basic of coverages, even though they're just as vulnerable, if not more so, to fire or some other calamity. The results can be disastrous.

Types of Coverage

Homeowners of relatively new homes have three types of progressively expensive coverage to pick from (HO-1, HO-2, HO-3, in industry lingo). A fourth (HO-4) covers renters, a fifth (HO-6) covers "unit" dwellers (people who own condominiums, coops, lofts, etc.), and a sixth (HO-8) covers older homes. No, I don't know what happened to HOs 5 and 7.

I've always felt homeowner's insurance is a great bargain considering the peace of mind it provides. In fact, it's affordable enough that most homeowners, us included, choose HO-3 insurance, which is the most expensive of the three. To give you some idea of how reasonable it is, we have $158,000 worth of coverage on our house, $16,000 for "other structures on residence property" (garage, shed, etc.), $110,000 for personal possessions, $32,000 for "loss of residence premises" (this will pay the bill at the Holiday Inn while our house is being rebuilt), $100,000 for each occurrence of personal liability, and $1,000 in medical payment for each occurrence of personal injury. Our annual premium for all this is only $455.

Renter's policies provide the same kind of coverage, minus coverage for the structure itself. It's equally affordable.

What's Covered

A good HO-3 homeowner's policy protects your home and possessions against just about everything. It will protect you from loss due to fire, lightning, wind and hail, smoke, vandalism, vehicle collision, theft, snow and ice, exploding appliances, burst pipes, and surges of electrical current. But that's not all. If there's a riot in the neighborhood and your home is damaged, you're covered. If that pesky volcano down the street erupts, you're covered. You're even covered if the Mir space station should land on your house.

What's Not Covered

Your policy won't cover damage from flood, earthquake, war, nuclear accident, and any other exclusion that may be specified. It more than likely won't cover any business-related property that's in the house (home office users, take note). Also, if you're one of those lucky couples who own a really old home—one that's loaded with charm but may be a little creaky in the rafters—you'll be relegated to HO-8 status. That means you may have trouble finding coverage against things like ice and snow damage, burst pipes, and the other calamities that frequently befall older houses.

Floater Policies

If you have certain possessions for which your standard policy doesn't provide adequate protection, you can add layers of protection with floater policies. For example, most homeowner's policies limit coverage for silverware to no more than $2,000. If you need more, you can buy additional coverage for about $5 per $1,000 worth of silver. The same holds true for jewelry and other valuables. Be aware, though, that some companies may require sales slips or professional appraisals of your property before they'll agree to insure it under a floater policy. It's understandable. The potential for all sorts of scams is obvious.

Make sure your floater policy will pay off under all circumstances, including just plain losing things (the industry calls this "mysterious loss").

Inventory Your Possessions

If your house burns down, are you going to be able to remember everything that was in it? Not likely. This is why making an inventory of your possessions is so important. Write down the serial numbers of your televisions, stereo, computers, and other electronic devices. Take photographs of your furniture, appliances, and other items. Even better, do a videotaping session of the entire house, room by room, closet by closet, and drawer by drawer. Don't forget the basement, attic, and garage.

Once you've completed your inventory, keep it stored in a safe-deposit box or other secure location outside your home. And keep it updated as you make new purchases by adding the receipts to the file.

Review Your Policy Regularly

Hopefully, your home will increase in value during the period of time you own it. Your insurance coverage must keep pace. If the house you bought for $150,000 two years ago would cost $175,000 to replace today, you'd better make sure your policy is changed to reflect that fact.

AUTOMOBILE INSURANCE

Americans both love and hate their cars. On the one hand, they're attractive and fun to drive. To some, they're also a symbol of wealth and achievement and even personality. On the other hand, they're horrid investments and expensive to operate and repair. Still, unless you live and work in a major city, life without an automobile is virtually impossible. And if you own a car, you have to insure it.

What Kind of Coverage Do You Need?

This will be determined more by the value of your car(s) than by anything else. Here are the basic types of coverage for automobiles.

Bodily Injury and Property Liability Insurance

Liability insurance is required by law of all car owners, regardless of the age or value of their cars. It covers injury caused by you to pedestrians, other cars, and the passengers in other cars. Conversely, if someone should run into you, their policy will cover injury or damage to you and your vehicle.

The amount of coverage you need will be tied to your vulnerability to a lawsuit if you cause an accident. The more assets you have, the more liability insurance you should purchase. Basic coverage should include $100,000 worth of coverage for each injured person, with a maximum of $300,000 per accident. If you have a lot of assets that could be pursued by a plaintiff's attorney, you may want to purchase even more.

Collision Insurance

Collision insurance covers damage to your car no matter what the cause. Your premium will depend on the age and value of your car and the deductible you choose.

Cars depreciate in value quite rapidly, and the need for collision insurance decreases right along with it. If you have a really old car, collision insurance makes no sense at all. This is because when you have an accident, your insurer will pay you either the cost of the repair to the car or the actual cash value of the car, whichever is less. If you're tooling around in a '76 Pacer (ah, the memories) and you smack into a tree, the insurer looks at the cost of repairs (several thousand dollars) versus the cash value of the vehicle (about $19.99). The result? You end up with $19.99, and your beloved Pacer ends up in the junkyard. So why pay the premiums?

Medical Payments Insurance

This coverage is for medical costs of the policyholder, family members, and passengers who are injured in an accident involving the policyholder's car, regardless of who caused the accident. It's fairly cheap, but may not be necessary if you have a good health insurance policy.

Uninsured Motorist Coverage

Despite the fact that liability insurance is required by law, there are a lot of people who don't have it. And they're usually the worst drivers on the road. Many have had their coverages canceled because of their poor driving histories. If one of these people should hit you, whether you're in your vehicle or just walking down the road, collecting for damages will be a nightmare. Uninsured motorist coverage protects you against such situations.

Comprehensive Coverage

Comprehensive coverage protects you and your automobile against anything your other policies don't cover—theft, the Mir space station or other falling objects, vandalism, collisions with animals, and many other risks.

Whether or not you need comprehensive coverage is really tied to the value of your car. If you have a late model car, you really should have it. You never know what can happen. For example, we live in an area with an extremely high deer population, and deer/car collisions are common. Last Thanksgiving weekend our daughter was coming home from a friend's house late one night and hit a deer right around the corner from our house. She was only going about 20 miles an hour, but the collision still caused about $1,500 worth of damage. Our comprehensive policy covered the repairs (less a $50 deductible).

Premiums

Insurance premiums are based on statistical probability. The greater the likelihood that a company will have to pay a claim on a policy, the higher the premiums for that policy. This is one reason why homeowner's policies are so reasonable. The likelihood of your house burning down, being vandalized, or being hit by a tornado or even the Mir space station is really quite small.

But people are always smashing into each other in their cars. That's why the premiums for automobile insurance are so high. Consider the fact that we can insure a $150,000 house for $455, but it costs us more than $2,000 to insure $30,000 worth of automobiles. It doesn't seem fair, but unfortunately it's a direct result of the prevalence of accidents in this country.

Many factors are calculated in determining premiums. If you live in a city you'll pay more than people living in rural areas. Different states have different insurance regulations, and these affect premiums. Age and sex are big factors. Our son recently turned 16 and began driving. He's now a member of the most feared demographic group on the road—16-to-25-year-old males—and our premium reflects it. The day he got his license our car insurance shot up $800 a year.

Your driving record will affect your premiums. If you have a history of speeding tickets, accidents, or drunk driving, you'll pay more than someone with a clean record. If your record becomes bad enough, you may even become uninsurable. And even the kind of car you drive will affect what you pay. The owner of an expensive high-performance car like a Corvette will pay a higher premium than he or she would to insure a Dodge Neon.

LIABILITY INSURANCE

Imagine this scenario. Nice old Mr. Jones, the man next door who's been like a grandfather to your children and a second father to you, suddenly falls off your back porch one day and breaks a hip. The next thing you know, this gentle widower is claiming your shoddy home maintenance is responsible for his fall and is suing you for a million bucks.

Can't happen, you say? Well, you're wrong. People sue each other every day for all sorts of things, including falling off porches. If you're sued, you'll need liability insurance to protect you.

You'll probably have some liability coverage through your homeowner's or renter's policy. There's just one problem. Even the best homeowner's policies only provide $300,000 in liability coverage, and people are being awarded settlements for many times that amount these days. And if you have your own business, your homeowner's policy won't provide any protection against liabilities related to your professional activities.

Personal Liability Insurance

For most people, personal liability insurance (also called umbrella insurance) is an affordable way to augment the liability protection provided by their homeowner's policies. Depending on your circumstances, a $1 million policy can be obtained for as little as $100 a year. However, the company that issues the policy may require that you also beef up your homeowner's as well. This is because umbrella insurance takes over when you've exhausted your homeowner's benefits.

It's called umbrella insurance because it's supposed to cover everything. If your dog bites Mr. Jones, if your kids knock him off the porch again, even if you run him over with your riding mower, you're protected. Read the fine print and make sure that's the case. Even your kids who are away at school should be covered. And make sure your policy includes legal defense expenses. Even if you're ultimately vindicated, defending yourself against a lawsuit can be a financial nightmare.

Professional Liability Insurance

Anyone who owns their own business—not just doctors—needs professional liability insurance. It should also be purchased by architects (buildings fall down on people), accountants (the decimal point gets put in the wrong place), engineers (whoops, shoulda used more steel), and anyone else whose professional activities could make them liable for personal or financial injury. Even if you work for someone else, you should evaluate your individual liability risk and find out how much coverage your employer provides. If it's not enough, get more. It's expensive, but it's absolutely essential.

The best place to start looking for liability insurance is through an agent specializing in small business coverage. Trade and professional associations are also a good source of information. You may even be able to purchase coverage through an association. And make sure any policy you're considering covers both your professional activities and your place of business. You never know when Mr. Jones might show up for a consultation and fall down the steps.

You also should evaluate your liability if you engage in volunteer work. If you're on the board of directors of, or even just donate your time to, an organization that's sued, it could end up costing you plenty. Neither your umbrella policy nor your professional liability policy will protect you. Find out what kind of liability you're exposed to and what kind of protection, if any, the organization provides its volunteers.

Mike: *I'm on the board of directors of our local youth hockey association. We have four hundred kids ages 5 through 18 flying around with sticks and smashing into the boards, the ice, and each other. When I was approached to join the board I asked them if they had liability insurance. They didn't. They do now.*

Jacquie: *I'm on two boards, the Community Arts Partnership and the Ithaca Players Guild. Neither group is faced with four hundred kids committing mayhem on each other either accidentally or on purpose. And while one board dispenses thousands of dollars to arts organizations and artists each year, the other is always struggling to make ends meet, in order to produce five theater performances a year. But you better believe I made sure when I joined each board that they had liability coverage. I'm happy to say they did, and do. You never know what kind of off-the-wall claim your group—and you as individuals—might be hit with. So best be prepared. We are.*

DISABILITY INSURANCE

As we mentioned earlier in the chapter, most people are quick to insure their lives but fail to adequately prepare for a disability, even though their chances of being unable to work due to a long-term illness or disabling injury are much higher than dying young. If you fail to replace the income lost from being unable to work, financial disaster will be just around the corner.

How Much Do You Need?

There are several factors to consider when evaluating your disability insurance needs. You need to find out how much it pays, how soon it starts after you're unable to work, and how long it lasts.

Most experts recommend that you should have enough disability insurance to provide you with 60 to 70 percent of your gross income. That will provide you with an amount approximate to your regular take-home pay because, as long as you're the one paying the premiums, the federal government will not tax your benefits. If you're buying your own policy, this is obviously not a problem.

But if your employer is paying your benefits, it's a big problem.

Is there a solution? You bet. All you have to do is reimburse your employer for the premiums and you're all set. It's not a major investment, just a few dollars a week for most people, but it can save you a lot of money down the road.

You should also make sure your insurance provides coverage until you're fully recovered or, if you're permanently disabled, until you reach age 65.

Where Can You Obtain Disability Insurance?

There are several sources for disability insurance.

Your Employer

Many people have some form of disability coverage through their employers. But the amount and duration of coverage will vary significantly. If you have a policy through your employer, evaluate the coverage. If it's inadequate, you can purchase additional coverage by purchasing either group or individual insurance.

Group Insurance

You may be able to purchase coverage through a group policy offered by a trade group or other association. Self-employed people can sometimes purchase disability insurance through their local Chamber of Commerce. These organizations purchase group policies to reduce premium costs just like large employers do. If you don't belong to such an association, it might be worth your while to join one just for this benefit.

Individual Insurance

If all else fails, you can always purchase an individual policy. It will be more expensive, but you'll be able to tailor it more to your exact needs than you would with a group policy.

KEEPING YOUR INSURANCE COSTS DOWN

Depending on the types of coverage you need, your insurance premiums can quickly add up and seem like a terrible financial burden. But there are some simple methods to keep your costs under control.

Shop Around
Insurance premiums are not carved in stone. In fact, they vary widely from company to company. Approach the purchase of insurance like you would any other big-ticket item, and shop around. Compare the offerings and coverages of different companies. Call a variety of insurance agents and let them get you some quotes. If you buy a policy from the first company you talk to, you're bound to spend more than you have to.

Buy All Your Coverage from One Company
Many companies will provide all your insurance needs—such as a package including life, disability, homeowner's, automobile, and liability insurance—and give you a discount for bringing all your business to them.

Keep Your Deductibles High
It's simple. The higher your deductibles, the lower your premiums. It can save you hundreds of dollars a year.

Buy from Highly Rated Companies
Insurers are rated according to their financial health, so you should buy only from companies that have high ratings. Getting a cheap policy is one thing. Finding out

that the company that sold you the policy doesn't have the money to pay your claim is something else altogether.

Adjust Coverage to Meet Your Needs

Your insurance needs will change over time. For example, there will come a time when you will need less life insurance or even no life insurance at all. If you're continuing to pay high premiums for coverage you don't need, you're wasting your money.

Protect Your Property

Antitheft devices in cars and alarm systems in homes will often result in premium discounts.

Check for Unnecessary Features

Insurance policies have all sorts of optional features that can drastically affect premiums. Make sure you read the fine print, and eliminate any features you don't need.

Don't Ignore Mail Solicitations

Not every piece of junk mail you receive should be immediately tossed into the recycling bin. You may periodically be offered insurance coverage that can really save you money. The trick is to carefully investigate the terms of the policy you're being offered. And investigate the company or organization behind the policy even more carefully. If you find they both check out, compare the terms with your current policies and with those of competitors. You just might find you've got yourself a great deal.

7

Getting Some Help:
Financial Planners and Advisers

Negotiating the sometimes perilous path of financial management is not for amateurs. Granted, your fiscal situation may not be as complicated as that of someone like Donald Trump (who must have at least one financial assistant devoted solely to alimony and child support distribution), but that doesn't mean the two of you won't need professional help.

BUILDING YOUR TEAM

For most people, a sound financial management team includes an accountant, a banker, a lawyer, a financial planner, and a securities broker (sometimes you'll be able to find professionals who can fill two or three of these roles). Depending on your situation, you may use the services of some of them on a regular basis. Months or even years may go by between consultations with others.

No matter how often you need them, don't underestimate—or underutilize—their knowledge. A lot of people find it hard to turn to others for advice. It's understandable. First of all, professional help costs money. Secondly, most of us think that if we do a little legwork, we can gather enough basic information to make us experts in accounting, banking, financial management, insurance, and other fields. It doesn't work that way. The only way to become an expert is to hire experts.

Where Are They?

The best way to find expert professionals is to ask your friends and business associates. People are especially critical of financial professionals, so those who stand out from the crowd quickly gain good reputations and become widely known. You can also check professional associations. Don't hire people who advertise. If they have to advertise for new clients, they're not very good at what they do.

Make a list with at least three candidates for each position you need to fill. Call each one and ask for a free consultation. If one objects, cross him off your list. There are plenty of other people out there who would be happy to have your business.

When you meet with a candidate, look at his office. Is it neat? That usually means he's organized. Does he take phone calls while he's talking to you? If so, it probably means he'll never give you, or your needs, his full attention.

Ask him about his professional affiliations and ongoing education. All professional fields are constantly changing, and pros who are worth their hourly fee make every effort to keep up. Listen carefully to your candidates' answers. Do they sound packaged, or are they responding honestly and thoughtfully? If you don't feel the three of you can communicate well, thank him for his time and leave.

Ask about fees. How much does he charge and why? Tell him exactly what you need him to do, and ask how many hours he thinks it will take. Before you leave, ask for the names of two or three clients. Contact them and ask about the professional's services. Has his work been satisfactory? Has he been efficient and responsive to his clients? Did they get along well? Would they hire him again?

Once you've decided on a professional, write a letter that spells out what you want the professional to do for you and what you understand the fees to be. Be sure to include a mechanism to separate yourself from the professional if you should decide your affiliation needs to end. It's not legally binding, but it does help avoid misunderstandings.

FINDING AN ACCOUNTANT

You may laugh at the idea of hiring an accountant. Many people do. They claim their financial situations are simple enough that they really don't need professional help.

They're often right. But there's one financial area in which almost everyone can benefit from some help—taxes. We all have to pay them, and we all complain bitterly about how much we have to pay. But a good accountant— one who keeps up with the ever-changing tax laws and absurd complexities of IRS rules—can make April 15 a lot less painful.

Accountability is critical when preparing taxes. A few years ago, *Money* magazine asked fifty different tax experts—CPAs, franchised tax preparers, and licensed enrolled agents—to prepare a return for the same hypothetical taxpayer. They all came up with different results. A year later the magazine repeated the test, and again everyone's results were different. In fact, only ten of the theoretical returns came within $500 of what *Money* and the IRS had determined was the right figure. If the pros had trouble figuring it all out, imagine what a botch job you'd be capable of.

Hire Only CPAs

When you look at candidates, whether you're looking for someone to just do your taxes or for more comprehensive accounting services, choose only Certified Public Accountants (CPAs). These people have earned their titles by undergoing extensive training and passing a rigorous three-day exam given by the American Institute of Certified Public Accountants, so they're universally respected in the business world. In fact, their training has as much to do with ethics as it does with accounting. They're licensed and, because they can lose their licenses, they invariably are straight arrows.

Another advantage to CPAs is that they are year-round professionals. When you go to a seasonal tax preparer, one who rents a storefront and is in business from January 15 through April 15, you're usually getting someone with just enough tax knowledge to get you in trouble. A CPA, on the other hand, can work with you year round to help you structure your finances to minimize your tax burden. They're also there to help you if the IRS questions your return.

The person you select should be experienced, but that doesn't mean he or she has to be tottering around with a cane. Many bright young CPAs will work for a large firm for four or five years and then go out on their own. You want someone who's energetic, responsible, precise, a perfectionist, and who can teach you a few things.

Mike: *What you really need is an accountant like ours. Rocco is pushing 70, grizzled and gruff, and smells like the old pipe he's always smoking. He also reeks with financial wisdom. He's been a CPA for forty years and there's nothing he hasn't seen.*

When we visit Rocco to talk about one thing or another, he goes over the papers we've presented him, sits back in his beat-up leather chair, and, squinting at us through a haze of smoke, announces his verdict of our financial affairs. Over the years,

he's said everything from "You did good" to "You're idiots."
And he's always been right.

FINDING A LAWYER

Your lawyer will be the single most important professional
you ever hire. He or she will help you buy and sell homes,
draft your wills, help you with estate planning, represent
you in legal actions, and in general serve as a trusted friend
and confidante. For this reason, it's absolutely critical that
you hire someone with whom you have rapport and absolute trust and confidence.

When you begin looking for a lawyer, keep in mind
you need a generalist, not a specialist. Your needs will be
broad, and your lawyer should have an equally broad area
of knowledge. But he or she should also be willing to refer
you to specialists if the need arises. For example, your
personal attorney may work with you in real estate transactions or planning a trust, but refer you to other lawyers
if you should be involved in a civil action. A good attorney
realizes the extent of his or her expertise. Those who don't
really do their clients a disservice.

We talked about the importance of the interview process earlier in this chapter. It's especially important in hiring a lawyer. The person you hire may at some point need
to know the most intimate details of your personal and
financial lives. You need to have someone you're comfortable discussing such topics with and whom you trust to
keep your personal matters confidential. The lawyer/client
relationship is based on trust, sensitivity, caring, intimacy,
and personal compatibility. Keep these traits in mind when
looking for someone to represent you.

Jacquie: *Our lawyer is a close friend who we met when
our daughters attended elementary school together. She's about*

our age, and we share a lot of the same interests. We've become friendly as couples and have vacationed together. And our daughters, although now in college, are still close and see each other when they're home on vacations.

Having such a strong personal relationship makes Mike and I feel confident with the professional relationship. We know that when we call her office (or home) she'll drop whatever she's doing to talk to us. And because she's already so intimately involved with our family, she can more readily assess our needs and concerns.

FINDING A BANKER

You really have two decisions to make—first, what bank you want to deal with, and second, whom within that bank to contact for reliable service when you need it.

You'll need to start by selecting a bank. You're fortunate, because banks today are more competitive than ever. Since they're virtually identical in their rules and interest rates, they've made service a priority to attract customers. They'll go out of their way to take care of all your banking needs—from checking and savings accounts to IRAs, CDs, and Keoghs to home mortgages and automobile loans. Many even offer brokerage services.

Because banks are so similar, you shouldn't evaluate them on the basis of their interest rates and fees. Rather, look to see who they're interested in having as customers. Some banks aim at small businesses. Others aim at young couples or senior citizens. If you're a young couple just starting out, you'll want a bank that has a good home mortgage program, offers a variety of credit cards and consumer loan options, and maintains a number of branch offices and ATM machines.

The size of a bank is another important factor. Although a bank whose main office is a downtown behemoth with a marble facade and ornate lobby is certainly more impressive than one whose main office sits out in a suburban strip mall between a pizzeria and a video store, it doesn't necessarily mean it will give better service. In fact, for most couples, dealing with a smaller bank provides the opportunity for more personal service. The bank employees will get to know you, and all your transactions will have a more personal flavor.

That gets us to the issue of choosing a banker. You need to find an individual who will deal with your problems personally and not delegate them to a teller or some other subordinate. Your banker needs to be learned, experienced, concerned about your needs, and willing to deal with your problems personally. The chances are you'll rarely need this kind of personal attention. But when you do, particularly if it's regarding a critical financial issue, you'll want to know there's someone who will respond to your need in a timely and sensitive manner.

FINDING A BROKER AND FINANCIAL PLANNER

When you begin to invest money, you're going to get involved with investment brokers and financial planners. A broker acts as the agent between the buyer and the seller of a security and charges a fee, called a "commission," for the service. A financial planner provides consultation and advice for a flat fee. Some have the impressive title "certified financial planner" and prominently include the acronym CFP on their business cards and advertising.

Many brokers also act as financial planners. They recommend certain securities based on the needs of each client. Full-service brokers recommend and sell stocks, bonds, mutual funds, investment certificates, annuities, and most other investment vehicles. Many work for big firms like Merrill Lynch and Kidder Peabody. Others work for tiny firms most people have never heard of.

Many couples prefer to work with just one broker. This is fine as long as the broker is knowledgeable in the securities you're interested in. Some brokers specialize in bonds or mutual funds but have only a rudimentary knowledge of other types of investments. If you plan to be more diverse in your investing, having several experts on your side is probably the more prudent approach.

Most brokers are honest, well-trained individuals who work hard on behalf of their clients and do their best to help them make money. But there are also brokers who are only interested in getting into your wallets by selling you whatever security they can get you to buy. Your long-term financial health is *not* on their agenda.

The Conflict of Interest Problem

A big part of the problem is that brokers are working for themselves, for their employers, and for their clients, and their clients' interests might not always come first. While the two of you may be trying to save to put your kids through college, your broker may be trying to earn money to put *his* kids through college, too. This can sometimes lead to conflict between broker and client.

This is because brokers work on commission. They only make money when you buy or sell a security. And it doesn't matter whether you make money or not. If a broker recommends a stock and you decide to buy it, he makes a commission on the sale. If the stock goes down in value and you sell it, he makes a commission again on that transaction. So while you've lost money on your little venture, he's made a tidy profit even though he gave you lousy advice. This has led many people to suggest that brokers should only make commissions when they steer you to investments that make a profit.

Searching for Good Financial Planners

When you begin to look for a financial planner, ask around for some recommendations. The best sources of information are people who are experienced investors. We have some former neighbors who won $8.4 million in the New York State Lottery a few years ago. He was a meat cutter in a grocery store, and his wife worked in the back office in a Kmart. We asked him if there was a downside to their good fortune.

"The biggest problem was we didn't know anything about investing," he said. "We had always lived from pay-check to paycheck and had a savings account, but that was about it. So I started talking to doctors and lawyers I knew, figuring they had money to invest. They introduced us to some people who have done a good job helping us manage the money."

When you're talking to financial planners, explain what your goals are and how long you have to reach them. If you're approximately the same age as the candidate, you may find you share a lot of the same goals. You might want to find out if they have children the same age as yours. If they do, it more than likely means they're already devising their own investment strategy to pay for college. Here are some other questions that will need answering.

How do they earn their income? If it's solely from fees, you're generally safe. But if a portion of their income comes from commissions on the sale of investment products, the person may be more interested in making sure you buy something than in helping you plan for your needs.

What's their hourly fee? This seems like a no-brainer, but you'd be amazed how many people either fail to ask beforehand or are just too intimidated to ask. Some financial planners charge as little as $50 an hour, and some charge several hundred dollars an hour. Generally speaking, though, you should be able to find good people for about $100 an hour.

What are their qualifications? How long have they been in the financial planning field? What did they do before that? What financial planning courses have they taken? All these questions will help you get some idea of how qualified they really are.

As we mentioned earlier, some financial planners will have earned the title "certified financial planner" and will wave their CFP flag as evidence of their competence. Don't get too excited. Anyone can become a certified financial planner by taking a mail order home study course and passing an easy test administered by the College for Financial Planning.

Do they offer other services such as tax services or legal services? If they do, beware. You want an expert, and these fields are too complex for a person to be competent in each. If you want tax advice, see a tax specialist. If you want legal advice, see a lawyer.

Do they carry liability insurance? *Liability insurance? A financial planner?* You bet. Financial planners can make mistakes that cost their clients a great deal of money. Sometimes they're liable for their errors. If they are, and it's your money that's been lost, the fact that they have liability insurance will guarantee you'll get your investment back. Investing wisely means minimizing risk. This is one way to do just that.

Have they worked with other clients whose investment goals are similar to yours? Ask for the names of other clients, then ask those people how the planner's advice worked out. Ask if they enjoyed working with the planner. The answers will help you get an idea of the planner's strengths and weaknesses.

You Need to Educate Yourselves

Once you find a good broker and/or financial planner, don't accept everything he or she says as gospel. You need to be proactive in your approach to investing and be able to discuss various options with your broker and understand the investment decisions that are made.

This means you need to educate yourselves. Read

about investment strategies. Pick up financial publications like the *Wall Street Journal* and *Barron's* and *SmartMoney* magazine. If you're proactive in your approach to investing, you'll be able to have much more constructive conversations with financial advisers and stockbrokers. You'll also feel a lot more confident in your investment decisions.

This may seem intimidating to you. Some people have a real aversion to dealing with money. To them, investing is a very daunting concept. If you're one of these people, we'll point out that we've seen many people like you who, once they got involved and began to educate themselves, became absolute financial addicts. It becomes a big game. In fact, we have friends who we consider to be more knowledgeable about investing than some of the stockbrokers we know. Once you get started, you may become like them, with your nose buried in the *Wall Street Journal* every morning.

Discount Brokers

Discount brokers charge a reduced commission for their services. They do this because they don't try to sell people investments, they just execute trades. They're popular with people who prefer to do their own market research and make their own investment decisions. If you get to the point where you're comfortable calling your own shots, use a discount broker. There's no reason to pay for a service you don't need. Here's a list of some of the biggest.

Accutrade (800) 228-3011
Ceres Securities (800) 669-3900
Charles Schwab & Co. (800) 435-4000
E*Trade (800) 786-2575
Fidelity Brokerage (800) 544-8666
Freedom Investments (800) 944-4033

Kennedy Cabot (800) 252-0090
Jack White (800) 233-3411
Muriel Siebert (800) 872-0444
National Discount Brokers (800) 417-7423
Quick & Reilly (800) 221-5220
Vanguard Discount Brokerage (800) 992-8327
Waterhouse Securities (800) 934-4410

Investment Clubs

If you like the idea of making your own decisions and don't mind the input of other investors, putting some money into an investment club might appeal to one or both of you. These are groups of people who pool their money to buy not just stocks but other securities as well. Some of them have turned in fantastic performances over the years.

Investment clubs have regular meetings where members discuss and vote on proposed investments. Members contribute an agreed-upon amount each month—sometimes as little as $10 or $20—to put toward investments and cover the cost of brokers' commissions. One of the benefits of these clubs is the chance to learn how other people approach investing. You may learn a few tricks you can apply to your private accounts.

8

A Home of Your Own: Buying Your First House

Owning a home has always been a part of the American Dream, and it still is the goal of most couples in the United States. When you own your own house, you have a little piece of the world that's entirely yours to do with what you will. It's your sanctuary, and you can stay there as long as you choose. You don't have to worry about landlords, about losing your lease, or about having to ask permission to drive a nail in the wall so you can hang a painting. You can hammer, drill, paint, paper, carpet, and landscape until you've created the home you've always wanted.

Home ownership is almost always a positive financial move. You build equity over time until you finally own the house outright. Plus the interest you pay on your mortgage is tax-deductible. But there are a lot of issues to consider when buying a home. We'll begin with a very important one.

ARE YOU BETTER OFF RENTING?

Home ownership isn't for everyone. Think about people who have careers that require them to move every year or two. The last thing they need to be dealing with is buying and selling houses each time they change addresses.

For one thing, they'd constantly lose money. Buying and selling homes is expensive. When you buy a house, you need to hire an attorney. You need to pay for a structural inspection to make sure you're not buying a house that's going to fall down around your ears the first time you slam the front door. You're also charged anywhere from 2 to 5 percent of the amount of your mortgage by the lending institution in "points" and "closing costs." Selling a home is expensive, too. If you use a realtor, you're going to pay him or her 6 or 7 percent of the selling price in commission. You're also going to need another attorney. In each case, we're talking about thousands of dollars.

The only way to offset those expenses is for the house to increase in value by an equal amount or more. But there are only a few real estate markets these days in which home values are appreciating like they did in the boom times of the 70s and early 80s. In some markets, the house might even decrease in value over the short term. For transient professionals, renting is clearly the better option.

Some people also have great rental arrangements that make buying a home a less attractive option. We know a number of people in New York City who live in rent-controlled apartments they could never afford if they had to buy them. Other people have "caretaker" arrangements where they live in a property for very little rent or even for free. Still others just stumble across great deals.

Mike: *We once fell into this group. From 1978 to 1984 we lived on a 5,400-acre property in the northeast corner of Maryland just inside the Pennsylvania and Delaware state lines. The property was owned by the State of Maryland and managed by its Department of Natural Resources. It had once been owned by a member of the DuPont family and included a half dozen* *or so old houses dating back to the early nineteenth century. We rented one of them for $350 a month, including utilities. It was a completely restored three-story stone house with a slate roof, spiral staircase, five fireplaces, and a huge yard. Plus we had the run of the property, most of which was closed to the public. It was the deal of a lifetime.*

During the six years we lived there, we were able to save a great deal of money because of our ridiculously low rent. Buying a home never entered our minds. We finally moved (and bought our first house using the savings we had amassed as a down payment) when our careers took us to another state. But if we had stayed in that area, we'd probably still be living in our old stone mansion and socking away a thousand dollars a month in mutual funds and other investments.

The bottom line is that owning a home is expensive. In addition to your mortgage, you're responsible for property taxes and school taxes. The sewer and water bill will arrive faithfully every three months. Plus there's the expense of maintaining the property. By contrast, when you rent, you pay the landlord every month and write a check for your utilities and that's pretty much it. Plus you're not tied down. If you want to move, you just do it. If you're a homeowner, your ability to pull up stakes is determined by your ability to sell your house.

HOW MUCH CAN YOU AFFORD?

Ah, the big question. Most of us have eyes that are bigger than our wallets and long for houses that are beyond our means. But you have to be careful. Just because a house is too expensive for you doesn't mean you won't be able to get financing. If you have a sizable down payment, a good credit history, and little debt, you may find a lending institution that's willing to loan you more than you can chew. The crunch might not come right away, but in time the pressure of other financial obligations can make that monthly mortgage payment more and more problematical.

Be realistic about what you can afford. If you plan on having children, remember that college educations are down the road (chapter 9 will open your eyes to *that* reality). You need to plan for retirement. Plus it's nice to have a vacation every once in a while. Sure, a nice house is important, but so are a lot of other things.

There are two factors that will determine how much house you can afford: the amount of money you have for a down payment and the amount of money you can afford in monthly mortgage payments.

The Down Payment

Depending on the requirements of the lending institution that provides you with a mortgage, you'll need anywhere from 5 to 20 percent of the purchase price of the house as a down payment. For argument's sake, we'll assume you'll need 20 percent, which is the case with most commercial lenders these days, particularly for loans to people who are buying their first homes. You'll also be charged "points" by your lender—loan origination fees that can be anywhere from 1 to 3 percent of the amount of your mortgage—plus additional closing costs that can add another percent or two. And don't forget your attorney.

Let's say the two of you find the home of your dreams and are able to meet the seller at a price of $150,000. Assuming a 20 percent down payment, you'll need a minimum of $30,000. If we throw in 4 percent for points and closing costs on a $120,000 mortgage and another $1,500 for your attorney, the figure becomes $36,300.

So we're talking about a sizable chunk of cash to become a homeowner. Later in the chapter we'll look at how you can come up with the money.

The Mortgage Payment

Before you start shopping for a house you'll also need to determine how much money you can afford each month for a mortgage payment. Here are three guidelines that real estate professionals use when helping buyers calculate this figure.

1. *Your monthly mortgage payment should be no more than one and a half times your weekly take-home pay.* Following this guideline, if the two of you make $800 a week after taxes, you can afford a maximum of $1,200 a month.

2. *Your monthly mortgage payment should be no more than 28 percent of your net monthly income.* Based on your $800 a week take-home pay ($3,200 a month), this guideline drops your recommended monthly payment to a maximum of $896.

3. *Your total monthly debt obligations should not be more than 35 percent of your gross monthly income.* This includes your mortgage, credit card payments, car loans, educational loans, and any other debts on which you make monthly payments. It does not include taxes, utilities, or insurance.

Do we agree with these formulas? Not necessarily. If you'll recall what we said in chapter 5, we feel the best way to determine how much you can afford is to begin with what you're currently paying in rent and then figure how you can add to that amount by cutting other expenses. This method allows you to determine the maximum you can *really* afford each month.

But does that mean you should go after the biggest mortgage you can afford? No, particularly if you have children to educate. Most people get into trouble because they try to live right on the edge of their financial means, maxing out on their mortgage payments and car loans and credit cards. If you scale back a bit, life can be more enjoyable.

Once you've determined how much you can afford each month, you need to translate that figure into the total amount you can afford to borrow. It's easy. Any realtor can provide you with the tables you need to get the answer. So can many financial publications. Libraries also carry books that include mortgage rate tables.

Here's an example. The following table shows how much you can expect to pay every month for each $1,000 you intend to borrow, depending on the interest rate and duration of your mortgage. It's an abridged version of what the professionals have, but it serves to give you an idea of how the tables work.

Payment Per $1,000 of Loan

Interest Rate	15-Year Mortgage	30-Year Mortgage
6.00	$7.48	$6.01
6.25	$7.61	$6.17
6.50	$7.74	$6.33
6.75	$7.87	$6.49
7.00	$8.99	$6.66
7.25	$9.13	$6.83
7.50	$9.28	$7.00
7.75	$9.42	$7.17
8.00	$9.56	$7.34
8.25	$9.71	$7.52
8.50	$9.85	$7.69
8.75	$10.00	$7.87
9.00	$10.15	$8.05
9.25	$10.30	$8.23

Let's say you're able to afford a maximum of $800 a month and plan on applying for a 30-year mortgage at 8 percent interest. A quick calculation using the figures above shows you that a $100,000 mortgage would cost you $734 a month. Adding incremental amounts of $1,000 to the mortgage, you discover that you can borrow up to $109,000 before reaching your $800 a month limit.

Now let's go back to that $150,000 house the two of you just fell in love with. If you can only afford a $109,000 mortgage, you're going to have to come up with at least $41,000 for a down payment, plus another $5,860 for closing costs and your attorney. If you can't raise that kind of cash, your only choice is to scale down your expectations and stay within your range of affordability.

As you can see, determining how much you can afford for a house is a delicate balancing act between the amount of money you have for a down payment and the amount you have for your monthly mortgage. Just remember that nothing is carved in stone when it comes to buying a house and that everything is negotiable. For example, if you don't have much for a down payment but can demonstrate to a lender that you can afford a large monthly mortgage, you may be able to reduce the amount the lender requires as a down payment.

GETTING THE DOWN PAYMENT

Okay. We've determined that buying a house requires a lot of money. The question then becomes how to come up with it. We'll begin with the most obvious.

Save, Save, Save

Put as much money aside as you possibly can. That means living on the cheap. Create a budget and stick to it. Cut back on meals out and trips to the movies. Learn to get by with one car instead of two. Don't buy new clothes unless they're absolutely necessary. Forget about stereo equipment, new furniture, health club memberships, new golf clubs, vacations, and other luxuries. And pay off the credit cards and put them away in the back of a drawer. You need to become obsessed with saving money and begin to look upon spending as a mortal sin.

You can also save money by finding a less expensive living arrangement. They may not be up to your standards, but Spartan living quarters can help you put together a down payment real quickly. After all, just because you can afford $1,000 a month for rent doesn't mean you have to spend that much. If you can find something adequate for half that amount, that means the other half can be invested every month. That's $6,000 a year, plus interest. It will put you into your house that much faster.

Where should you put all the cash you're setting aside? The best place is in mutual funds and short-term (one to three year) bonds. You also should keep a portion in a money-market fund so you have access to emergency cash. The important thing is to keep your money in investments that are liquid, meaning you can withdraw the funds when you need them. When that magic day finally comes and you've amassed the amount you need to start looking for a home, you're going to need to cash in your investments quickly.

Borrow Money from a Retirement Account

If your firm allows it, you can borrow money from a 401(k) or some other retirement plan. When it works, this is a good strategy because the interest you pay on the loan goes back into your account. Just remember you're going to have to add your repayment to the amount you're going to borrow for a mortgage. Make sure you can afford it.

Withdraw Money from a Retirement Account

In this case, you don't have to pay the money back. But you do have to pay income taxes on it, and if you're younger than 59½, you'll also pay a 10 percent penalty for early withdrawal.

There is one relatively new exception to this. The Taxpayer Relief Act of 1997 introduced an IRA with a new wrinkle. The Roth IRA allows you to withdraw money without penalty or tax libility five years after you open the account. This makes the Roth an excellent source of money not just for a down payment on your home, but also for children's college educations, automobiles, and other big-ticket items. (See Chapter 10 for more detailed information on the Roth IRA.)

Work Out an Equity Sharing Arrangement

Unless you live in a severely economically depressed area, your house should increase in value over the period of time you own it. In some markets its value may increase dramatically. You can put this potential profit to work by agreeing to split it with an investor in an equity sharing arrangement. The investor puts up most or all of the down payment for the house, but you pay the mortgage. When the house is sold, the investor gets back the down payment and a portion of the profit from the sale of the house. The exact percentage he or she receives is negotiated at the outset of the arrangement.

Don't Forget Mom and Dad

If all your siblings are educated and out of the house and your parents have the money, they might be happy to give you the down payment. In fact, it can often make sense for them from a tax standpoint. They can give you $10,000 a year tax-free ($20,000 if the money is from both of them). In doing so, they're giving you money you would have eventually received from their estate but avoiding the taxes that would have been due.

FINDING A MORTGAGE LENDER

Many, many financial institutions offer mortgages. In fact, you can probably drop into your local bank and get a mortgage without much problem. But that doesn't mean you'll get the best interest rate. That's because not all lending institutions put the same priority on making mortgage loans. Those for whom mortgages are a small priority usually charge relatively high interest rates. Those that count on mortgages for their business have better rates.

For this reason, the best place to get a mortgage is a mortgage bank. Mortgages are their business, and they're set up to be as competitive as possible. The best ones are those backed by the Federal Housing Authority and the Department of Veterans Affairs. After that, your best bets are credit unions, savings and loan associations, and then commercial banks.

SELECTING A MORTGAGE

Mortgage shopping used to be easy. You'd get a conventional 30-year loan at the going interest rate and that was that.

Not any more. Finding a mortgage today means sifting through a whole variety of options to find one that works best for you. Here are the most popular choices.

Adjustable-rate Mortgages (ARMs)

The interest rate of an adjustable-rate mortgage rises and falls with overall interest rates. This means your monthly mortgage payments will also fluctuate. Living with an adjustable-rate mortgage can be unnerving and requires that you be able to afford the payments when interest rates rise. There are built-in ceilings to ARMs, however, so at least you know going in that your interest rate, and therefore your monthly payment, will never rise above a certain point. Your lender will be able to provide you with the numbers for such a worst-case scenario.

The main benefit of ARMs is that, over the long haul, they're often cheaper than fixed-rate mortgages, particularly when interest rates are high at the outset of the loan. When you first take out the mortgage, you'll be paying two or three points below what you'd pay for a fixed-rate mortgage, so you're enjoying savings right off the bat. But be assured that over the course of the mortgage, there will be times when you'll be paying a lot more than that fixed-rate mortgage. At some point, however—it might take a year (good news), five years (not so good news), or ten years (absolutely horrible news)—interest rates will begin to decline, and you'll get back to where you started. If you're lucky they'll drop even lower than where they were when you started.

Is an ARM a gamble? Yes, to a degree. If interest rates rise sharply and remain at high levels for a long period of time, you're going to pay a lot more than you would with a fixed-rate mortgage. But if inflation and interest rates remain relatively stable, or rise dramatically for only short periods of time, ARMs are a great deal. They're best for people who need a smaller monthly payment in the early years of their mortgage or those who only plan to be in their house for three or four years.

Fixed-rate Mortgages

A fixed-rate mortgage provides a loan at a fixed rate of interest for a certain period of time, typically fifteen to thirty years. Your monthly payments will always be the same, regardless of what happens to interest rates. To many people the security of a fixed-rate mortgage is preferable to the unpredictability of an adjustable-rate mortgage.

Fixed-rate mortgages are best for people who aren't

anticipating an increase in income or who couldn't afford a higher payment than a fixed-rate mortgage offers. They're also good for retirees who are living on fixed incomes. When it comes to choosing between an ARM and a fixed-rate mortgage, the best advice is this: If interest rates are 9.5 percent or lower, go with a fixed-rate mortgage. If they're higher than 9.5 percent, go with an ARM, *but only if you can afford the maximum monthly payments.*

Graduated Payment Mortgages (GPMs)

A graduated payment mortgage provides even lower initial monthly payments than an ARM. They're so low, in fact, that they don't even cover all the interest due each month, so your total indebtedness to the lender actually increases at first. Eventually the monthly payments begin to increase and you start to nibble away at your principal as well as interest.

GPMs are only for people who need absolute rock-bottom payments during the first year or two of their mortgage. But they also need to have confidence that their income is going to rise quickly enough to meet the inevitable increases in their payments. If you have a GPM, the time may come when you want to refinance, so it's important to make sure there's not a prepayment penalty associated with the loan.

Renegotiable Mortgages

These mortgages are twenty- or thirty-year loans that get renegotiated periodically, typically every two, five, or ten years. They're then rewritten at the current interest rate. In this sense they're similar to ARMs. Where they differ is that an ARM is guaranteed for the term of the loan, while there's no guarantee that a lender will renew your renegotiable mortgage. If you've fallen on hard times and the lender doesn't want to renew, you'll have to find a new source of financing. If you can't do that, you may have to sell your house to pay the balance of the mortgage.

Renegotiable mortgages are really only attractive when interest rates are very high and you're confident that nothing will happen to ruin your creditworthiness.

Balloon Mortgages

A balloon mortgage also offers low fixed payments early on, usually for one to seven years. At the end of that period, the entire balance comes due in one enormous "balloon" payment. Most lenders will then refinance, provided your payments have been on time.

Balloon mortgages are great for people who don't expect to be in their homes for more than two or three years. They're also good for people who intend to move up to a more expensive home after only a few years. The key to balloons is to make sure you can refinance when the big payment is due. Otherwise, you may have to sell the house to make the payment.

Again, Don't Overlook Mom and Dad

Your parents or some other relative may be willing to lend you the money. To them, the return on investment will be greater than they'd be able to earn with a certificate of deposit, money-market fund, or other conservative investment. And if you're lucky, they'll be willing to meet you in the middle and lend you the money at lower than prevailing interest rates. It can be a great deal for all of you.

Jacquie: *My father held our mortgage when we bought our first house. He's done the same for both my brothers over the years, hence his nickname "The Big Al Savings and Loan." We arranged a conventional thirty-year loan and paid a point and a quarter below what we'd have paid for a bank mortgage. Plus we didn't have to pay points.*

When we moved a few years later, my father was nearing retirement and needed to have his money in more liquid investments, so we got a conventional mortgage from a bank. The Big Al Savings and Loan was definitely the better deal.

SHORT-TERM OR LONG-TERM?

The duration of a mortgage can be anywhere from a year or two up to thirty years or more. Most traditional home mortgages are for thirty years, and yours will more than likely fall into this group. But is it to your advantage to pay it off sooner?

The answer is a resounding yes. Mortgage loans cost people an astonishing amount of money in interest. For example, let's say you have a mortgage of $100,000 at 10 percent interest. If you pay it off over 30 years you'll pay a total of $316,080 over that time. But if you cut the duration of the mortgage in half—to fifteen years—you'll only pay $193,500. So the sooner you can pay off the mortgage, the sooner you can direct that money toward income-producing investments. You'll also be accruing equity in your home at a faster rate.

Obviously, the repayment terms you choose will be dictated by your personal financial situation. You may find that a thirty-year mortgage works best for you. Just remember two important things: 1) You can put extra money toward your mortgage payment at any time to reduce both the principal and the total amount of interest you'll pay, and 2) you often can elect to pay biweekly rather than monthly. This strategy alone will save you an enormous amount in interest. Consider the thirty-year, 10 percent, $100,000 mortgage we just discussed. If you were to divide your monthly payment into two biweekly payments (twenty-six payments a year, which actually allows the mortgage to be paid off in twenty years and ten months), you would pay only $237,605. That's $78,475 less than if your payment was monthly and over thirty years.

WHAT KIND OF HOME IS BEST FOR YOU?

Once you know how much you can afford, you can start house shopping. But what kind of house do you want? Do you want to be in a city neighborhood, the suburbs, or out in the country? Does an older home appeal to you, or do you want something brand new? Do you want a single-family house, a multifamily home with a rental unit, or a condominium? Do you want to be near schools and shopping? How many bedrooms will you need? How many bathrooms? How big a yard?

If you're a young couple and planning on having children, you'll want to carefully consider your future needs. You'll definitely need an extra bedroom or two and probably at least two bathrooms. A yard will be important, as will proximity to schools. Check into the school district of any home you're considering. Does it have a good reputation? Are the facilities adequate? Are class sizes reasonable?

Length of stay is another important consideration. If this house is just a step in your game plan to ultimately land in your dream home, you'll want to carefully consider its resale potential. In fact, it should be one of your most important criteria. Being stuck with a white elephant has ruined the plans of many people who are eager to move on.

As you may have guessed, buying a house can be a source of tremendous stress and friction in a relationship. It's important to sit down together early in the process and map out your wants and needs. If they differ, try to make compromises. And don't rush. Buying a house will be one of the biggest, if not the biggest, financial moves you'll make together. Take your time and make sure your final decision will make you both happy. After all, this is *home* we're talking about here.

WORKING WITH REALTORS

When you start looking at homes, you'll more than likely be using a real estate agent. Just be aware that they work for the seller of a home. Sellers pay realtors 5, 6, or even 7 percent of the selling price to find a buyer, and this means the realtor is going to act in the seller's best interests, not in yours. The more money a realtor can get for a house, the happier the seller will be and the more money the realtor will earn in commission.

It's an odd situation. Even though they work for the seller, realtors spend the majority of their time with potential buyers. They'll spend hours and hours driving you around to look at various houses that are for sale. They'll call you at all hours of the day and night. They'll get to know all about you and your family. They eventually may start to seem like a member of your family.

Just remember the real nature of the relationship and know that in conversations between the realtor and the seller—conversations that occur when you're not around—you're looked upon as a sacrificial lamb. Keep your relationship with realtors friendly but professional. And don't lay all your cards on the table. You know the maximum you can afford to pay for a house. Keep it to yourself. If you find a place that you absolutely love, and you think your ultimate offer will tip the scales in your favor and land you a deal, then make it known. Otherwise, keep that number in your back pocket.

If you choose to, you can enlist the assistance of a buyer's broker to represent you in the transaction. These people will deal with the seller and the seller's realtor, do the negotiating, and deal with a lot of the annoying paperwork involved in buying a home. They charge either an hourly rate or a percentage (2 or 3 percent, usually) of the selling price of a home.

WHERE ELSE CAN YOU LOOK?

Most houses today are sold through realtors, but there are other sources you should look into. Many sellers, outraged at what they consider to be the exorbitant fees of the real estate industry, will try to sell their homes themselves. Realtors call these people "Fizbos," which is a loose acronym for the term "For Sale By Owner." As you can imagine, they hate Fizbos.

But for you a Fizbo can be a great find. In their minds they're already saving 6 or 7 percent of the purchase price by not paying a commission, so they might be willing to come down in price more than a seller who's represented by an agent. Some Fizbos, particularly retirees who are looking for a steady cash flow, will agree to hold all or part of the mortgage.

Two other sources of houses are auctions and foreclosure sales. Auctions are sometimes held by people who want to move their properties quickly. They also occur when a person with no close relatives passes away and they've made no provision to pass the property on. Foreclosure sales are held by banks to sell properties they've seized from people who could no longer make their mortgage payments. Some surprisingly good deals can sometimes be found.

Mike: *My sister and brother-in-law bought their house at auction. She was out riding her bicycle one Saturday morning and rode by the house and saw a sign saying there was to be* *an auction that afternoon. She immediately fell in love with the place and pedaled home as fast as possible to tell her husband. They arrived at the sparsely attended auction right on time and two hours later they owned a house. They were the only bidders and got it for a song.*

The house is an old stone place in Chester County, Pennsylvania, that was covered with stucco. Over the years, they've pulled the stucco off, pointed the stone, put on an addition, and installed beautiful landscaping. They could sell it tomorrow for five times what they paid for it.

MAKING AN OFFER

Once you find the house of your dreams, the real fun begins—negotiation. Just remember that no seller expects to get what he's asking for a house. Nor should you expect him to accept your first offer. Arriving at a price is a tedious, frustrating game that usually ends up with both parties meeting somewhere between the seller's asking price and the buyer's initial bid.

Let's say you can afford a $150,000 house. If that's your top price, start looking at houses in the $160,000 to $175,000 range. If you find one you like for $165,000, make an offer of $140,000. Typically, the seller will counter by lowering the price a bit. You'll respond by jumping up your offer a bit. This back and forth will continue until you either get the house for the price you can afford or the seller stands firm at a higher price (most sellers need a certain amount to finance their next move; just as you have a maximum amount you can afford to spend, they'll have a minimum amount they can afford to accept). If the deal stalls, you'll just have to continue your search.

This is not to say that miracles don't happen. People sometimes find sellers whose houses have been on the market for a long time and who finally take much less than they'd hoped for just so they can get on with their lives. Some sellers have time or financial pressures that make them eager to make a deal. These people are called "motivated sellers" in real estate lingo, and they're often good folks to stumble upon. With any luck, you'll do just that.

A HOME-BUYING CHECKLIST

• Once you decide to buy a house, work hard to accumulate the down payment. Make a budget and stick to it. Live frugally and cut out all unnecessary expenses. Get rid of all your other debts in anticipation of successfully applying for a mortgage. And don't overlook other ways of raising the money.

• Once you have the down payment in hand, figure out how much of a mortgage you can afford. But don't forget your other financial obligations down the road.

• Discuss what kind of house you want before you begin your search. It's better to have your arguments at home than in the backseat of a realtor's car.

• Don't rush. Be slow and methodical in your search. The more time you spend inspecting houses and neighborhoods, the happier you'll be with your ultimate choice.

• Shop around for mortgages and choose one that best suits your financial situation.

9

Starting the College Fund

There's been little in this book thus far that we would consider alarming. Most financial challenges are relatively straightforward and can be conquered with careful planning and disciplined behavior.

Now it's time to get scared. This chapter looks at what for most couples will be the biggest investment of their lives—paying for college. It's more expensive than ever and will only get more so. Putting their children through college will be *the* biggest financial hurdle that most young couples will face during their lives together. For many, the total cost will exceed the value of their homes, especially if they have two, three, or four or more children to put though school.

It is a daunting challenge. But if you start saving early—and wisely—and take advantage of financial aid and other sources of assistance when the time finally arrives, meeting the costs of just about any college should be within your reach.

HOW MUCH WILL YOU NEED?

For years, the cost of college increased at roughly the rate of inflation. But since around 1980, it's increased at three times the rate of inflation. Today, the cost of just one year at an Ivy League university or one of the nation's other premier institutions is more than $30,000. Even many state universities, which for years were considered the backbone of our higher education system, cost $10,000 or more a year.

How much will you need when your children are ready? It depends on their academic accomplishments and professional goals as much as anything else. There are roughly three thousand colleges and universities in the United States, and their costs vary greatly, ranging from pricey private universities, to more moderately priced state universities, to downright affordable local community colleges. And while everyone wants to send their children to the best schools, the fact is that only the very top students get into the Princetons and the Stanfords and the MITs. You may find that your children will be quite content and able to get excellent educations at a much less expensive school.

To get an idea of just how expensive college might be, take a look at the following chart. Based on the current ages of your children, you can get the projected costs of four years at both private and public institutions when your kids are ready to enter college. The numbers assume a 5.5 percent annual increase in costs. With any luck, the actual increases will be less. But if recent history is any indication, they could just as easily be higher.

Obviously, the older your child, the less you'll have to pay. If you have a child who's 15 and a freshman in high school, you'll pay close to $47,000 for the average public university and just over $108,000 for the average private university. But if you have a newborn staring expectantly up at you from the crib, the numbers will really put you on your heels. In eighteen years, you can figure on shelling out more than $100,000 for four years at a public university and more than $240,000 for a private university. If that private university is a member of the Ivies or one of the other dozen or so most prestigious schools, you're probably looking at even more.

The Average Cost of a Four-Year College Education

Child's Current Age	Public University	Private University
18	$40,000	$92,000
17	$42,200	$97,060
16	$44,520	$102,400
15	$46,970	$108,030
14	$49,550	$113,970
13	$52,280	$120,240
12	$55,150	$126,850
11	$58,190	$133,830
10	$61,390	$141,190
9	$64,760	$148,960
8	$68,330	$157,150
7	$72,080	$165,800
6	$76,050	$174,910
5	$80,230	$184,540
4	$84,640	$194,680
3	$89,300	$205,390
2	$94,210	$216,690
1	$99,390	$228,600
Newborn	$104,860	$241,180

There is some good news, however. Most of you won't need to raise the complete cost of your child's education. The average student today pays only about 60 percent of his or her college costs with savings and unsubsidized loans. The rest is covered by grants, scholarships, and subsidized loans.

Still, it's important to remember that having a healthy chunk of money set aside will increase your child's options when it comes time to apply to colleges. Colleges are more than willing to chip in to help you put together a financial package that will cover your costs. In fact, they're remarkably generous. But they do expect you to carry your share of the load. So your ability to pay will be a deciding factor in opening a lot of doors.

WILL YOU HAVE ENOUGH?

Speaking of scholarships and loans, another factor that will determine how much you'll need for your children's college educations is your socioeconomic status. If you're wealthy, you obviously won't have a problem. The cash flow will be there. If you're poor, you probably won't have too much of a problem, either. Colleges are clamoring for talented students from underprivileged backgrounds and toss scholarships at them by the handful.

But if you're a member of the middle class, you may be in trouble. The middle class is the socioeconomic group that has been hit hardest by skyrocketing college costs. While wealthy families can afford to pay their own way, and poor families are having their way paid for them, middle-class families often are finding themselves priced out of the market.

As college costs have gone through the roof over the last fifteen years, the middle class has had to contend with a shifting economy that for many has resulted in stagnant or even downward economic mobility. At the same time, they've had to continue to pay for significant portions of their children's college expenses, and they're finding it harder and harder to make ends meet. There is legitimate concern that higher education is gradually becoming unattainable to this huge segment of the population. If the trend continues and college does indeed become unrealistic for more and more students, the ramifications for the future of the nation are enormous.

A study by the National Institute of Independent Colleges and Universities illustrates just how daunting some parents see the prospect of sending their kids to college. While a third of the parents in the study said they would like to send their children to a private college, fewer than half of those expected to be able to afford it. The study also revealed some other interesting facts.

- Sixty-two percent of parents expected to use personal savings for college, but only 50 percent reported saving on a regular basis.
- Twenty-three percent said they were unable to save and didn't expect to be able to start in the immediate future.
- Of those who were able to save, the average amount put aside was just over $500 a year.
- Nearly 40 percent expected their children to receive scholarships or some other form of financial assistance.
- A third expected to take out loans to pay for college.
- Thirty-one percent expected to pay with money earned while their children are enrolled in college.
- Forty percent expected their children to contribute to the costs of college.
- Only a quarter of parents expected to seek state and federal programs as potential sources of funding.
- Most favored a tax incentive plan that would give them a tax credit for money put aside for college.

So if you're a member of that large group of Americans who scrape by from paycheck to paycheck, who aren't poor but for whom luxuries are rare, the challenge of paying for college is enormous. You need to plan very carefully and begin saving as soon as possible.

THE KEY? START INVESTING EARLY!

Unfortunately, there's no magic formula to help you pay for college. But there is one very concrete rule: *Start investing as early as possible, and be diligent in putting money aside on a regular basis.* The reason is simple: Investing for college is best approached as a long-term endeavor, and the longer you have to save, the easier it will be to pay the bills when college finally arrives. In fact, our advice to couples who plan on having children is to start a college fund as soon as they make the decision to become parents, even if they plan on waiting a few years before they actually bring their first newborn home. It's going to take that long to raise the money.

It's often hard to do. A lot of couples say to themselves, "It's eighteen years away. We have plenty of time." It's particularly difficult to put money away for college when you also may be trying to save money for your first house, a new car, or some other big-ticket item. If you've recently graduated from college yourselves, you may be paying back student loans you used to finance *your* educations. And you may simply be enjoying your first serious paychecks and treating yourselves to clothes, vacations, and other luxuries that you deferred for so long.

But college has a way of sneaking up on you. What was once eighteen years can quickly become ten years or six years or four years. Many unfortunates suddenly wake up to realize their son or daughter is about to enter high school and they've done nothing to prepare for the expenses of college. The result is usually panic and a mad dash to catch up.

They may try valiantly, but they'll never make it. What they'll end up doing is borrowing heavily. As a result, they'll carry a huge debt load well into their fifties and even their sixties. Instead of being able to travel and relax after their children are out of the house, they'll be struggling to pay off college bills.

The bottom line is you're going to pay one way or another, so you might as well do it right and start putting the money aside while your children are babies.

WHAT ARE THE BEST INVESTMENTS?

Your goals in saving money for college should be to maximize your savings and minimize your risk. College funds are not something to gamble with. The safest place to put your money, of course, is in savings accounts, certificates of deposit, and money-market finds offered by banks. These are federally insured and risk free. The downside is they don't earn much interest.

Your investment strategy needs to be a bit more aggressive. We're not suggesting anything as radical as flying to Atlantic City or Las Vegas and going for the Big Score. But there are other investments that, chosen carefully, can help you fill your college coffers more quickly. Here are your best bets.

Bonds

Bonds are relatively secure and risk-free investment vehicles, which is why they're the most commonly held kind of security. When you buy a bond, you're essentially loaning the issuer of the bond your money for an agreed-upon length of time, anywhere from a few months to thirty years or more. In return, the issuer agrees to pay you regular interest payments at an annual rate determined beforehand. These interest payments can then be reinvested, either in additional bonds or in other investments. When the bond "matures" at the end of the agreed-upon length of the loan, you get back your original investment (the "par" value).

Bonds are issued by all sorts of entities. States and cities issue them to finance the construction of large public projects like airports, schools, and stadiums. Corporations issue them to raise capital for expansion. Even the federal government issues them to raise money for all sorts of things, including paying down the national debt. Bonds are rated according to the reliability of the issuer, so it's almost impossible to lose your money if you buy those that are rated highest. The safest bonds of all are U.S. Treasury bonds, which are backed by the federal government and therefore considered totally risk-free.

One of the most popular bonds with people who are saving for college are zero-coupon bonds. Zeros are popular because they're sold at a deep discount to their face value. They're discounted because they don't pay interest to the bondholder. For example, a ten-year $1,000 zero-coupon bond that pays 10 percent would only cost you around $380. You'd receive nothing during the life of the bond, but upon maturity you'd receive $1,000.

With careful timing, you can purchase zeros that will mature just as each year's tuition comes due. If you're really on top of things, you'll start buying fifteen-year zeros when your children are still in preschool. Fifteen years later, as they walk through the doors of their college dorms for the first time, you'll be redeeming your zeros to pay their tuition bills.

There is one downside to zero-coupon bonds. Even though you're not actually receiving the interest they earn each year, you're still liable for federal income taxes on the amount you would have received. On the other hand, that means that when the bonds mature, you don't have to worry about taxes and can put the entire amount toward college costs.

Once you purchase a bond you don't have to hold on to it until it matures. You can always sell it—and sometimes for a profit—on the enormous bond market that operates on Wall Street. This is because bonds fluctuate in value as interest rates rise and fall. For example, if you purchase a bond that pays 9 percent and interest rates fall to 5 or 6 percent, that bond is going to be an attractive investment to a lot of people, and they'll pay you more than par value for it. Of course, the opposite is also true. If interest rates climb, the value of your bond will decrease. If they climb so high that you want to unload the bond and put your money elsewhere, you'll have to accept less than what you paid for it.

Stocks

When you buy stock you become a part owner in the company whose stock you purchase. As an owner, you ride the fortunes of the company, for better or for worse. If the company does well, you may receive healthy dividends—periodic per-share payments—from the company. The value of the stock will also climb. If the company does poorly, dividends decrease—or even stop altogether—and the value of the stock also decreases.

So stocks are a more risky investment than bonds. Despite this fact, more than 50 million Americans own stock. One reason is the long-term profitability of the stock market. Despite periodic crashes (do the years 1929 and 1987 ring a bell?) the stock market has outperformed every other form of investment over the last seventy-five years.

Almost all stock falls within one of two categories—common and preferred.

Common stocks are the basic ownership shares in a company. They're purchased by a wide variety of individuals and institutions and are continually traded among investors; each day, hundreds of million of shares change hands. One of the biggest trading days in history at the time—October 20, 1987, the day after the market crashed and lost 22 percent of its value—saw more than 600 million shares traded as investors struggled to staunch their wounds.

The owners of common stock receive periodic dividends. There are no guarantees on how much a dividend will be; they fluctuate with the company's performance. The stock price also fluctuates with performance. The lucky investor will see his stock steadily increase in value at a rate that outperforms other investments. The unlucky investor will watch his stock become worthless as the company goes down the tubes and eventually out of business. But at least his losses will stop there. Fortunately, shareholders are not responsible for a company's debts.

Preferred stocks are also ownership shares that are traded by investors. But they differ from common stock in several important ways. One, the dividend is guaranteed and is paid before the dividends for common stock are paid. Two, the dividend doesn't change, no matter how poorly—or wonderfully—the company performs. And three, the value of preferred stock increases more slowly than the value of common stock.

Stocks are popular because they offer the opportunity for greater growth than bonds, whose return is carved in stone. This has been particularly true over the last ten years, as the stock market has taken a bull ride to record highs almost weekly. During that time, many companies have seen their stock double or even triple in value. They've been heady days indeed for stock owners.

But investing in single stocks does carry an amount of risk that many people prefer to avoid. That's why the next type of investment is so popular.

Mutual Funds

Mutual funds offer many of the same earning opportunities as single stocks, but with less risk. Why? Because rather than investing in a single company, mutual funds use their investors' money to purchase many, many securities that are "bundled" into a single fund. Investors then buy shares in the fund. Mutual funds take the "strength in numbers" approach to investing and operate under the assumption that the majority of the securities in the fund will perform well enough to negate the effects of the few that don't.

There are currently more than six thousand mutual funds with total assets of more than $1.5 trillion available to investors. Some are aggressive "growth" funds that invest in exciting young start-up companies and carry a relatively high amount of risk. At the other end of the spectrum are funds designed to guarantee a certain income and carry almost no risk. They might invest in "blue chip" companies like DuPont, General Motors, and IBM. In between are funds with varying degrees of potential growth and varying degrees of risk. The safest—and therefore least profitable—mutual funds make short-term investments in groups of money-market funds.

Some mutual funds invest solely in stocks, some solely in bonds, and some in both. Some funds specialize in overseas companies, and others invest only in domestic corporations. There are funds that invest solely in specific industries, such as biotechnology or communications. There are even funds designed to mimic the performances of certain indexes like the Standard and Poor's 500, an index of 500 of the nation's largest companies.

Mutual funds earn income for their investors in three ways—payment of dividends received from the securities owned by the fund, payment of capital gains realized from trading securities in the fund, and increases in the value of the shares. And, if you wish, you can elect to have the proceeds reinvested in additional shares. Some mutual funds have up-front charges, called "loads," that can be quite expensive and cut into your profits. Avoid such funds. There are plenty of excellent "no-load" funds on the market that don't charge such fees and will only charge about 1 percent of the value of your investment in annual service fees.

One reason mutual funds are so attractive is the professional management they receive. They are overseen by fund managers whose sole job is to scout the horizon for promising new investments that can be added to the fund. At the same time, they weed out poor performers that have slowed the fund's growth. And since most fund managers are compensated according to how well their funds perform, you can have every confidence that they're throwing themselves wholeheartedly into their jobs. The more money they make, the more money everyone invested in the fund makes.

Even though they're generally safer than single stocks, mutual funds still have varying degrees of risk. They also have a level of return commensurate with the amount of risk they carry. The most common types of mutual funds are listed below, from highest risk to lowest.

Small capitalization funds are the most aggressive of all mutual funds. They invest in the stocks of young companies that have the potential for rapid growth. Because they have a high potential return, they also carry the most risk. If you like a wild ride and the excitement of watching an investment rise and fall like a kite on a windy day, this type of fund will provide it.

Growth funds are also designed to pursue a high rate of return and carry a similar level of risk. But rather than invest in small start-up companies, they buy the stock of larger, more established companies.

Growth and income funds are more conservative than small capitalization funds and growth funds. They are designed to provide a good return, but to reduce risk they invest in both stocks and bonds. Their share values tend to be more stable than those of growth funds. Because they're designed to provide income as well as growth, they usually pay a lower return.

Income funds are even less risky. They're designed to guarantee an income and generally invest in bonds.

Tax-exempt funds are also designed to guarantee an income. They invest in securities that are exempt from federal income taxes, such as municipal bonds. The level of risk is quite low.

Money-market funds are the most risk-free of mutual funds. They also generally provide the lowest return.

As an individual investor, you'll need to decide what your financial goals are and what levels of risk you're most comfortable with. If you have a long period of time until your children enter college, you might decide to put some money into aggressive growth funds and see what happens. If you have less time, conservative growth and income funds might be more to your liking. If you've already managed to put together a considerable nest egg and you're looking for minimal risk and are content to live with a lower return, bond funds, tax-exempt funds, and money-market funds may be your best strategy.

Real Estate

It's often overlooked as a strategy to save for college, but real estate can be a wonderful way to build equity. One method of saving is to buy a rental property. You have to crunch the numbers carefully, but if you purchase the right property, the rent will cover your mortgage, taxes, and maintenance costs and still leave you with a profit that can be invested in stocks, bonds, or mutual funds. And hopefully, the property will increase in value while you own it, adding to your profit.

Our daughter who's away at college rents a house with two other girls. We happened to meet their landlord on a recent visit. He's a young man who owns a carpet cleaning business and invests in rental properties on the side. He uses a very strict formula in deciding whether a potential property will work for him.

"If I can't put a third of the rent in my pocket, I won't invest in the property," he said. "I know what the rental market is in this town and that dictates how much I can invest in each property. Mostly I try to find houses that need a bit of work. Once I fix them up I can get a good price for them and then sell them down the road for a lot more than I paid for them."

A similar strategy that's popular, particularly in college towns and other communities with a high demand for apartments, is to buy a home that has a rental unit attached. Once again, rent from the unit can cover most, if not all, of your costs and frees up a great deal of investment income that can be earmarked for college.

Mike: *One of my real regrets is that we didn't buy a house with a rental unit when we moved here ten years ago. With two colleges full of students and transient faculty members, the rental market in our town is enormous.*

Since we've lived here I've met many people who own such properties. Often the apartment is a small wing of the house that was either part of the original floor plan or that some enterprising homeowner added later. Some are attic or basement units. Others are duplexes in which the owner occupies one side of the house and renters occupy the other. The rental units have their own entrances and allow both the renters and the homeowners to enjoy their privacy.

With the rent covering a large portion, if not all, of their mortgages, these people have been able to steer impressive amounts of money toward investments. Few will have problems paying for college when the time rolls around.

Jacquie: *I'll have to shoulder most of the blame for this one. Mike suggested a house with a rental unit when we were looking at homes, but I absolutely refused to consider it. I thought having a tenant would be terribly intrusive and I didn't want to give up my privacy. I was concerned about loud music* *and comings and goings at odd hours. I also didn't want someone coming to the door every time there was a problem.*

I was probably wrong. Of all the people we know who have rental units, only two or three have had bad experiences—the inevitable "tenants from hell" who trash their apartments or suddenly move out owing two or three months' rent. Most have had great tenants and also forged great friendships. One woman we know ended up marrying the guy she rented to. It was a real easy transition. He just carried his stuff out one door and into another.

Another investment worth investigating is a real estate investment trust (REIT). REITs are companies that own, manage, and develop properties such as shopping malls, apartment complexes, and resorts. As of early 1997 there were around 300 publicly traded REITs with a combined market value of around $70 billion. At least a third of them have been created since 1993, and the largest have capitalization of more than $1 billion.

Although REITs are not completely new to the investment world, their performance in 1996 attracted a lot of attention as they outperformed the Standard & Poor's 500 by more than 50 percent, with a 36 percent return, as opposed to the S&P 500's 23 percent return. Two REITs, Patriot American Hospitality and Starwood Lodging, had gains of 75 percent and 92 percent, respectively.

Another characteristic of REITs that has investors swooning is their stability in a falling market. They showed this ability in the July 1996 downturn, and they weathered the last quarter of 1987 fairly well. They're also popular because of their high dividend yield (the annual dividend divided by the share price). Because they are required to distribute 95 percent of their net earnings to shareholders, yields can be 8 percent or more. Many investment analysts expect them to provide a total annual return of 13 to 15 percent over the next five years.

KEEP INVESTMENTS IN YOUR NAME

One common mistake parents make when putting money aside for college is putting the accounts in their children's names. This isn't a problem at first. You can open a custodial account in your child's name and until age 14 the first $650 of the child's interest income is tax-free. The next $650 is taxed at 15 percent, and anything over $1,300 is taxed at your rate.

Once your child reaches age 14, however, all college accounts should be in your names only. There's a very good reason for this. You're going to be applying for financial aid in another three or four years, and when the federal government assesses your needs, they view your assets and your children's assets differently. Because you're parents with many financial responsibilities such as a mortgage, other hungry mouths to feed, and possibly other children to educate, the government expects you to contribute only around 6 percent of your assets each year to meet college costs. Your children, however, don't have such financial burdens, so they're expected to contribute 35 percent of their assets plus a portion of their income. The wisdom in keeping their assets to a minimum is obvious.

PREPAID TUITION PLANS

As this book was being written, nine states—Alabama, Alaska, Florida, Kentucky, Massachusetts, Michigan, Ohio, Pennsylvania, and Texas—had implemented prepaid tuition plans that allow people to lock in a college education tomorrow at today's tuition rates. Twenty-one other states had legislation pending to implement their own programs. Since they began in Michigan in the mid-80s, an estimated 500,000 families have bought prepaid tuition contracts.

Prepaid tuition plans have advocates and critics, and both sides make some good points. Let's take a look at some of their arguments.

How Do Prepaid Tuition Plans Work?

Prepaid tuition plans are the reversal of the old Buy Now, Pay Later approach to purchasing something. There are slight variations from state to state, but the basic idea is this: Rather than paying a higher tuition when your child enrolls in college, you lock in the average current tuition rate at the public institutions in your state by giving the money to the state while your child is growing up. When your child graduates from high school and enrolls in college, the state makes up the difference between the guaranteed tuition you already paid and the current average tuition at its state-supported institutions.

How does the state afford it? Simple. It invests the money you and other parents have given it and uses the earnings to cover the difference between the two amounts. If it earns more than that, the state makes a profit, since it's only guaranteeing you the cost of tuition when your child enrolls in college. So—in theory, anyway—everybody comes out ahead. The college gets its money, you pay less for tuition, and the state can possibly earn a profit.

The Advantages of Prepaid Tuition Plans

The biggest advantage of prepaid tuition plans is that they operate like forced savings plans. For some people, particularly those with poor money management habits, this is a benefit. They don't have to pay the money in one lump sum and can make weekly or monthly contributions. They can even have the money deducted from their paychecks. At that point, saving for college becomes something they really don't even have to worry about anymore. The money's being put away, and they know it will be there when they need it.

Another advantage to prepaid tuition plans is that the money put into the plan is tax deductible when your child redeems it to pay for tuition. It's also backed by the individual states, so there's virtually no chance you'll lose it.

If you're like most people, a couple of questions immediately come to mind. The first is, Are there limits on where my child can attend college? In most states the answer is no, your child can enroll in a variety of public and private institutions throughout the United States and the money will be applied to the tuition cost.

The second question is, What happens if my child doesn't get accepted or decides not to go to college? In that case you have two options. You can transfer the tuition credits to another family member for their education, or you can receive a refund.

The Disadvantages of Prepaid Tuition Plans

The big argument against prepaid tuition plans is obvious. When examined from a purely economic perspective, they're a lousy investment. The rate of return on the money you give the state is limited to the increase in tuition between the time you invest the money and when you use it for college. In other words, if tuition rises an average of 5 percent annually during that time, that's your annual return on investment. Meanwhile, if the state has earned 10 or 15 percent annually with the investments it's made with your money, it's keeping the extra money as profit.

Another problem is that some states guarantee to pay the existing tuition when your child enters college. Others only guarantee an *estimated* tuition that's determined at the outset of the plan. If the estimate is low, you're out of luck. And regardless of whether the agreed-upon tuition amount is current or estimated, it's the tuition at *state* institutions. That means if your child wants to attend a private college or university, you're going to have to come up with a lot more money. At that point, the money you lost by not doing your own investing will loom large indeed.

Yet another problem can arise when, for whatever reason, you seek a refund. You'll only get a very small portion of the interest the money has earned, and there may be ridiculous conditions attached to even getting that. In Florida, for instance, you'll earn only 5 percent on your money, and you'll only get that if your child wins a full scholarship, becomes disabled, or dies. Otherwise, you just get back the amount you put in, with no interest at all. If you've been socking money into that plan for ten or fifteen years, you're going to be extremely unhappy.

DON'T NEGLECT YOUR RETIREMENT FUNDS

Remember, you have a life, too. Once you retire, you're going to want to be able to do all the things you've looked forward to for so long. So don't put all your savings into investments for college. Make sure you contribute to your 401(k)s, IRAs, Keoghs, or other retirement plans, too. Chances are retirement will be almost as costly as putting your kids through college.

But that's just one reason to beef up your retirement accounts. We'll discuss another, equally good reason in the next section.

BORROWING AGAINST YOUR ASSETS TO PAY FOR COLLEGE

When the government assesses your financial situation to determine how much financial aid you'll qualify for, it ignores two very valuable assets: your home and your retirement funds. You can have a million dollars in your retirement accounts and own a mansion worth another million, but as far as the government is concerned, they don't appear in your financial aid profile.

This opens the door to two excellent strategies for reducing the assets the government *does* consider: one, pay down your mortgage as much as possible, maybe even pay it off completely, and two, put as much money into your retirement accounts as possible. By doing so, not only do you increase your chances for more financial aid but you also create two sources of equity from which you can borrow to meet college costs.

Borrowing against Your Retirement Funds

Your retirement accounts can be a source of funds from which you can borrow to pay for college. The great thing is that when you do, you're borrowing the money from yourself, so the interest you pay on the loans goes right back into your own accounts. It's a win-win situation with three big "ifs." If you can't keep up with the repayment schedule, your loan to yourself will suddenly be considered a withdrawal and you'll have to pay income taxes on it. If you're younger than 59½ when that occurs, you'll also be assessed a penalty. And if you leave your employer for a new job, the borrowed amount will come due immediately.

Borrowing against Your Home

You can also borrow against the value of your home by taking out a home equity loan. These loans are becoming a popular strategy to pay for all sorts of expensive items, including college tuition. They have several advantages. One is the fact that the interest on the loan is tax deductible, unlike the interest on a conventional loan. They're also easy to get. A bank will usually be quite willing to spot you the money because it has your home as collateral. If you default, the bank sells your home to get its money back.

Most home equity loans can be taken for up to 70 percent of the equity you have in your home. Let's say your home is worth $150,000 and you have $50,000 left on your mortgage. That means you have $100,000 in equity in the home, $70,000 of which can be borrowed to pay for college. That kind of money can come in real handy.

GRANTS, SCHOLARSHIPS, AND FINANCIAL AID

As we pointed out earlier in the chapter, the average student today pays about 60 percent of his or her college costs with savings and unsubsidized loans. The rest is covered by grants, scholarships, and subsidized loans. In 1996, nearly 70 percent of the students enrolled in America's colleges and universities received some form of financial aid. About 75 percent of the financial assistance came from the federal government. The rest came from the states, individual schools, corporations, foundations, and other sources.

Financial aid is designed to make up the difference between what a student and his or her parents can pay and the actual costs of college. As you would expect, it can be applied to tuition, fees, books, and other academic expenses. But what a lot of people don't realize is that it can also cover living costs like housing, food, and transportation. Also, not all financial assistance is designed for undergraduates in four-year programs. There are programs for graduate and doctoral students. There also are programs for students attending vocational and trade schools.

Financial aid comes in many forms and from many different sources. The most desirable are grants and scholarships. These are gifts, really, because the money does not have to be paid back. Grants are almost always based on financial need. If they're federal or state grants, they're provided by tax dollars. Scholarships, on the other hand, are usually awarded by colleges, universities, corporations, private foundations, and other organizations. If they come from schools, they're usually from money generated by endowment. They differ from grants in that they're usually given as a reward for academic, societal, or athletic achievement.

Other forms of financial aid include government-provided low-interest loans and work-study programs in which the student works a certain number of hours a week at a campus-based job.

Most students who apply for financial aid are offered a combination of all these types of assistance. The awards are "packaged" by college financial aid officers in an amount sufficient to cover that portion of the costs that parents and student cannot afford.

When the time comes, you should apply for every kind of financial aid you can think of, no matter how much money you make. The worst thing that can happen is you'll be turned down. But you may be surprised to discover you qualify for some assistance. You should also research grant and scholarship opportunities. There are tens of thousands of sources of grants, scholarships, low-interest loan programs, work-study programs, and other kinds of financial aid out there. There are so many, in fact, that millions of dollars in grant and scholarship money go unclaimed every year.

Mike: *We've been fortunate enough to learn firsthand how scholarships work. Our daughter attends a state university in the Midwest, where, because of her excellent SAT scores, she is allowed to pay in-state tuition rather than out-of-state tuition. This saves us about $6,000 a year. She also is a National Merit*

Scholar, which provides her with $750 a year from the National Merit Scholarship Corporation. But the biggest benefit she's received was one we didn't learn of until she actually arrived on campus for her freshman year. To entice talented kids to their schools, the State University Board of Regents awards National Merit Scholars who attend their state universities $5,000 a year.

Because of all this, we've only had to pay a fraction of what we had anticipated for her college education. In fact, depending on the timing of the scholarship payments, there have actually been a few times when, much to our delight and the amazement of our friends, the university owed us money and sent us a check.

A SAVING FOR COLLEGE CHECKLIST

- Time is on your side, IF you start early. Start saving as soon as possible, even before your children are born.
- Create a budget and stick to it.
- Invest in mutual funds, bonds, and other conservative investments that provide healthy growth over time. If you also choose to invest in individual stocks, make sure that no more than 20 percent of your portfolio is devoted to stocks. Don't forget the benefits of real estate.
- Keep investments in your name.
- Investigate grant and scholarship opportunities.
- Apply for financial aid.

10

Starting the Retirement Fund

Ah, retirement. Does the word conjure visions of undulating fairways and pristine golf greens? Aqua waters glimmering off the bow of a luxury liner? Shafts of sunlight slanting through stately, lacy birch, viewed from a hammock swaying gently on a woodsy cabin deck?

If it does, you're not alone. Most Americans assume they're entitled to a well-cushioned, leisurely retirement. They consider it a basic American right. After all, their parents worked hard, built a secure savings, then retired to their personal version of "The Life of Riley," so why shouldn't their children expect the same?

Why indeed. The truth is we live differently than our parents did, and always have. In fact, we live as well as or better than our parents did, and have become accustomed to a more lavish standard of living. But that free-spending lifestyle comes at a much higher cost. And even with the two incomes that have become almost a necessity to maintain that lifestyle today, couples are finding it harder to save. Especially for something as far distant as retirement and as unacceptable a concept as old age.

THERE'S REASON TO BE WORRIED

A recent article in *USA Today* noted that 31 percent of baby boomers surveyed are worried they aren't going to have enough money to live well throughout their retirement. In fact, money worries top their list of retirement concerns. And they have good reason to be worried. Financial experts agree most Americans today simply aren't saving enough to finance their retirement.

Marcia Novotny, 40, worries about funding her retirement. She's a therapist, her husband's an accountant. Their joint income is just over $150,000 a year, but they haven't managed to save more than a pittance over the years, and that in their company pension plans. Not enough, Marcia fears, for a comfortable retirement.

"Like most of our friends, we live day-to-day, year-to-year. We're not stupid, we know we should be saving more, and we even once sat down and calculated what we think we'll need to finance a decent retirement," she said. "But the reality is, we just can't seem to get ahead enough to put money away. It's hard to skimp today to save for tomorrow, especially when tomorrow's light-years away. Let's face it, we all like to live too well, and we don't want to deny our kids."

And there's more cause for concern. Retirees generally plan on two key sources of income in addition to their own savings—Social Security and pensions. But the Social Security system is on the sick list; some even have predicted its imminent demise. If inflation, increased longevity of Americans, and the wave of baby boomer retirements on the horizon don't kill it off, it will have to be doctored into a new form. Already, older boomers will have to work until age 66, not 65, to get full Social Security benefits. Younger boomers will have to wait until 67.

On top of that, private pension plans are going broke and being dismantled. But not to worry. In this chapter we'll take you step-by-step through the process of establishing and maintaining your retirement fund. And if you follow these steps, we guarantee you'll have sufficient funds to float whatever boat you choose in your salad days.

START YOUR RETIREMENT SAVINGS EARLY

While it's true it's never too soon or too late to start saving for your retirement, one rule of thumb is the 20/20 rule: To save for twenty years of retirement, start your retirement savings fund no later than twenty years before you plan to retire.

Three things will affect how much money you can accumulate for your retirement:

- the amount of time between now and your retirement, in which your savings can be earning money
- the amount of money you can invest in your retirement fund
- the rate of return you can get on that money

Obviously, the earlier you start to invest for retirement, the less you need to invest and the less risk you have to take. In other words, you won't need as high a rate of return.

ESTABLISH YOUR GOALS

Like any other kind of planning and strategizing, you should start retirement planning by establishing your goals. What kind of dreams do you have about retirement? Do you see yourselves traveling to exotic places? Buying a cottage at the beach? Getting a long-delayed law degree? Starting a new career? Set down your goals and estimate the costs they'll entail. Soon you'll need to figure out exactly how much money you'll need to finance your retirement, so any costs connected with pursuing new, postretirement dreams must be included.

Jacquie: *One word of caution here. In this chapter we're focusing on the financial implications of retirement. But while* *we're on the subject of goals and lifestyle, I feel compelled to offer some advice: Be sure you know what you're getting into when you retire, and I don't mean just financially. I mean understanding exactly what kind of retirement lifestyle will satisfy both of you.*

Someone close to me who shall go nameless retired happily at age 65 after a lifetime of hard work at a job he loved and felt fulfilled by. He expected to enjoy a retirement life on the links and puttering around the house, with winter months in Florida. But a few weeks after the retirement party he started taking long naps in the morning and again in the afternoon, then heading up to bed by 9 at night. It was hard to move him off the sofa in between.

Gifts of beer-making kits and art supplies did nothing to alleviate what was clearly postretirement depression, and a severe case of it. What finally worked was coming to an understanding of the fact that for him, his job was a vital part of who and what he was as a person, and how he enjoyed spending his time.

The solution: He went back to work part-time, just a few hours a week. He was lucky that he had that option—not everyone does. But what's important is to remember to plan ahead, figure out exactly what you do and don't want in your retirement lifestyle, and prepare for it.

And in a shameless plug, if you want to read more on this subject, let me suggest my book, The 21st Century Entrepreneur: How to Start a Retirement Business (Avon 1996).

Mike: *I'm so embarrassed. She has no shame. But she's right about figuring how you want to spend your retirement days before you decide how you're going to finance your retirement. You never know. I have a secret hankering to buy a golf course and run it, of course spending as much of my own time as possible on the links. If I decide I'm really serious, I guess it might not be a bad idea to discuss it with you-know-who, who I'm sure will have some very explicit thoughts on the subject. But I have to admit, the thought of that conversation worries me.*

YOUR LIVING EXPENSES WILL BE REDUCED

Don't forget that your cost of living is likely to be less during your retirement years. For one thing, while you'll still need to continue to save in order to cover rising costs later in life, including those that come with aging and health care concerns, you probably won't need to save as aggressively as you have been.

You probably won't need as much insurance as you've been carrying, either. For example, you may feel comfortable dropping life and disability insurance. On the other hand, you may need Medigap health insurance to cover the gap between what Medicare pays and actual medical costs, as well as long-term care insurance to cover a nursing home or home health care costs.

You'll also be saving on work-related expenses during retirement. You won't be buying those business suits, train tickets, parking permits, and lunches out. And unless you decide to continue working, you won't be paying Social Security taxes. All of these can add up to substantial savings.

And finally, don't forget that you'll most likely be a senior citizen when you retire. That means that come age 55, you'll be eligible for travel discounts, reduced rates for cultural and community events, some newspaper subscriptions, and all kinds of goodies. Okay, you have to face up to the idea of being "senior," but get over it, already. Senior discounts can help you keep your overall living expenses down, so take advantage.

YOUR LOCATION WILL MAKE A DIFFERENCE

Location, location, location. Every realtor and every retailer knows location makes a difference. But prospective retirees should remember the same thing, because where you live will have a substantial impact on your finances. If you're considering relocating, whether to the mountains, the Sunbelt, or just to a smaller house in the suburbs, you need to consider the move from a tax standpoint—in terms of both property and income taxes.

You need to determine which state, or states, will impose income tax on your earnings. And there may be gift or inheritance taxes to consider as well. This can be an opportunity to lower your overall tax burden, but be careful. You may need professional help in sorting out the tax implications before you make any move.

FIGURE OUT WHAT YOU'LL NEED

Once you've set your retirement goals and figured out where and how you want to live, you need to determine exactly how much you'll need to achieve that lifestyle. One rule of thumb says that to live comfortably you'll need 75 percent of your preretirement annual after-tax income. Let's say that's $50,000.

Next, determine the annual rate of return you expect from your investments. Experts say 8 percent is reasonable, but you have to cut that rate in half to factor in inflation. Next, divide the $50,000 by 4 percent. The answer, $1.25 million, is what you need in your retirement pot on your last day of work.

If that number sends shivers down your spine, don't collapse into a puddle yet. Remember, if all goes as you anticipate, you'll probably have income from a company pension plan and Social Security. A pension could provide about 18 percent of your final pay, while Social Security could replace roughly 31 percent. So if you think you'll need $50,000 a year in retirement, this additional income could provide almost half that amount. Of course, we wouldn't count on Social Security or your pension.

Here's another way to calculate your postretirement financial needs using the 75 percent rule:

1. Calculate your total current gross annual income from all sources.

2. Subtract your annual savings, including capital gains, contributions to retirement funds, and reinvested dividends.

3. Write down the subtotal, which is the amount you currently spend.

4. To figure out what you'll need when factoring in inflation, count the number of years you have until retirement, and, using the table below, come up with a multiplying factor.

5. Multiply the current annual figure you came up with by the inflation factor (for example, $50,000 x 1.2= $60,000). This gives you the amount you'll need to live on annually in retirement dollars.

6. If you estimate living about twenty years or so in retirement, about the average lifespan if you retire at age 65, the total amount needed is $1.2 million, very close to the previous calculation.

Inflation Factors

# Of Years until Retirement	Multiplying Factor
5	1.2
10	1.6
15	1.9
20	2.4
25	3.0
30	3.7
35	4.7
40	5.8

DETERMINE CURRENT EXPENSES

Next, you need to determine more definitively what your retirement living expenses will be. To do this, you first need to list your current expenses. You already did this in chapter 3, so go back to your financial notebook and take out that worksheet. This tells you what you currently spend both monthly and annually. But you also need to estimate what you're going to be spending both monthly and annually in retirement.

Estimate Retirement Expenses

Run down the same list again, calculating what you'll probably spend on these items, both monthly and annually, in retirement.

Say you currently spend $1,200 a month on your mortgage, but plan on moving to Florida, where you expect your mortgage payments to be cut in half. Under monthly estimated expenses for your mortgage, you would then write $600. To come up with a yearly total just multiply $600 by 12 for an annual expense of $7,200.

Don't forget, though—these numbers are only estimates, and every couple going through this process will come up with different figures. If you're not sure yet if you're going to be moving, or what a particular expense might be, but you're pretty certain it'll be lower, just take the current number for that item and multiply by 0.75. Say you're currently spending $1,000 a year to put gas in your car and $800 to park at work. You know you won't be parking regularly in retirement, but you're not sure how much less you'll be driving. So drop the $800 and multiply the $1,000 by 0.75, and assume your transportation expenses will drop to $750 per year in retirement.

Don't forget, too, that you'll probably see increases in some expenses in retirement. For example, many couples end up spending more on entertainment, hobbies, and leisure time activities in retirement than they did when they were working.

Now tally up your monthly and annual estimated retirement expenses. Remember, these are figured in current dollars. To be safe you need to take inflation into account. That means multiplying your numbers by the same inflation factor you used for your earlier calculation.

Let's say that, according to your earlier calculations, you'll be spending $7,200 a year in retirement on your mortgage. That's in current dollars. But you're not planning to retire for twenty more years. Checking the inflation table, you see that the inflation factor for twenty years is 2.4. You multiply $7,200 by 2.4, and what do you get? In future dollars, you'll probably be spending $17,280 a year in mortgage payments.

Tackle your expenses again, this time writing down what you estimate you'll be spending monthly and annually in both current and future dollars.

	Monthly	Monthly	Annually	Annually
EXPENSES				
Mortgage/rent				
Utilities				
Gas/oil				
Electric				
Water				
Sewer				
Property taxes				
Home maintenance				
Car payments				
Car/commuting expenses				
Maintenance/repairs				
Gas				
Commuting fees/tolls				
Credit card/loan payments				

Insurance premiums	____	____	____	____
Life	____	____	____	____
Health	____	____	____	____
Disability	____	____	____	____
Home	____	____	____	____
Liability	____	____	____	____
Other	____	____	____	____
Income taxes	____	____	____	____
Employment taxes	____	____	____	____
Food	____	____	____	____
Clothing	____	____	____	____
Medical expenses	____	____	____	____
Child care	____	____	____	____
Education	____	____	____	____
Entertainment	____	____	____	____
Vacations	____	____	____	____
Alimony	____	____	____	____
Gifts	____	____	____	____
Personal needs	____	____	____	____
Charitable contributions	____	____	____	____
Savings/investments	____	____	____	____
Emergency fund	____	____	____	____
Vacation fund	____	____	____	____
Investment fund	____	____	____	____
Other	____	____	____	____
Other payments	____	____	____	____
Total Expenses	____	____	____	____

This may seem like overkill, but it will give you a good idea of exactly what you'll need to meet your expenses in retirement. The next step is to figure out where you are now in terms of eventually meeting those needs.

Figure Out Where You Are Now

In calculating what you'll need to live on in retirement, you probably assumed you'll be working and saving between now and whenever you hope to retire. We're going to continue our retirement planning based on that assumption, but beware: No job is totally secure in today's business climate.

In fact, experts agree that in the future, most people won't work for a single company most of their lives as their parents did. Rather, for a variety of reasons, they'll work for a succession of companies at a succession of jobs and maybe even change careers several times in the course of their work lives.

So while you shouldn't count on your job or income stream being secure and increasing automatically over the years, you need to plan to remain employed and maintain that income stream in some way to fund your retirement. It'll be up to you to stay on the path we set out.

Right now, though, your next step is to figure out your starting point. That is, where you are now. The only way we can accurately chart the best way to get you where you want to go is by knowing exactly where you are now. Your starting point is your net worth, which you calculated in chapter 2. Those worksheets and calculations should still be in your financial notebook for easy reference. If not, review chapter 2 and redo the calculations outlined to establish your net worth.

Now, you've figured out how much you're going to need to fund your retirement and you know where you are right now. The next step is to figure out how to achieve your retirement fund goals from this starting point. Don't forget, though, that in addition to your savings from this point you should be able to count on some help from Social Security and a pension fund.

Before we go any further in strategizing how to accomplish your retirement fund goal, let's take a closer look at how much help you can expect from Social Security and pension benefits and how much you will have to save yourself.

To figure out how big that gap is going to be, use this easy formula:

1. Earlier in this chapter you calculated your estimated annual expenses in retirement, in inflated dollars. Write that figure down.

2. Take your estimated Social Security income and your estimated pension income and add them together.

3. Subtract this combined figure from the number you wrote down in step 1.

4. Take that number and multiply it by the personal inflation factor you used earlier, referring back to the Inflation Factors table on page 225.

5. The number you arrive at is the amount of income you'll need in retirement that you *don't* have covered.

6. Generally, for every $1,000 of annual income you'll need to fund retirement, you'll need at least $17,000 in savings/investments to keep up with inflation. If you're planning on retiring at age 65, multiply the figure from step 5 by 17 to see how much investment savings you're going to need in inflated dollars. If you're planning for early retirement, multiply by 20.

HERE'S THE SCOOP ON THE MANY RETIREMENT PLANS

This is where we get down to the nitty-gritty of sorting out the different investment options you have in funding your retirement, including Keoghs, IRAs, 401(k)s, ESOPs—among others. The list is seemingly endless.

Company-Sponsored Retirement Plans

Let's start with company-sponsored retirement plans, known as pension plans. Pension plans are old hat. In the United States they date back to 1636, when the settlers of the first colony at Plymouth established a military pension.

American Express created the first corporate pension plan in 1875, and today almost two-thirds of the workforce is covered by some form of pension.

If your company has a pension plan—and many don't—be sure to participate. You're entitled to join your company's pension plan no matter what your position or salary. But many workers don't participate, in part because they don't understand how the retirement plans work. In fact, it's estimated that as many as 60 percent of workers don't participate in a company-sponsored plan. That's a shame, since company-sponsored retirement plans can make a huge difference in your ability to retire comfortably.

Jacquie: *Don't just participate on automatic pilot, either. Many pension plans offer employees a wide variety of investment options, so get actively involved. Both Mike and I have pensions with the Teachers Insurance and Annuity Association-College Retirement Equities Fund through Cornell University, our current employer. I'm also vested in a pension fund from my twenty years at the Gannett Company.*

I'm embarrassed to confess that the first couple of years we were covered by TIAA/CREF we took the automatic pilot route and accepted the basic investment package offered, since it involved no decision making. In our defense, it was a very busy time in our lives, and we were too stressed to make any other decisions. Then our brains kicked in, and we took the time to sit down and really look at our options and make some decisions. Now, I'm happy to say, we have a good, diversified mix of investments, and we regularly review their performance.

We've got our money in a 401(k) (from Gannett), a 403(b), a TIAA stock fund, a CREF stock fund, a CREF bond market fund, and a CREF global equities fund. Right now it works for us, but we'll continue to evaluate and change the mix if something better comes along or if circumstances change.

Mike: *I'm more than embarrassed. I'm furious with my-*

self for taking the easy way out for a couple of years. It really cost us money. Learn from our mistake and don't let inertia cost you.

A word of caution here, though. When Jacquie gets going she sometimes goes too far in her enthusiasm. Yes, we regularly review the performance of our investments. And we'll make changes if it appears prudent. But don't jump in and out of investments whenever the wind blows, or you'll get nowhere fast. You need to give your investments time to grow. So do your research well before you make your decisions, and then let them work for you.

How Company-Sponsored Plans Work

A qualified plan is one in which an employer both sets up and contributes to the employee's retirement plan. In return, employers get substantial tax breaks. Non-qualified plans are those in which employers don't qualify for tax deductions because they don't contribute money to the plan, just set it up. Whether your company offers a qualified or non-qualified plan, the money invested in your plan remains tax-free until you withdraw it.

With defined benefit plans, your company does all the funding. You don't have to put in a penny, but you also have no say in how the money in your plan is invested. That's totally a company call. How much money you actually receive at retirement is based on a formula that takes into account your compensation, as well as how long you've worked for the company. When retirement day arrives, your monthly retirement income is calculated and paid out according to that formula.

Most companies use one of three formulas for calculating retirement benefits: the final pay formula, career average formula, or flat benefit formula. While they vary, each takes into account both salary and length of service.

You can't participate in a defined benefit plan unless you've worked at the company a certain number of years—that is, unless you're vested. Vesting periods vary from company to company, but it's important to know what yours is.

In the case of defined contribution plans, the employer, employee, or both make contributions to your retirement account. These plans can be 401(k)s, 403(b)s, SEPs, employee stock ownership plans (ESOPs), etc.

Defined contribution plans are very popular. That's because the company doesn't have to shoulder the full burden of funding your retirement plan. Additionally, the company isn't solely responsible for deciding how the monies in your fund are invested; you have a say in the matter.

In her book, *The 21st Century Investor: How to Invest for Your Retirement* (Avon 1997), Deirdre Martin suggests that you ask your employer, or the employee benefits representative, the following questions about your plan:

- What's the name of the plan being offered?
- Will I have to pay any fees to participate in the plan?
- As simply as you can, would you please define the plan for me, as well as what it means for me as an employee?
- Do I have any choice in where and how I can invest my money in this plan? Can I change my mind about those choices anywhere along the line? And if I do, are there any costs and fees that will be passed on to me for doing so?
- What are those choices? Do you have printed material on the different choices that I can take with me?
- How much money can I put in the program annually? Is there a cap? Is the money deducted automatically from my paycheck? If not, how do I contribute to the account?

• Will my employer be making any matching contribution to the plan? If so, how much? What determines the amount of those contributions?

• How well have the investments available to me in this plan performed in the past? What sources can I use to compare how these investments have performed so I know which investments are worthwhile?

• If I leave the company, do my defined contribution monies go with me? Can I leave them here? What are advantages and disadvantages of each?

• Must I contribute annually? Or can I occasionally stop making contributions depending upon my financial situation?

• If I have any more questions about the plan, who is the most appropriate person to speak to?

As is the case with any investment, the performance of your defined contribution plan depends on how much and how long you and/or your employer contribute to the plan; how well the pension monies are invested; and how well the stock market performs during the investment period.

The good news with defined contribution plans is that all employee contributions are vested immediately. If you leave the company, the money *you've* put into the plan goes with you. That can happen in three ways: it's placed in a new retirement plan via a rollover (taking money from one retirement account and putting it in another without incurring any taxes and/or penalties); it's disbursed to you in a lump sum distribution; or it stays with your old employer until you're ready to retire.

Here's a look at the most commonly used defined contribution plans:

401(k)s

In 401(k)s money is taken directly from your salary and placed in a tax-deferred retirement plan. You don't have to pay taxes on that money until you retire. Usually, you decide how to invest the money.

Plans in which your employer matches your contribution (sometimes as much as 50 cents for every dollar you contribute) are a special boon to your retirement fund. Unfortunately, that "free money" is only guaranteed yours if you stay with the company. If you leave, 100 percent of the money you put into the account is yours, but the money your employer puts into it may or may not go with you, depending on company policy. Check it out.

Your 401(k) money can be invested in a number of ways: in mutual funds, which are diversified portfolios of stocks, bonds, and money-market instruments, individual stocks and bonds, and any number of other instruments.

The downside of 401(k)s? There are limits to the amount you can contribute annually. In 1995, an employee was allowed to contribute up to 15 percent of his or her salary or $9,240, whichever is less. And you can't touch the money in your 401(k) until you're age 59½. If you need to withdraw the money sooner, you'll pay a 10 percent penalty. You're also penalized if you leave the money in too long, or if you take out too much during any given year. And finally, you have to pay Social Security taxes on your 401(k) contribution.

403(b)s

403(b)s are just like 401(k)s, except they're for people who work for charitable or nonprofit organizations, such as social welfare offices and churches.

Your contribution is deducted directly from your salary, and your employer may contribute as well. Most plans prohibit employees from contributing more than 5 percent of their annual salary to the plan. A second kind of 403(b) is a TDA, or tax-deferred annuity. These are simply tax-deferred investments.

Like 401(k)s, your employer offers investment options

for 403(b)s. The drawbacks, too, are similar. With 403(b)s you must pay Social Security on your contribution, and their performance is contingent on the investments you've chosen.

Experts say that many employees' investments don't earn what they should because people are afraid of taking a risk. The safe investment is probably not going to earn you the biggest return. For example, more than 50 percent of people invest the money in their 401(k)s in fixed-income securities, where long-term return is subject to interest rates and inflation. What they should be doing instead is putting more of their money into stocks and stock mutual funds—those with a track record of good returns. But only 25 percent of people participating in defined contribution plans own stock or stock funds.

ESOPs

ESOPs, or Employee Stock Option Plans, are those in which you invest in your employer's stock. They give employees a stake in the company's success, beyond just their own job security. An estimated 11.4 million employees in the United States participate in ESOP plans.

On the pro side of ESOPs is the fact that you don't spend your own money to buy company stock. Instead, your employer buys it for you through plan contributions. When you retire, you can take either a cash payout or receive your pension proceeds in stock certificates.

On the con side, you have little or no control over your investment, since the company itself *is* the investment. If the company does well and the stock's riding high at retirement time, you can cash in. But if the company's not doing so well, neither will you.

Helpful Hint

If you're part of an ESOP plan and your only current investment for retirement is in company stock, be sure

you look into other investment options as well. It's important to diversify your investments. If you don't, it could
spell disaster.

Keoghs

A tax-deferred Keogh plan is available if you're self-
employed or if you moonlight. That means you can invest
in your company's 401(k) plan, but at the same time invest
in a Keogh any money you earn moonlighting. Like pension plans mentioned earlier, Keoghs can be either defined
benefit or defined contribution plans, or both. Four kinds
of Keogh plans are available:

• **Profit-sharing Keoghs,** in which you can contribute and deduct from your taxes up to 13.04 percent of
your self-employment earnings up to $30,000. You decide
how much or how little money you want to put in each
year. If you have a bad year, you don't have to contribute
at all.

• **Money-purchase Keoghs,** where the maximum
that can be contributed is up to 25 percent of your annual
self-employed earnings, with a ceiling of $30,000. How-
ever, once you pick a percentage, you're stuck with it.
Generally speaking, if you have a bad year and can't make
that contribution, you'll be in trouble with the IRS.

• **Combination Keoghs,** where money-purchase and
profit-sharing Keoghs are combined. The good news is
you can be more flexible in the amount you contribute
each year. First, you set up a money-purchase plan with
a guaranteed annual payment of whatever percent you
choose. Then, you establish a profit-sharing plan to receive whatever money you bring in above that established
percentage. You may want to start off with a profit-sharing
Keogh and add the money-purchase plan later, when
you're assured of making more money.

- **Defined Benefit Keogh,** which provides you with a fixed annual income when you retire. You pick the annual pension you want, then contribute the amount needed to reach that goal. You may contribute up to 100 percent of your self-employment salary annually, if necessary. The tough part is figuring out what to contribute each year. To aid in that process, you're required to consult an actuary *annually* to review your plan and determine how much you have to put away the following year to meet your goal. A copy of the actuary's report must accompany your tax return. It'll cost you to consult the actuary and to maintain this kind of Keogh. But if your income drops, you can dissolve the Keogh immediately and roll the money into an IRA.

While most people maintain a single Keogh account, you may establish several Keoghs to do different things, provided you don't exceed the annual ceiling. For maximum flexibility, we suggest opening a Keogh with a mutual fund group. We also suggest having a fixed amount withdrawn from your bank account each month and deposited directly into the Keogh—an enforced form of savings.

With all types of Keoghs, you're penalized if you withdraw money before you're 59½, and withdrawals are mandatory when you turn 70. But unlike other plans, you can continue putting money into a Keogh after age 70½, and you can borrow against funds accumulated in the plan if you need to, with certain restrictions.

Finally, if you have employees, they must be included in your Keogh plan. If you contribute 20 percent of your earnings to the plan, you're also required to contribute 20 percent for each employee covered by the plan. An actuary will also determine how much you must contribute to your employees' Keoghs, based on your net profit.

SEPs

A SEP, or Simplified Employee Pension, is another option for the self-employed or employees of small companies, especially those who can't invest a lot of money each year. SEPs work much like Keoghs, but they are preferred by small business owners because employees own and manage their own accounts. Employers save money, since they don't have to pay someone to administer the program. All they have to come up with is their contribution. Currently, the most an employer can contribute to a SEP is 15 percent of the employee's wage or $22,500, whichever is less.

SEPs are easy to administer. You don't have to file an annual report with the IRA the way you do with a Keogh, and you can change the amount you contribute annually to accommodate both good and bad business years. If you find a new job, you can roll your SEP money into an IRA without incurring any penalty, although you can't roll a SEP into your new company's retirement plan.

IRAs

IRAs, or Individual Retirement Accounts, are retirement plans for individuals who are employed, or for individuals married to someone who's employed. The maximum you may contribute to an IRA annually is $2,000, or $2,250 into separate, spousal IRAs if one of you isn't employed. You can open an IRA with less than $2,000, and you don't have to put money in it every year. On the other hand you should, since IRAs are one of the best tax-deferred retirement vehicles on the market.

IRAs are similar to some investment plans listed above. You pay a 10 percent penalty if you withdraw money from your IRA before you're 59½, in addition to any taxes due. You must start withdrawing money from your IRA at 70½, although you can continue to invest $2,000 a year in a nonworking spouse's plan until he or she reaches that age.

Your IRA can be invested any way you choose, in individual stocks and bonds, as a simple savings account, or a mix of mutual funds. You can change your mix of investments each year, or even set up a different IRA each year if you like. The decision is yours and yours alone.

To simplify your record keeping, however, we suggest that you set up your IRAs in one place, whether it's a bank or a brokerage house. That way, while you may have many different types of investments, you'll have only one statement to keep track of.

If you're starting your retirement fund early, you should consider investing your IRA in riskier, high-growth investments like mutual funds or growth stocks, then switching them to safer investments closer to retirement. But if you're getting close to retirement—in your early sixties—you may want to avoid IRAs, since the law requires you to start withdrawing money from your IRA by age 70½. That doesn't give you much chance for a good return on your investment, even though you may save some on taxes.

Be sure to shop around before opening your IRA, as there are fees associated with opening and maintaining these accounts. While some brokerage houses will waive fees if you put a certain amount into the account, generally you'll pay between $10 and $50.

One thing to keep in mind. Accounts opened before December 19, 1993, are insured up to $100,000 each, whether you have one IRA or twenty. But accounts opened after that date are insured up to $100,000 total. This means that if you have two IRAs worth $200,000 apiece in a bank that goes under, you're entitled to just $100,000. That's why some people open up each IRA in a different bank. They feel that keeping track of different IRAs at different institutions is worth the insurance it provides. That insurance applies only to bank deposits, though. Mutual funds and other investments *aren't* insured.

While you can't borrow from your IRA as you can with some pension plans, you can use the money during a sixty-day period, once a year. You can withdraw the money, use it, or open a new account with the full amount you withdrew before that eight-week period is up. If you miss the deadline, you'll have to pay a penalty.

The Roth IRA

Recently, a new IRA hit the market, courtesy of the Taxpayer Relief Act of 1997. The Roth IRA (named after Delaware Senator William Roth) is similar to most IRAs, with a few delightful exceptions. The biggest is that it provides tax-*free* income rather than tax-*deferred* income; when you withdraw money from your account, you pay no taxes on it.

The second bit of good news is that you can begin to withdraw money from a Roth IRA once the account is five years old. This makes the Roth an excellent investment strategy not just for retirement, but also for saving for a home, paying college tuition, and any other big expense you know will be coming down the pike in a few years.

Another difference between the Roth IRA and traditional IRAs is that you don't have to begin to take your money out at age 70½. If you choose, you can let the money sit for years, accumulating additional tax-free interest. You can also continue to make contributions to the account. And if you should pass away before the account has been emptied, the balance can be passed on to your children.

The law also allows you to convert a traditional IRA into a Roth IRA, provided your adjusted gross income is less than $100,000. (That's for both single people and married people who file joint returns, by the way. If you're married and file separately, you won't qualify. Once again, married people get the shaft.) However, you'll pay the tax due on your old IRA before you put the money into the Roth IRA, so the initial value of the Roth will be less than that of the IRA you're converting.

As with traditional IRAs, you can contribute up to $2,000 a year to a Roth IRA. (Married couples can contribute $4,000.) You can also contribute to both kinds of IRAs, as long as the total contribution doesn't exceed $2,000.

All this is great news. But, predictably, there is a downside. Unlike traditional IRAs, your Roth IRA contributions cannot be deducted from your gross income for tax purposes. If you make $45,000 and contribute $2,000 to a traditional IRA, your income for tax purposes is $43,000. If you contribute the $2,000 to a Roth IRA, you still pay taxes on your total income of $45,000.

So which kind of IRA is better? The answer depends on a number of factors, including current and future tax rates, the return on investment, and the length of time in the investment. Financial planners and investment counselors have Roth IRA "calculators" that will help you weigh their merits against those of traditional IRAs.

Social Security

As we mentioned earlier in this chapter, if you're counting solely on Social Security to fund your retirement you're in trouble, since the system may not even survive into the twenty-first century. But in case it does, there are some things you should know about it.

The system is funded by money withheld from your paycheck, as well as the paychecks of everyone else who works. It's designed to provide a guaranteed monthly income for those who are retired or disabled, their families, and their survivors should they die.

To qualify for Social Security, you need to have paid FICA taxes. You also need to have accumulated forty "credits" if you were born after 1928. In 1995, a credit was given for every $630 earned. However, no worker can accrue more than four credits a year, no matter how much money he or she earns. The dollar amount per credit is adjusted each year to reflect cost of living increases. So, too, is the maximum income on which you must pay Social Security taxes. Once you earn those forty credits, you're in.

The monthly payment you receive when you retire is based on what you've earned during your highest-paying thirty-five working years. That means the more money you make over the course of your career, the more you'll get back from Social Security. If you've paid the full amount of FICA each year and wait until you reach full retirement age before you begin collecting, you'll be eligible for the largest benefit Social Security offers.

You can start collecting Social Security when you're 62, but in that case the amount you receive will be smaller than if you waited until age 65, when you're eligible for full benefits. Those between ages 62 and 65 can work while collecting Social Security, but with some restrictions: You can only earn up to $8,040 without affecting your benefits. After that, for every $2 you earn, $1 in benefits is withheld. If you're between 65 and 69, you can earn up to $11,160 without cutting into your benefits, but for every $3 you earn, Social Security will withhold $1. Once you hit 70, you're golden. You can make as much income as you are able to and still collect your full Social Security benefits.

Once you qualify for Social Security benefits, you get them for as long as you live. And your spouse can collect as well. Spouses are eligible to collect 50 percent of your full retirement benefit at age 65, or 37.5 percent if they're between the ages of 62 and 65. If you're a woman and your spouse dies, you can switch from collecting on your own to collecting as a survivor if that makes you eligible for a larger benefit. By waiting until you turn 65, you receive 100 percent of your spouse's benefit. The same is true for men whose wives receive the higher Social Security benefit: should your wife die, you can get 100 percent of her benefit if you're 65 or older. You cannot collect two benefits, however.

The law's straightforward on taxing benefits. It says:

- If you're single and your income level is between $25,000 and $34,000, 50 percent of your benefit will be taxed. If you make over $34,000, 85 percent of your benefit is taxed.
- If you're married but living apart and filing separate returns, it's the same as above.
- If you're married and your income is between $32,000 and $44,000, 50 percent of your benefit it taxable. Earn above $44,000, and 85 percent of your benefit will be taxed.

Helpful Hint

If you want to check on how many credits you've earned or how much you've paid into the system, call 1-800-772-1213 and request a Personal Earnings and Benefits Statement. After filling it out, you return it to the Social Security Administration (SSA). SSA then sends you an estimate of what you can expect, based on your age and salary.

MAKE THE MOST OF THOSE RETIREMENT PLANS

Now that you're fully briefed on what retirement plans are available to you, it's time to learn more about the investment tools, or products, you can use to make the most of those plans—and get the biggest bang for your retirement bucks. Get ready for your eyes to glaze over—we've got a lot of ground to cover here, and there's no way around it if you're serious about investing for your future. Just put on a big pot of high-test coffee and grit your teeth.

And don't worry too much about the details. This laundry list is just an attempt to get you a bit more comfortable with the investment tools that are out there. Plenty of good books have been written on these individual tools, and you can refer to them when you're ready. And don't forget. You've already accomplished the most important assignments in your retirement planning: You've figured out where you are and where you need to go. When push comes to shove and it's time to put your money down, you can do more specific research yourself or hire a financial planner to guide you.

For now, keep in mind that there's no such thing as risk-free investment. Instead, the key is just how much risk you are willing and able to take. Some of that depends on timing—how quickly you need to earn a return on your investment—but a lot depends on your personality. That is, how much risk are you comfortable with? (Remember our discussion in chapter 2?)

Some of these investment products pose relatively low risk. Others are high risk. You may want to choose some from column A, some from column B, or you may be a real gambler and prefer the (excuse the expression) "go-for-broke route." Whatever approach you end up opting for, you need to know more about these products before you get down to the nitty-gritty of selecting the ones that will fund your retirement.

ANNUITIES

Tax-deferred Annuities

An annuity is a contract you make with an insurance company. Most people choose deferred annuities, in which you give money to the insurance company, either in a lump sum or over a period of time, for the purpose of building up a retirement fund. The insurance company invests your money, then pays out your benefit when it's time to collect. Since deferred annuities are, essentially, retirement plans, the money in them is tax-deferred.

There are basically two types of deferred annuities: fixed and variable. Fixed-rate annuities promise a predetermined rate of return, although that rate can be reset over the years. That means if the market drops dramatically, the earnings projected for your investment can plummet.

To safeguard against this, most fixed-rate annuities have a guaranteed minimum rate. Unfortunately, this minimum rate is rarely any higher than the prevailing savings rate at the time. Since generally fixed annuities don't keep up with inflation, they're considered a more conservative investment than variable rate annuities.

With variable annuities you decide how your money is invested. It's similar to a 401(k) plan, except that the monies you invest in an annuity already have been taxed, which isn't the case with a 401(k). The investment selection may be limited.

Naturally, there are pros and cons to deferred annuities. The pros:

- You're not locked in to one type of plan—you can pick and choose.
- Unlike earnings on other investments, the money doesn't count as income when it comes time to figure out if your Social Security benefit is taxable.

- You can put in as much money annually as you choose.
- You don't have to start withdrawing after 70.

The cons:

- The fees for maintaining tax-deferred annuities can be quite high.
- The money you invest is not tax deductible.
- You're penalized for withdrawing money before age 59½.

When the time comes to collect on your annuity you can choose lump sum withdrawal or regular payments. With a lump sum withdrawal, you must pay all the taxes up front. If you choose to take the money in regular payments, taxes are owed on a portion of each payment you receive, based on the insurance company's calculation—a much smarter choice.

Immediate Annuities

Immediate annuities work just the way they sound: You give a lump sum to an insurance company, and they start making monthly payments to you immediately. The size of your monthly annuity check is based on your age, the amount of your investment, and estimates made by the insurance company on how much your investment will earn. Since your estimated monthly payout will vary from insurance company to insurance company, it pays to shop around for the best rate.

Many couples like immediate annuities because they don't have to worry about managing the money themselves—the insurance company does that. Obviously, that's a negative for those who like control. Immediate annuities offer a guaranteed monthly income, which many retirees find reassuring. Since you've already paid taxes on the money used to fund the annuity, more than half of the income is usually tax-free.

There are downsides, though: The annuity contract is irrevocable—no chance to change your mind. It's up to you to decide how much money to put into the annuity, although most experts recommend you invest no more than a quarter of your total retirement savings. If the insurance company you've signed with goes belly-up, you're out of luck—another reason it pays to shop around. And, if you purchase your annuity at a time when interest rates are low, chances are that your payments may not keep pace with inflation.

Basically there are three types of immediate annuities:

- **Joint and several annuities.** This is paid over your lifetime, as well as the lifetime of your beneficiary. Though the monthly payouts tend to be smaller, the payments stretch over a longer period of time. But if your beneficiary dies, it doesn't alter the amount of your payment, which remains small. So you need to live longer to recoup your investment. No problem, right?
- **Single life annuities.** These are paid out each month for as long as you live. You can expect a bigger payout each month, but if you die, your survivor gets nothing. If you and your partner have been using the annuity to help meet basic expenses, this can be a problem.
- **Life or period certain annuities.** These are payable for either a fixed amount of time or for your lifetime. The monthly payment is less than you'd receive with a single life plan, but if you die before the fixed term ends, your survivor continues to receive the monthly payments.

BONDS

Bonds are loans that you make to either a corporation, the U.S. government, or a municipality. They, in turn, provide you with interest payments, which you receive from the time the bond is purchased until it matures or is sold, whichever comes first. Interest payments usually are made every six months. Depending on what type of bond you've purchased, payments may or may not be taxable. Currently, the income from corporate bonds can be taxed, while the income from municipal bonds is tax-free. Monies invested in treasury securities are exempt from state and local taxes but not from federal taxes.

Bonds generally appeal to conservative investors, as they offer regular, fixed payments until the bond matures. When the bond comes due you get back its face value, which you can reinvest.

Bonds are considered a less risky form of investment than stocks, but there are still some risks. The risks depend on the length of time until the bond matures, interest rates (which can affect bond prices), and the seller of the bond (which affects its quality).

A bond with a longer maturity period is considered riskier, but its potential yield is also greater. It's also risky to sell a bond before it matures, as you may not recoup your original investment.

Bond Ratings

Most bonds are given a rating to alert investors to their relative quality. Triple A is the highest rating, given to bonds that carry little risk. The issuers are considered stable and dependable. Double A bonds also are high quality, but carry a slightly higher degree of risk. Single A bonds are of high to medium quality, but are extremely vulnerable to market conditions. Triple B bonds, or Baa bonds as they are sometimes known, are good for the short term but do not perform well over a long period. They're considered to be of medium quality.

Any bond bearing one of these ratings is considered worthy of investment by both Moody's and Standard &

Poor, two of the best-known agencies for rating bonds. It's possible for a bond to be NR, or non-rated, as well. NR bonds often offer investors higher returns than triple A rated bonds. You might want to look into investing in a non-rated thirty-year maturing bond.

Helpful Hint
There are many types of bonds, each with plusses and minuses. To be sure you don't end up with your investment in the minus category, get all the information available on a particular bond before you decide to invest. Find out:

- what kind of bond it is—government, corporate, or municipal
- who is issuing the bond, as well as how and where the money you're investing in your purchase will be spent
- if and how the bond is rated
- the bond's maturity date
- whether the income you receive will be tax-free
- if the bond has a "call date," the earliest date at which the bond's issuer can redeem the bond before its maturity date
- the bond's price and its face value, or the amount the bond will be worth when it reaches maturity

CERTIFICATES OF DEPOSIT

Certificates of deposit, or CDs, are deposits made with a bank or savings and loan for a specified period of time. The institution generally pays a fixed rate of interest for the term of the certificate, with rates often increasing with the term of the deposit.

CDs are considered extremely conservative investments, just a step above your basic bank savings account. And since they're not as liquid as money-market deposit accounts, they should pay a bit more in interest. Despite offering a relatively low yield, CDs are quite popular. That's because they're easy to open, they're relatively safe (federally insured up to $100,000), and they're available in a range of maturity periods, including one, two, three, six, and twelve months, to two and one-half, five, and ten years.

FUTURES AND OPTIONS

Many couples shy away from futures and options as extremely high-risk investments. They consider them high-stakes gambling, and in a way that's true. But if you have a taste for gambling and take some reasonable precautions, you can also win big bucks with futures and options. It's your call.

Futures are investments wherein it's mandatory to buy or sell a specific commodity (from grain to oil) on a certain day for a certain price. Options, on the other hand, simply give you the *right* to buy or sell a specific product (like stocks or bonds). Like futures, options must be sold at a preset price during a specific period of time.

Most of the risk in investing in futures and options is the result of leveraging. Leveraging is the use of a small amount of money for the purpose of investing in a product of much greater value. This allows you to buy what's known as a futures contract. Investing in futures contracts allows you to put down 10 percent of a contract that carries a total worth of thousands of dollars. This 10 percent down payment is crucial: You're betting, or gambling, that the value of your contract will increase. If your contract gains by as little as 10 cents, the value of your investment jumps by $10. Since it's possible for futures contracts to gain by as much as $100, the potential exists for the value of your investment to increase to $10,000.

Unfortunately, the reverse also is true. If the value of your contract drops, you still have to fork over the full remaining amount owed on its purchase despite the fact that it's worth much less than you gambled on. Thus, you can find yourself thousands of dollars in the hole.

Jacquie: *This is one investment area in which Mike and I just don't see eye to eye. I strongly recommend taking some risk and investing in either options or futures. Okay, you can lose some money if you're not careful. But you can also make BIG bucks if you take care, do your research, or seek the guidance of an expert in the field. Like my brother.*

John's one of three partners in an options trading business with seats on the Philadelphia and New York Stock Exchanges. He learned the business from his partner—his father-in-law—and he learned it well. To put it conservatively, they make money hand over fist. Okay, they win some and lose some, as all traders do, but at the end of the year when they tally up, his share alone is well into six figures. If you can find a broker who's got a good track record at investing in options or futures, by all means ride their coattails for as much as you can afford.

Mike: *This is one area where Jacquie gets carried away with sisterly love. Yeah, her brother makes mega-bucks riding the options market. But he's investing mega-bucks to do it and can ride out the downs as well as the ups in order to come out ahead. Most small investors—like us—can't do that. Nor is it easy to find a broker with a good, solid track record in those kinds of high-risk investments. Remember, this is your retirement fund we're talking about here. I couldn't be more opposed to risking your retirement—or ours—in the quagmire of the options and futures game.*

COMMODITIES

Commodities are things we use every day, like wheat, gasoline, sugar, and corn, and you can invest in them via both futures and options. What you're doing is gambling on what these items will cost in the future. You make a profit by buying or selling futures contracts in a specific commodity. The commodities market is driven by supply and demand, so if an item is in short supply, its price will be high. If it's easy to come by, its price will drop.

Futures contracts are used to minimize risk and to protect against unforeseen disasters in the market. Let's say a tornado wipes out the wheat crop in Kansas. If the flour and bread manufacturers have been wise, they'll have invested in wheat futures at a low price, well before the tornado drives the price of wheat sky high. The people who produce commodities try to estimate what the demand for their product will be, but they run the risk of losing money if they over- or underestimate supply and demand.

No question about it. You can win big in a very short time if you can afford to invest in futures, options, and commodities. But most financial advisers recommend that couples who need to build a solid retirement fund—and who don't have a huge windfall they can comfortably lose—steer clear. It's gambling, plain and simple, and the dice can roll either way.

LIFE INSURANCE PRODUCTS

We covered life insurance in chapter 6, so we won't make more than a brief mention here. Keep in mind that life insurance products offer couples yet another way to accrue tax-deferred retirement savings.

MORTGAGE-BACKED SECURITIES

They may sound like a good old family, but Fannie Maes, Ginnie Maes, and Freddie Macs actually are the three most common types of mortgage-backed securities. Mortgage-backed securities are bonds that are secured by "pooled" home mortgages. Banks and savings and loans make mortgage loans, which they then "pool" together. Units in the pool are sold to investors, who receive payments, or distributions, of both interest and principal as the loans are paid off.

Any pool of mortgages that provides investors with periodic payments is known as a "pass through." Generally speaking, most mortgage-backed securities are issued by federal institutions. As we noted earlier, the most common are:

- The Federal National Mortgage Association (FNMA, or "Fannie Mae")
- The Government National Mortgage Association (GNMA, or "Ginnie Mae")
- The Federal Home Loan Mortgage Corporation (FHLMC, or "Freddie Mac")

Mortgage-backed securities offer high yields, but most couples can't afford to invest in them, as they often require a big investment up front—as much as $20–$25,000. The exception is Ginnie Mae mutual funds, which more of us can afford. Read on.

MUTUAL FUNDS

Investing in mutual funds may be your best bet, because they allow you to begin saving for retirement without putting a whole lot up front. They take in monies from all kinds of investors and invest those monies in all kinds of funds, from stocks to bonds, to money-market funds and more.

Because most mutual funds don't invest in one area, like just stocks or just bonds, they're considered to be a diversified product. While shares in mutual funds can be purchased by many investors, the decision on what the fund is invested in—what constitutes the fund—usually is made by an individual or a team of portfolio managers.

The great thing about mutual funds for the average investor is that while you get to decide how much risk you want to assume, you don't have to worry about managing the fund: fund managers do that for you. There's also plenty of information available on how the funds work, what their investments are, and how they've performed in the past, so you really can pick and choose yourself, without having to pay for outside advice.

Open-end Mutual Funds

Two types of mutual funds are available: open end and closed end. Most mutual funds are open ended, meaning shares in them are always available because they place no limit on the number of shares they create. Currently, some 5,300 different open-end mutual funds are listed.

You can purchase shares through the mutual fund company itself, or through a banker, broker, or financial planner. Such funds publish a prospectus, which explains in detail how the fund invests. These are updated annually and should be examined carefully before you invest.

When you invest in an open-end mutual fund, you receive a share of the dividends, as well as any profits that might be earned from the sale of securities. You can receive this money in cash, or reinvest it in additional fund shares. Payouts may be monthly, quarterly, or annually.

While all mutual funds seek to make money for their investors, different funds have different formulas for fulfilling that objective. Some invest for growth, others for income, others try for both. There are also many different types of mutual funds available, some with high risk, some with low risk. Here are some of the most common open-end mutual funds available.

Low- to Middle-risk Mutual Funds

Money-market mutual funds. These usually invest in low-risk, low-return products like CDs and Treasury notes. They're best if your goal is protecting your capital or profiting from short-term interest rates.

Tax-exempt money-market mutual funds. These, too, will keep capital safe and help you earn tax-exempt interest over a short period of time. Most tax-exempt money-market mutual funds invest in short-term municipals.

International money-market mutual funds. These invest in foreign governments and CDs, as well as other short-term paper. Many investors believe they can earn a higher return than if they'd invested domestically.

Short-term bond, taxable or tax-exempt mutual funds. These funds purchase corporate, government, or tax-exempt bonds that can come due from one to five years. Not too risky, they're worth investigating if you want to keep your capital safe while trying to earn a higher return than a money-market fund offers.

Intermediate-term bond, taxable or tax-exempt mutual funds. Similar to those listed above, except the maturity dates of the bonds involved are from five to ten years, not one to five. These funds offer a higher yield than the shorter-term bonds, but they are more subject to market fluctuation.

Long-term tax-exempt bond mutual funds. These mutual funds invest in tax-exempt municipalities in the fifteen- to thirty-year maturity range. They have the potential for earning a high tax-exempt income but are moderately risky, because money can be lost if the bonds are sold before they mature.

Long-term taxable bond mutual funds. These are invested in corporate or government bonds that come due in fifteen to thirty years. They have the potential to earn a substantial dividend, but you pay taxes on them.

Ginnie Mae mutual funds. These invest in pools of home mortgages backed by the government. They can earn you a nice income and give you a periodic return on the capital you've invested.

Global bond mutual funds. These aim for a high bond income, investing in the bonds of both domestic and foreign countries and companies.

International bond mutual funds. These are the same as above, but funds are invested only in foreign countries and companies.

Mixed-income mutual funds. These are just as the name implies—a mixed bag investing in money markets, bonds, and dividend-paying stocks. While these can earn less than straight bonds, the yield from the stocks involved might compensate.

Income mutual funds. These take money markets out of the mix above and invest just in stocks and bonds. They offer more opportunity for growth than mixed-income mutual funds.

Balanced mutual funds. These mix some stocks and some bonds with preferred stocks, and are moderate-risk funds that grow at a reasonable rate and earn a reasonable income.

Mid- to High-Risk Mutual Funds

Zero-coupon bond mutual funds. These invest in discount bonds which pay no current interest. They're safe only if the bonds are allowed to come to maturity, and aim to accrue high bond income. You can make a lot of money by speculating on falling interest rates, but if rates rise, you'll lose.

Equity income mutual funds. These invest in stocks that pay high dividends, like utilities. You do run a risk of losing if the market falls, but they usually grow at a decent pace and can earn investors a decent income.

Growth and income mutual funds. These invest in stocks that pay out high dividends *and* show a lot of growth. But they offer more growth and less income than equity funds.

Fixed portfolio asset allocation mutual funds. These are a mix of assets like cash, stocks, bonds, etc., all with the goal of limiting loss while seeking decent growth.

Flexible portfolio asset allocation mutual funds. These invest in mixed assets as well, but the portfolio keeps changing to reflect the best markets at the time.

Option income mutual funds. These invest solely in stocks that have call options, or an option to buy, written against them. Those who buy call options are hoping that the price of their investment is going to go up. These funds aim to gain a higher income than most stock funds offer.

Convertible mutual funds. These invest in preferred stocks (ones that guarantee dividend payments, although payments don't rise if the company does well) and bonds, which can then be converted into common stocks. They generally provide a higher yield on common stocks, but the yield is less on bonds.

Fund of funds mutual funds. Okay, we admit it. This is getting out of hand. But these are mutual funds that invest in other mutual funds. With a moderate to high risk, the earnings are average.

Index mutual funds. Index funds imitate the stock market by allowing investors to buy stocks that represent the specific market as a whole. They tend to mirror the behavior of the market.

Higher Risk Mutual Funds

Conscience mutual funds. These purchase stock in "moral companies" only. For example, before apartheid was dismantled in South Africa, these funds would not have invested in companies doing business there. While good for the conscience, these funds aren't always good for the pocketbook. They tend to be high risk, because the investments they can make are limited, and they have average growth.

High-yield bond, taxable or tax-free mutual funds. These funds invest in low-rated and junk municipal and corporate bonds, in hope of netting a high income return. The risk comes from bond defaults and major declines in market value.

Global equity mutual funds. These invest in stocks of both domestic and foreign companies, in hope of earning worldwide capital gains. If markets fall, you risk substantial loss.

Growth mutual funds. These invest in foreign and domestic stocks whose earnings have a tendency to skyrocket, seeking to earn big international capital gains. But their performance is tied in to how well the dollar performs, and that can be a crapshoot.

International equity mutual funds. These invest in stocks of foreign companies. You can earn international capital gains, especially if the dollar falls.

If you think this list of open-end mutual funds is endless, you're right—we could go on. There are even higher risk funds than the ones we already listed, but for most couples interested in building a relatively safe retirement fund we don't recommend them. We should talk a bit about closed-end funds, however.

Closed-end Mutual Funds

Closed-end mutual funds offer a limited number of shares to investors. Once those shares are purchased, that's it, fund closed. Closed-end funds can only be purchased through a broker and tend to be much riskier than open-end mutual funds. While they invest in just about everything, they're best known for bonds and international investments.

If you really are interested in a bigger risk and want to know more about closed-end funds, we suggest you consult a broker, since you'll have to do that anyway if you decide that's the way you want to go.

The Lowdown on Mutual Fund Fees

Naturally, the privilege of investing in mutual funds doesn't come free. Depending on the fund, you can be assessed sales charges in a variety of ways. If you've had even half an ear cocked to the investment scene in recent years, you've probably heard the phrases "no load," "front end load," and "back end load." They don't refer to a heavy equipment crew.

A load is just a sales charge. If you invest in a mutual fund that carries a front end load, you're required to pay the sales charge before shares in the fund are purchased. Back end loads are the charges you pay if you choose to sell the investments. With low load funds, the sales charge is considered to be below industry standards. And no load funds have no sales charge, but you still don't get off free. That's because all mutual funds require you to pay annual fees and expenses on the shares you own in the fund.

Helpful Hint

If you're interested in investing in mutual funds, you should check out the "NAV" connected with various funds. NAV stands for Net Asset Value, which is the per share price of the mutual fund. NAVs are calculated daily, according to the market worth of the fund's total assets, minus liabilities, divided by the total number of shares outstanding in the fund.

Before investing in any mutual fund, find out:

- what "family" the fund belongs to
- what the fund's investment objective is (Be sure the one you're looking into is compatible with your investment needs.)
- where the fund invests its money
- what the sales charge will be, if any, as well as whether it's front, back, low, or no load (Check the annual fees.)
- how long the fund has been around, who manages it, and how long they've been doing so

Then, get a copy of the fund's prospectus and read it. If it's still Greek to you after reading this book, ask your broker, a financial adviser, or someone connected with the fund to help you.

REAL ESTATE INVESTMENT TRUSTS

Real estate investments trusts, or REITs, are funds that invest in residential, commercial, and industrial real estate—shopping centers, office complexes, and apartment buildings. Like mortgage-backed securities, REITs pool money raised from investors and invest it in different properties. REITs are publicly traded stock funds, so they're traded on most major stock exchanges as well as over-the-counter.

REITs can be a good investment for several reasons. First, they allow you to become a part owner of several pieces of real estate, which you probably couldn't do on your own. REITs also promise capital appreciation, since you could make a profit any time you choose to sell your shares. Of course, if the market turns bear, you could lose money, since REITs tend to follow stock market trends rather than real estate trends.

REITs are easy to invest in and easy to shed. If you decide to sell your REIT, all you have to do is call your broker and tell her to sell—a whole lot simpler than owning real estate directly and having to put your property on the market.

Best of all, REITs tend to yield more than other types of stocks, and they perform well over the long haul. They're legally required to give shareholders 95 percent of each year's profits in the form of regular dividend payouts. Provided the properties in which you've invested remain profitable, you should have a guaranteed source of income.

There are three types of REITs: Equity REITs, Mortgage REITs, and Hybrid REITs.

Equity REITs use investors' funds to snap up income-producing properties—any property with rent-paying tenants. These are the best choice for those who want to produce an income stream, as well as those interested in capital appreciation, especially when you consider that the typical yield for these is between 4 and 7 percent. Equity REITs are usually inflation beaters, since in most cases real estate values tend to rise over the long term rather than drop.

Look for REITs that buy and manage their own properties, as well as focus on specific types of real estate or regions. Avoid REITs that spread their investments across the country and mix and match residential, industrial, and commercial purchases, as their rates of success generally are lower.

Before investing in an Equity REIT, read the prospectus and make sure it's been operating—and moderately profitable—for at least five years. Avoid REITs that finance dividend payments through cash reserves or sale of properties. Instead invest in a REIT with a track record of increasing profits, whose monies are derived from the rental income of the properties cited in the portfolio.

Mortgage REITs buy mortgages on commercial properties and generate profits by charging interest to the buyers and developers to whom they've lent money. While their potential yield often is higher than that of Equity REITs—between 6 and 10 percent—they tend to own fewer properties, so the potential for capital appreciation is much less.

One major concern with mortgage REITs is that if the borrowers default, the value of your stock in the REIT will fall. Unlike Equity REITs, these REITs tend to behave more like bonds than the real estate market, which means there's little room for diversification.

Hybrid REITs are a combination of Equity REITs and Mortgage REITs: They own property AND make loans. While hybrid REITs offer a higher yield than Mortgage REITs, their potential for capital appreciation is less than that of a straightforward Equity REIT.

REVERSE MORTGAGES

Reverse mortgages tap the equity you've invested in your home to provide you with a steady source of income. It's really pretty simple. First, a lender—usually a bank—agrees to lend you money against the value of your house. You don't pay any cash up front: All closing and insurance costs are included in the loan. You also don't pay any interest on the borrowed money. That's paid when the loan is settled.

How much you get monthly is determined by how much equity you've built up in the house, your age, and the age of your spouse. No matter how much you get, those monthly checks roll in as long as you live in the house. If the loan ends up being worth more than the value of your house, the loss is absorbed by the lender.

The loan comes due if you die or decide to move. Generally, the house is sold, with the proceeds from the sale going toward repayment of the loan, plus compounded interest. The balance of the money goes to you or your heirs. Some lenders also offer what's known as equity reserve, which provides that when the house is sold, a guaranteed 10 to 20 percent of the equity in the home remains yours or your heirs'. Obviously, in that arrangement, you get less on a monthly basis.

You don't have to get the money monthly, either. You can choose a lump sum payment, or a line of credit, which allows you to draw what you need.

A reverse mortgage is a great deal. It allows you to remain in your home while providing an income. Better yet, the payments don't count as straight income, since what's really going on is loan payment. That means no Social Security or income tax.

There are drawbacks, of course, including the high rate of interest you pay on the loan. Another negative is that if you leave the house you've got nothing, unless you use the equity reserve provision or the credit line payment.

Be sure you get an indefinite-term reverse mortgage rather than one with a fixed term—unless you have a definite place ready to go to at a specific time, or you can accurately predict your own demise. Otherwise you'll be out on the street. And reverse mortgages work best for older retirees, say 75 and up. Otherwise your monthly check amounts to peanuts. Also, before you consider investigating this option, be sure you want to stay in the same house when you retire.

STOCKS

Stocks still remain one of the all-time best investment tools. That's because some stocks pay dividends, which means they provide you with an income while allowing you to live off your capital. And stocks historically have provided real growth over the long term. There's no question the stock market fluctuates over the short term, but over a long period of time, stock values usually rise. That's why they're excellent inflation busters.

As a stockholder, you become a part owner in a business or corporation. Stocks usually are either income stocks, which pay dividends, or growth stocks, in which you don't expect to earn dividends but instead count on a higher stock price and earnings that rise quickly.

Most stocks are categorized as either common or preferred. Common stocks are those in which you're buying an ownership share of a corporation. The interest you hold in the company is known as equity. When the company in which you've invested makes a profit, you share in the success by earning dividends. Investors make money in the stock market when the price of their shares goes up, making their investment more valuable. But since common stocks offer no performance guarantees, your investment is at risk if the company in which you've bought shares does poorly.

Preferred stocks function much like common stock, but payments of dividends to shareholders are guaranteed before dividends on common stock. That means they're safer than common stock. But if the company does well and earns a profit, your dividend remains the same. While the price of preferred stock tends to rise more slowly, stockholders have a better chance of recouping their investment if the company fails than they would if they'd invested in common stocks, where you can lose everything.

Like bonds, stocks are rated, or ranked. The highest rank a stock can carry is an A+; the lowest, a D. In addition, corporations themselves may offer different classes of stocks. Some offer what's known as P shares, which means ownership in a specific subsidiary of the company.

Others carry a letter, whether it's A, B, or C, and are used for specific investment purposes, with each carrying its own dividend policy.

Many companies offer their shareholders DRIPs, or dividend reinvestment programs. These let the investor acquire more shares in the company by "reinvesting" their dividend money.

There are two ways of investing in stocks: you can pick them yourself, or you can buy into a mutual fund. Unless your brother is a stockbroker and you're on good terms, it's best to buy stocks through a mutual fund. But whichever route you choose, make sure you find out:

- the name of the company or corporation
- which stock exchange(s) it trades on
- the rank of the stock (check Moody's, or the Standard & Poor Stock Guide)
- whether the stock is common or preferred stock
- whether it pays a dividend, and if it does, how much and whether it's gone up or down over time
- how actively the stock is traded
- whether the company offers DRIPs

Helpful Hint
Stocks are best as long-term investments.

TREASURY BILLS

Treasury bills are short-term investment bonds that mature in three months, six months, or one year. Generally they're used by the government to raise money for immediate spending at significantly lower rates than most bonds. They're not cheap: The minimum investment usually is $10,000. Your profit is the interest earned by the difference between the discount buying price and the amount you'll be paid when the bill hits maturity.

Say you send the government a certified check for $10,000 for a Treasury bill, or T-bill, due to mature in one year, which is selling at $9,000. Treasury sends you a check for $1,000. When your bill matures in a year, you get a check for $10,000, the face value of the bill. So the $1,000 you got when you bought the bill was pure profit.

T-bills, considered a risk-free investment (although technically there's no such thing), are exempt from state and local taxes. You can also defer federal taxes. If you buy a T-bill that's due to mature in the next calendar year, the income interest you earn can be paid then, too. One caution: The taxable profit is not the discount check you first get from the government; it's the money you make when the bill matures.

NOW YOU'RE READY TO BEGIN

If you're still with us after all this, congratulations. You've just proven you can get through anything, no matter how often your eyes glaze over. Seriously, though, there may be nothing as important in your life as the need to plan properly for a secure retirement. After all, it's the culminating stage of life and one for which you've earned a good measure of ease and enjoyment. You want to be sure you can afford it. And now that we're all living longer and in better health than ever before in the history of humankind, you want to be doubly sure you'll be able to afford it all the way to the end.

With this chapter under your belts you're ready to get started saving and investing for retirement. Remember, you're going to need 75 percent of your preretirement income to live on during retirement—maybe $50,000 in current dollars, or about $1.25 million in future dollars. That's a lot of beans, any way you slice it. But we've discussed the many kinds of retirement plans out there and how they work, and the investment tools available to help you make the most of those plans. Just do it, as they say.

Your next step, then, is to determine your investment strategy—figure out what tools and techniques will take you where you want to go. Your strategy, as we mentioned earlier, will be determined in part by how much money you need to generate between now and retirement, and how much time you have to generate it.

First though, we offer these tips on investing:

- Stick to basics. Don't risk investing in futures and commodities if stocks and bonds will do the trick.
- When thinking long-term growth, stocks are the way to go. While the stock market fluctuates over the short term, over the long term stocks have continually proven to rise in value, much more so than bonds.
- Invest in stocks through mutual funds. If you're a stockbroker, you can pick stocks yourself. But if you're not, you should leave it to the professionals—mutual fund managers.
- Invest on a regular basis. Putting money into mutual funds at fixed intervals is a good way to save money for retirement.
- Diversify. Stocks are the way to go for the long term, but don't forget about the short term. You also need to invest in products that will protect your money during the market's down years. Your portfolio definitely should include your home (which provides equity); stocks; money-market mutual funds for more immediate savings; and bonds and dividend-paying stocks for a source of ever compounding interest.
- Reinvest dividends. Not all stocks yield dividends. But if yours do, avoid the temptation to go on a spending spree. Instead, reinvest and buy more stocks.

DECIDE ON YOUR ALLOCATION OF ASSETS

You're going to invest in stocks and bonds, but you need to find the right mix. Asset allocation is the practice of dividing your money among stocks, bonds, and other financial instruments, and letting the money earn maximum profits. How you allocate the assets in your portfolio will have a direct bearing on whether you end up with sufficient money to fund your retirement.

Forget about "beating" the market by buying and selling before prices rise and fall. The market rises and falls unpredictably—that's a basic fact of life. Therefore, which assets you buy is more important than when you buy them. By mixing and matching assets that rise and fall at different times, you can minimize your investment risk.

So, when picking your portfolio, remember:

- Try to own as many assets as you can via mutual funds.
- Diversify by making different types of investments.
- For long-term economic growth buy U.S. as well as foreign stocks.
- For stability, invest in short- to medium-term bonds, as well as financial instruments that can be liquidated quickly, like short-term T-bills and money-market mutual funds.

Whatever combination of stocks and bonds you decide to buy, be sure your portfolio includes a mix of U.S. stocks, medium-term bonds and cash equivalents, like the money-market mutual funds and short-term T-bills mentioned earlier. Then, perhaps, invest in a REIT, as well as foreign stocks, foreign bonds, and gold.

If you're starting early you can experiment a bit with what works best for you and what you can have the most fun with. The key now is to regularly keep track of the performance of your retirement fund and make changes as needed to suit your needs. Like a garden, your retirement fund needs to be watched, watered, and weeded regularly for it to grow into a thing of beauty.

Now, to ensure you're able to enjoy this lush, beautiful, well-nourished retirement together—as a couple—read on to chapter 11. There you'll find a brief discourse on the fine and noble art of compromise.

11

The Art of Compromise

Whether you've been together ten years or ten weeks, you're probably already well aware that in order to survive as a couple you're going to need to learn the art of compromise. If you've managed to survive five years or more together, you've probably been practicing the art of compromise with some degree of success, perhaps without even realizing it.

But despite the cliché, practice doesn't necessarily make perfect. Having read this far in this book you clearly feel a compelling need to get your financial house in order. And that means your financial house has been at least somewhat messy, disordered, or just plain out-of-whack. A word of warning here: For any couple, the decision to clean house financially can give a whole new meaning to the words *stress, discord,* even, perish the thought, *divorce.*

Okay, pretend we never said it. Put it right out of your minds. But be prepared. If you decide to undertake this financial house cleaning and put your family finances on a sound, businesslike basis, you'll be in for some rocky times unless you actually become a MASTER in the art of compromise. Because once you decide to invest in your future, as you've already read in this book, you not only must marry your disparate money styles but you also have a seemingly unending series of financial decisions to make, at every stage of your lives.

And let's face it. When couples have decisions to make they usually can come up with at least two opposing views on which decision is preferable. So they need to compromise. Or, to put it in the businesslike terms a full financial partnership demands, they need to make a deal. And to achieve the compromise—to clinch the deal—they must negotiate.

NEGOTIATE YOUR WAY TO A MORE SATISFYING LIFE

In this chapter, then, we'll give you some tips on how to negotiate successfully, so you can achieve the compromises necessary to keep your financial partnership afloat. But you should look at these negotiating tips as a sort of bonus, too. While they're designed to help you master the art of compromise that your financial partnership requires, you can use them in your business, professional, and personal life as well.

If, as someone once said, "life is a series of negotiations," these tips can help you negotiate your way to a more satisfying life. Remember, the end result of a negotiation will be a compromise of sorts, and that means both parties to the negotiation need to feel they've won something. You know, the old "win-win" strategy.

Usually in a negotiation the wins don't come out totally even. That is, one party, or partner, may win bigger this time, the other partner may win bigger next time. The important thing is to be sure each partner legitimately can lay claim to a measure of "win." You absolutely want to avoid the disaster a "win-lose" result can bring to your relationship.

So what does it take to be a good negotiator? Good negotiators are proactive; they don't accept the status quo without trying to make it better. They actively try to change situations for the better and go after what they want in life and in business. Keep in mind, though, that the best negotiators do that while finding a way to make their opponent—either their partner or another party—feel good about the result, too.

So you negotiate to get what you want in life and in business—to get a better deal. But some people are reluctant to negotiate because they fear they might lose. In other words, if you risk trying to win a negotiation and fail, that means you lose, right? Wrong. First, we repeat: Good negotiators try to end with a "win-win" situation, not "win-lose." Second, failure to win a negotiation doesn't necessarily mean you actually lose something. In most cases, if you're unsuccessful in a negotiation you probably just have to accept the status quo. Or, in a win-win situation, both parties accept less than they wanted but something usually better than the status quo.

Look at How Tom and Robyn Did It

Let's recall our spender versus saver personality conflicts from chapter 2. Say Tom, a spender, desperately wants to buy a Harley-Davidson motorcycle in the spring for his 30th birthday. He has wanted one all his life, and thinks if he doesn't do it by 30 he'll never manage it and will regret it his entire life. And, he points out, he wants to buy his bike before he gets too old to enjoy it.

But Tom's wife, Robyn, is appalled he would even consider spending a good chunk of their savings on a vehicle that not only isn't essential to their lives but in fact would be primarily a leisure-time activity. Robyn points out they need to continue saving for a house and start a college fund, because they're expecting their first child in the spring, just about the time that Tom wants to indulge his first midlife crisis.

A good negotiation would end with a compromise deal that went something like this: Tom agrees to delay purchase of the bike for one year while he puts some money each week into a special bike savings fund. He agrees some of that money will come out of his own discretionary spending money. He also agrees to buy a less expensive bike than he had his heart set on.

Robyn agrees to delay the start of the college fund one year, until after the bike purchase. She also agrees to forego one dinner out each month as a contribution to the bike fund. After all, she says, she'll enjoy riding on it too, occasionally, after the baby is born.

They both agree it's important to continue saving at the same rate for the purchase of their house, which is probably three years down the road. They've decided to save longer so they can purchase a little more house than they could if they rushed into it.

In the end Tom and Robyn are both happy.

HOW DO YOU BECOME A GOOD NEGOTIATOR?

To become a good negotiator you need to change the way you think about negotiating. Most people think of negotiating as a formal process, usually involving a business deal, where opponents sit down on opposite sides of a big boardroom table to resolve weighty matters. And if they think of themselves as negotiating at all, it's in terms of major, formal life events such as buying a house or a car. And then it becomes such a big deal, so to speak, they get strung out about it.

You probably don't think of yourselves as negotiators, but think again. Don't you resolve small issues on a daily basis through conversation? Something like this?

Jacquie: "Can you stop at the market on the way home from work and pick up milk? I have a meeting and will be running late."

Mike: "Okay, but will you call the plumber to fix the

garbage disposal and make an appointment for the dog at the vet?"

Sound familiar? Sure it does. That's negotiation and compromise, even though we generally don't think about it that way. There's no big mystery to it. Negotiating really is just going after what you want. And that usually means asking for more than the other person wants to give. You need to be willing to ask for more to be a good negotiator. You also need to know what you want, and what the other party is likely to want. That way you can figure out how to end with a deal—a compromise—that leaves both of you feeling satisfied.

THREE KEY RULES FOR GOOD NEGOTIATING

There are three basic rules for success in negotiating:

Rule #1: Know Yourself

It's most important to know what end result you want to achieve through negotiation—in other words, what you want. Ask yourself, too, if it's worth your time and if it's important to you. Be sure to set a specific goal to work toward. That way, as part of the negotiation, you can be prepared to make concessions in other areas less important to your goal.

But it's also important to know yourself—how you tend to respond in certain situations, what makes you crazy, what makes you lose focus, when you're most awake and sharpest.

For example, are you sluggish in the morning and hit your stride about 4 P.M.? Do your negotiating at that time, if at all possible. Does whining send you into a frenzy that destroys your best efforts at self-control? If you're aware of that, you can guard against it.

If you're fully aware of your own personality traits and responses, you're going to be better able to negotiate, no matter who your opponent is. And of course if your opponent is your partner, you not only know full well how you tend to respond to his or her negotiating style but you also should be able to predict what that style will be. Which leads us to Rule #2.

Rule #2: Know Your Opponent

On the surface, in terms of this book, Rule #2 would appear easy. After all, we're talking about couples here, so your opponent is your partner. In theory, there isn't anyone you know better, right?

It's a little more complicated than that. But remember also that we're trying to give you advice that will help you negotiate successfully with anyone on any subject, not just your partner.

Rule #2 doesn't mean being able to read someone's mind or predict exactly how that person will respond in a given situation. Rather, for the purposes of a negotiation, it means determining if there's a discrepancy of power between you and your opponent. If there is, you must seek to minimize that imbalance of power—level the playing field—in order to achieve a successful negotiation. If you fail to even out the perceived imbalance of power, you run the risk of having such issues as ego and status muddy and even block the negotiation. In fact, you run the risk of failure.

Stephen M. Pollan and Mark Levine, in *The Total Negotiator*, suggest you can better know your opponent and minimize any imbalance of power by answering four questions: What information do I need? With whom should I negotiate? Are there side issues that could cause problems? And, what do I share with my opponent—where can we find common ground?

Sam and Winona offer an example of how Rule #2

can relate to a couple's financial partnership. Sam is a very conservative investor; a saver, really, rather than an investor. They've been married ten years but just started a real financial partnership six months ago. Until then Sam handled all their finances, and he still believes he's the expert, not Winona.

Winona is a risk-taker who has limited knowledge of finance. But since she started taking an interest in their partnership, she's been dying to invest in commodities futures. She thinks she can make them a lot more money than Sam is earning with the CDs he's invested in.

If neither Sam nor Winona has any negotiating skills you can picture the discussion. They may avoid bloodshed—after all, they've been married ten years. But they won't avoid a bitter battle and maybe a few weeks of cold silence. But let's say Winona has been reading this book. She knows that the balance of power lies with Sam, and she knows she'd better level the playing field before the negotiation begins.

So she bones up on the current status of their finances. She analyzes how much money they're saving and investing each month. She researches the commodities market and then, as a fallback, researches a variety of mutual funds that offer an exciting mix of investment options.

Before their next weekly family finance meeting she adds "investments" to the agenda. She's ready. At the meeting she says she investigated investing in the futures market for a potentially greater return than they're getting on their CDs. But, she adds, after thorough research she determined the risks are too great and suggests they invest a portion of their investment/savings budget in a medium-to high-risk mutual fund.

Sam objects, so she lays out her research materials, showing the track record and rate of return on the various mutual funds. She asks his help in selecting one as an experimental investment.

Winona has done her homework. She knew her opponent and leveled the playing field by doing sufficient research to even the balance of power between them. And she was willing to settle for less than her original goal and less than total control. In the end Sam sees no way they can lose, and goes for the deal.

Rule #3: Know the Situation

This rule is a bit more difficult to follow because each situation is different. In some ways it involves a little bit of both Rules #1 and #2. You need to put what you know about yourself and your opponent, and what each of you wants, into the situation. Then figure out what elements of the situation impact your goals and those of your opponent. From there it's just a question of finding the best path to a win-win conclusion. And the best way to get better at all this? That's not rocket science: experience.

THERE IS NO RIGHT OR WRONG IN A NEGOTIATION

Notice that we haven't used the words *right* and *wrong* in discussing negotiation and compromise. That's because they simply don't apply here. There's your position and goal and your partner's position and goal. It's irrelevant whether you think your partner's goal is wrong. That's still the point from which he or she is negotiating. The key is to find a way to get what you want while still accommodating your partner's needs, at least to the point where you both achieve a measure of satisfaction.

To that end, then, avoid using words like *right* and *wrong* in your negotiations. Be sure to use language that is noncritical and inclusive. Avoid starting all your sentences with "I," and avoid an accusatory tone. This advice might seem basic, but when you're in the heat of battle you'd be surprised at what you find yourself saying and doing.

Body language is important, too. Be open and relaxed. Signal with your body that you're in control of yourself and the situation. Don't bite your nails or tap your feet, or tap on the table with your pencil. That kind of body language signals distress, and can give your opponent some leverage in your negotiation.

TEN BASIC TIPS FOR SUCCESSFUL NEGOTIATIONS

In summary, here are ten basic tips that will help you achieve successful negotiations, in life as well as in your financial partnership:

1. Make your goal specific. That way you're more likely to achieve it.

2. Be sure you understand your opponent's objectives.

3. Don't attempt to negotiate for things that aren't readily negotiable.

4. Decide whether the potential outcome outweighs the time and cost of negotiating.

5. Eliminate or minimize any perceived discrepancies in the balance of power.

6. Negotiate only with someone with the power to make a deal.

7. Prices are invitations to buy, not statements of value.

8. Terms of a deal are as important as dollars.

9. Be sure your body language is relaxed and avoid critical or accusatory language.

10. Aim for a win-win compromise.

Jacquie: *This advice is distilled from therapy, research, and twenty years of marital battles over everything from finances to kids to the color of the toilet paper. Okay, we're slow learners, but we got there in the end. You might think it seems manipu-*

*lative or somehow sneaky to bring these techniques to your rela-
tionship, financial or otherwise, but that couldn't be farther
from the truth.*

*I know, your relationship is based on truth and trust, right?
So is ours. But there's nothing dishonest or untrustworthy about
these tips. They're simple, commonsense techniques to help you
learn to work together for a common goal—to compromise. Believe me, your future financial health may depend on that one
word more than any other in this book.*

Mike: *Jacquie's right. The two of you will experience any
number of occasions where you seem to be at opposite ends of
the spectrum on one financial issue or another. Keep the lines
of communication open, respect one another's opinions, and do
your best to meet somewhere in the middle. Also, remember
that money is just one of many relationship issues that require
the art of compromise.*

*We both wish you well in your financial future together,
and we hope this book will be helpful to you for many years to
come. May your investments stay strong, may you and yours
stay healthy, and may the financial gods walk with you always.
Oh, and most important—don't forget to have fun.*

INDEX

A

accountants, 167–68

accounts, setting up, 41–43, 111

American Life of New York, 145

Ameritas Low-Load, 145

amiable personality, 9, 10, 30–31

analytical personality, 9–10, 30

annuities
immediate, 247–48
tax-deferred, 246–47

automobile insurance, 155
collision coverage, 156
comprehensive coverage, 157
liability coverage, 156
medical payments coverage, 156–57
premiums, 157–58
uninsured motorist coverage, 157

B

Bankcard Holders of America, 77

bankers, 170–71

bankruptcy, 68–69, 101
Chapter 7, 102–3
Chapter 13, 103
forms of, 101–3
meaning of, 101

Barron's, 77, 175

Barron's Financial Tables for Better Money Management, 122

blended families, 20–21
financing, 21–23

bonds, 202–4, 248–49
hints concerning, 250
ratings, 249–50
U.S. Treasury, 203
zero-coupon, 203

budgets, 52–53, 111–12
analyzing cash flow, 53–57
definition of, 52
easy credit and, 58–59